Art of the American Automobile

The Greatest Stylists and their Work

This edition first published in the United States in 1995
by SMITHMARK Publishers Inc.,
16 East 32nd Street, New York, NY 10016.

First published in the United Kingdom in 1995 by
PRION, an imprint of Multimedia Books Limited,
32-34 Gordon House Road, London NW5 1LP.

Text copyright © Nick Georgano 1995.
Copyright © Multimedia Books Limited 1995.

ISBN 0-8317-0677-5

Printed in Italy

SMITHMARK books are available for bulk purchase for
sales promotion and premium use. For details write or
call the manager of special sales, SMITHMARK
Publishers Inc., 16 East 32nd Street, New York,
NY 10016; (212) 532-6600.

All rights reserved. No part of this book may be
reproduced or transmitted by any means, electronic or
mechanical, including photocopying or recording, or by
any information storage or retrieval system, without
permission in writing from Multimedia Books Limited.

All correspondence concerning the content of this
volume should be addressed to the publishers.

HALF TITLE
Henry Ford and his 1896 Quadricycle.

TITLE PAGE
Bill Porter and his 1995 Buick Riviera.

Art of the
American Automobile

The Greatest Stylists and their Work

BY

Nick Georgano

with photographs by

Nicky Wright

SMITHMARK

DISCARDED

PENN YAN PUBLIC LIBRARY
214 Main Street
Penn Yan, New York 14527

CONTENTS

CONTENTS

ART OF THE AMERICAN AUTOMOBILE

INTRODUCTION

L ike this picture of a razor edge on a British Bentley? Maybe you don't know why – you just like cars. If the picture pleases you, you're getting a charge out of art – the automobile as art.... These words were written by Fred Horsley in his book, *Dream Cars*, published in 1953. We feel that he expected readers to be surprised that they would be pleased by an art form. "What, me, a down-to-earth auto enthusiast who was dragged unwillingly around art galleries when I was a kid, turned on by art?"

Yet art is not just to be found in galleries and museums, but in almost everything we use and look at every day. Tableware, refrigerators, food processors, TV sets, all kinds of furniture — all have an input from the stylist as well as the engineer. This is especially true of the automobile, which has to sell on its appearance as much as on its mechanical qualities. Just as much as a house or a garment, a car is a statement of what the owners think of themselves, and how they would like others to think of them.

Every car ever made has a style of some sort, even if it is of the most plain and functional kind. Sometimes attractive lines spring from purely practical considerations, which can be called functional art. For example, the first military Dodge trucks and vans of World War II were compromise machines with military front ends and fenders, and hoods and cabs of civilian design. Then the military demanded a wider track to improve stability, the hood was redesigned with a lower profile, and the cab became a soft top. Instantly, a more aesthetically satisfying vehicle resulted; in addition to being a fine army truck, the Dodge T214, of which more than a quarter of a million were made, was a more attractive design to look at than its predecessors. The Jeep was also an example of a machine with purely practical parameters and no positive artistic input, which also contrives to look "just right."

People have admired cars since the first examples chugged down the road, but the auto was not recognized by the art world until 1951, when the

◁ 1955 CHEVROLET BEL AIR (LEFT)
AND 1959 CHEVROLET BISCAYNE
In the four years separating these two cars, the front has become much bolder, with a higher grille, larger headlights and projecting overriders.

▽ 1928 AUBURN CABIN SPEEDSTER
Streamlining has won out over a good rear view (below) in this striking design.

▽ 1953 KAISER DRAGON
A bold rear end styled by Howard Darrin (below right).

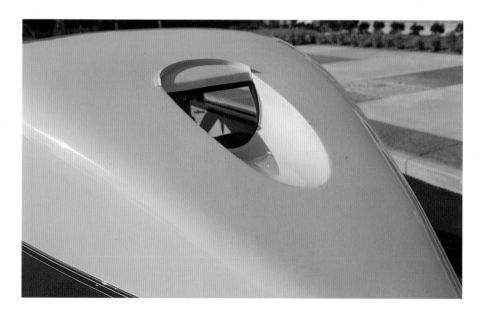

Museum of Modern Art in New York staged an exhibition "concerned with the aesthetics of motorcar design," featuring eight examples of cars chosen for their excellence as works of art. The oldest was a 1930 Mercedes-Benz SS and the youngest a 1949 Cisitalia coupe by Pinin Farina. Of the eight, three were American – a Cord 810, a Lincoln Continental, and a Jeep, the latter hailed as "a beautiful tool for transportation." Since then, numerous shows and *concours d'elegance* have been held around the world, of which the premier event must be the annual show at Pebble Beach, California.

Throughout its history, the automobile has been an amalgam of form and function. The ideal form is constrained by the mechanical elements and, in the case of mass-production cars, by the economics of manufacture and sales. The individually styled custom car may sacrifice less to function, but surely the challenge of producing a car which is economical to make, has appeal to the widest possible market, and yet still looks wonderful is the greater achievement. That is why, in this book, we have devoted the bulk of the pages to artists who sold successfully to a mass market: Harley Earl, Bill Mitchell, Bob Gregorie, Frank Hershey and the others. By creating memorable shapes out of metal, these men have given pleasure to millions through an art form without barriers, true people's art of the twentieth century.

Nick Georgano
Fall 1994

▽ 1936 851 BOAT-TAIL SPEEDSTER
Gordon Buehrig's classic (below left) was the closest the U.S. industry got to a European-type sports car in the 1930s.

▽ 1955 CHRYSLER C-300
A bold instrument panel and steering column gearshift were typical of 1950s' design.

▷ 1940 LINCOLN CONTINENTAL
Lincoln's waterfall grille was the work of Bob Gregorie, but the car was inspired by Henry Ford's son, Edsel.

△ FRANK DE CAUSSE (1879-1928)
One of the first stylists to establish a personal reputation,
de Causse was lured away from the French firm of Kellner
in 1914 to head Locomobile's custom body department.
He later designed the radical 1925 Franklins.

CHAPTER ONE

THE COACHBUILT ERA

"The dictates of good taste in automobile design cannot be observed when frequent changes in body features occur."

Frank de Causse

I N THE BEGINNING, the auto builder's concern was with making his machine go rather than look good. Up to 1900, the artistic element put into the automobile was negligible; engineering was all. This is particularly true in the United States, where cars were derived from the ubiquitous buggy, owned by a wider section of the populace than were any horse-drawn vehicles in Europe. Two- or four-horse carriages, some very ornate, were in Europe owned by royalty and the wealthy; middle-class professionals such as doctors might have a two-wheeled trap, and the poor walked, or if they were lucky, used a bicycle. Public transportation was also well organized by the 1890s in most European countries, with close-knit rail services operating from the country and suburbs into large cities. In the U.S. a higher proportion relied on their own transportation which, typically, was provided by the one-horse buggy. This conveyance was strictly functional,

with no styling considerations, as were the early buggy-derived autos by such pioneers as the Duryea brothers, Haynes, Winton and Packard.

From 1900 on, the more expensive European cars such as Panhard and Mercedes began to be imported, mainly by wealthy East-coasters, and within a few years their influence started to be seen on domestic productions. Thus the Pierce Motorette, a typical short, high, two-passenger buggy when it appeared in 1901, became the Pierce Great Arrow three years later, when it had a front-mounted engine under a proper hood, and a frame long enough to accommodate a four- or five-passenger body. Wheelbases grew by an average of 15 to 20 inches between the 1903 and 1904 models of many American cars. By 1909 the Motorette had become the Pierce-Arrow, the first in a long line of one of America's most illustrious makes.

Styling was certainly a factor in auto design in the early years of the twentieth century, but it was mainly a function of convenience rather than art for

its own sake. For example, a longer wheelbase made the car look lower and sleeker, but its main purpose was to allow for a larger body with a side entrance rather than the clumsy rear-entrance tonneau imposed by a short wheelbase. The styling of fenders could make or mar an auto, but their main purpose was to protect the passengers from mud and dust, increasingly important as speeds rose every year. In August 1903, *The Horseless Age* reported "… the bulk of orders, therefore, go to the maker who offers a car of satisfactory appearance… at the lowest possible price." Note that they talk of "satisfactory appearance," not "revolutionary," "breathtaking," or even "elegant"; such adjectives were to come later.

An important development which was more concerned with style than practicality was the position of the engine in the frame. As engines grew in length, with fours and then sixes increasingly popular in the years 1903 to 1908, the front of the engine projected ahead of the front axle, and

◁ ▽ 1929 DUESENBERG MODEL J BOAT-TAILED SPEEDSTER

This car has a body by Walter Murphy of Pasadena, the best-known West Coast coachbuilder. This style has come to be known as the "boat-tailed speedster," but Murphy's own description was Disappearing Top Torpedo Convertible Coupe. At least five were built, and the three survivors each have slight differences in the shape of the lower end of the rear deck. Murphy publicity said that "the car is unusually fast because of its effective streamline." Behind the passenger compartment was a rumble seat for one. This is the oldest of the survivors; another car, from 1931, was originally owned by Cliff Durant, son of General Motors founder Billy Durant, then later by oil tycoon J. Paul Getty and novelist John O'Hara.

OWNER: AUBURN-CORD-DUESENBERG MUSEUM

◁ ▽ The earliest Model J radiator did not have any shutters, but these soon appeared on most cars from mid-1929 onwards. The design of the radiator and mascot (an option not seen on all Model Js) was probably by Al Leamy, though he has never been directly credited.

consequently the radiator was farther forward still, in line with, or even ahead of the leading edge of the front wheel. This gave the car a heavy appearance, the very reverse of speed and elegance. About 1907 most designers began to position the engine farther back in the frame (some, such as Mercedes, had never pushed it forward), reaching an ideal position where the radiator was directly above the front axle. This was not ideal technically, for it transferred weight rearwards, reducing steering control and allowing for less body length. Nevertheless, the set-back radiator became an established icon for anyone who laid claim to elegance of design and remained so until the early 1930s. Then engines began to move forward again, to give greater body space, and elegance retreated. Most people would agree that, for example, a 1939 Packard V12 is less aesthetically satisfying than its predecessor of 1930. Dave Holls, former director of design at General Motors, observed recently that 1932 was the last year of the classic look. "After that

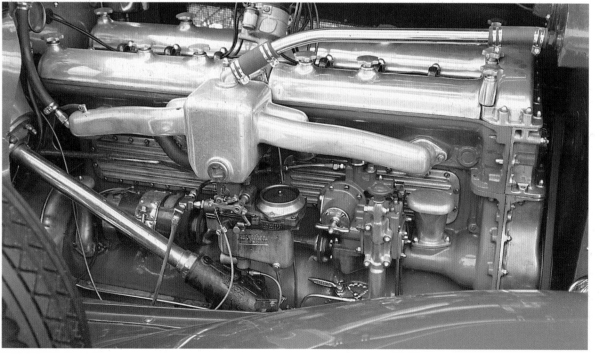

◁ △ ▷ 1929 DUESENBERG MODEL J
The Duesenberg Model J engine was a remarkable piece of machinery with a twin-cam in-line eight engine of racing pattern. Made to Duesenberg's design by Lycoming, another company in Cord's empire, it had a claimed output of 265hp, boosted to 320hp when a supercharger was used. These figures have been disputed but it seems likely that they were achieved on the test bed without accessories. It far exceeded any other American car at the time of its introduction in 1928; the Cadillac V16 of 1930, with a larger displacement, gave 175hp. The external exhaust manifold pipes were characteristics of the supercharged Model SJ, but were a popular cosmetic accessory on non-supercharged cars such as this one.
OWNER: AUBURN-CORD-DUESENBERG MUSEUM

◁ The instrument panel was described by its makers as one of the beauty spots of the car. The surface was of brass, finished in engine-turned oxidized chromium plated strip. All the instruments have black dials with white numbers. The speedometer read to 150mph and the tachometer to 5,000rpm, though maximum power was developed at 4,200rpm. Other instruments included a water temperature gage, brake pressure gage, ammeter, gasoline gage, altimeter, carburetor choke, ignition lock, and lights for oiler, oil change and battery water.

OWNER: GILMORE CAR MUSEUM, KALAMAZOO, MICHIGAN

single point in time, cars grew more streamlined. In 1932 every car was a jewel."

In recent years the process has reached exaggerated lengths, with a short hood, long body, and the radiator grille some 36 inches ahead of the axle.

THE COACHBUILDER'S ROLE

During the automobile's first 20 years, styling evolved almost anonymously, with no individual names becoming famous. The lead in styling was often given by the great coachbuilding houses, which could be loosely divided into three groups. First, there were the established firms which had made horse-drawn carriages, dating back into the nineteenth century. Doyen of them all was Brewster, founded in 1810 at 52 Broad Street, New York City, not far from the present site of the Stock Exchange. It later moved uptown to Broome Street, then Broadway, and in 1910 to a considerably larger factory in Long Island City. Its slogan was "Carriage Builders to American Gentlemen," and it catered to generations of prominent families, often continuing the family color scheme from carriage to automobile. Its first automobile body was on a Barrett & Perret electric car in 1896.

Other carriage makers in the first category were J. M. Quimby & Sons of Newark, New Jersey,

△ △ ▷ 1929 DUESENBERG MODEL J DUAL-COWL
PHAETON BY LEBARON
This style was first seen on the 1916 Locomobile which
Frank de Causse designed for Rodman Wanamaker, and
was a popular style on the Model J, being made by
Derham, LeBaron and Union Body, as well as by
Murphy. The curved panel in the front door was a
continuation of the design on the hood. It was known
as the "LeBaron sweep panel" and was copied by other
coachbuilders including Weymann and La Grande.
OWNER: GILMORE CAR MUSEUM, KALAMAZOO, MICHIGAN

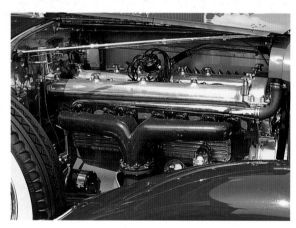

△ Exhaust side of the Duesenberg Model J engine,
showing the two aluminum camshaft covers. The inlet
valve shaft is on the right side of the engine, the
exhaust shaft on the left. Four valves per cylinder made
a total of 32 valves. The camshafts were driven by a
2-inch silent chain from a transfer gear, which itself
was driven by a second chain from the crankshaft.

founded in 1834; the J.B. Judkins Company (founded as Judkins & Goodwin in West Amesbury, Massachusetts, in 1857); Biddle & Smart of Amesbury (1870); Derham of Rosemont, Pennsylvania (1884); and Healy of New York City (1890). Most of these companies built their first bodies on automobiles close to the turn of the century and were well-established by 1910.

The second category comprised companies set up after 1900, mainly to build automobile bodies and staffed by graduates from the older coachbuilding firms. They included Locke & Company of New York City (1902); Brunn of Buffalo, NY (1908); and Willoughby & Company of Utica, NY (1908).

Finally, there were the companies wholly of the automobile era, dating from the 1920s and often located on the West Coast. These included Murphy and Bohman & Schwartz, both located in Pasadena; Don Lee Coach & Body Works of Los Angeles; LeBaron of Bridgeport, Connecticut; and Rollston of New York City.

By and large, progress in styling came from the second and third types of coachbuilder, for the inheritors of the coachbuilding tradition tended towards conservative lines. Their innovations were confined to luxury interior items such as flower vases, washbasins and electric lighting. Healy made some unusual interiors including the "beamed ceiling" in which the framework of the roof was exposed. Sometimes it was finished in natural wood color, but more often was painted to match the headlining fabric, or even covered with the fabric. Healy also pioneered built-in vanity cases.

A practical innovation by the conservative Brewster company was the antiglare windshield. A vertical screen gave a lot of glare from street lights and shop windows, and to eliminate this Brewster came up with a double shield, the lower part canted forward and the upper sharply backwards. A later and simpler version had a single pane sloped forward. Both were patented and adopted by other coachbuilders, including Holbrook, Judkins, the New Haven Carriage Company, and Rolls-Royce

ART OF THE AMERICAN AUTOMOBILE

△ LeBaron built dual-cowl phaetons on both short and long wheelbase Duesenberg chassis. This is on the short (142½-inch) wheelbase; the longer (153½ inches) made for a better balanced appearance. More dual-cowl phaetons were made than any other open-body style on the Duesenberg J chassis.

▷ The Duesenberg motif was an option, and seems to have been used more on open-bodied cars than on sedans and limousines. No nameplate or monogram appeared anywhere on the exterior of the car. Its shape was thought to be sufficient identification.

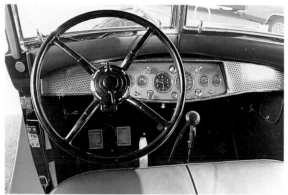

△ ▷ 1931 CADILLAC V16 WITH TOWN CAR BODY BY FLEETWOOD.

Founded in 1912, Fleetwood was located in the Pennsylvania town of that name, though in 1929 it set up a new plant in Detroit. Bodies for the V16 Cadillac came from both factories, those from Pennsylvania being distinguished by their vertical V-type windshields, as on this car. Detroit-built Fleetwoods had one-piece windshields at a slight angle.

OWNER: AUBURN-CORD-DUESENBERG MUSEUM

◁ The dashboard and instrument panel of the 1931 Cadillac V16. The panel is flanked by sheets of turned aluminum.

ART OF THE AMERICAN AUTOMOBILE

Custom Coachworks, which took over Brewster in 1926. Before long, fashion dictated a slight rearward slope to the windshield, and the unorthodox Brewster designs became obsolete, but they were examples of innovation from a coachbuilding house.

Some stylists worked as consultants to coach-builders who merely executed the designs. The best known of these was LeBaron, Carrossiers Inc., founded in 1920 by two young draftsmen, Thomas L. Hibbard and Raymond H. Dietrich. They met when both where working at Brewster, and they decided to set up a consultancy which would provide body designs which could be sold outright or for a percentage of the selling price. The name LeBaron was chosen simply because of its French sound. Both men were Francophiles, and indeed Hibbard had tried unsuccessfully to obtain a discharge from the Army during World War I in order to take a job with the prestigious Paris house of Kellner. Their first important commission was from William Durant, who had recently purchased Locomobile. He wanted to cut the expense of an in-house Custom Department (headed by Frank de Causse, who later became a consultant with commissions from Franklin), and at the same time keep a choice of up-to-date body styles.

At first LeBaron provided designs to two Bridgeport companies that were the main suppliers of coachwork to Locomobile, the Blue Ribbon Body Company and the Bridgeport Body Company. In 1924 the two firms merged and adopted the name LeBaron, which thus became a bodybuilder rather than simply a consultancy. Ray Dietrich was vice-president, chief engineer and sales manager, but Hibbard was only an associate as he had moved to Paris to form a partnership with Howard Darrin. In 1926 LeBaron was acquired by the Briggs Mfg. Company of Detroit, which was one of the largest body builders, with customers including Ford, Chrysler, Essex, Hudson, Overland and Willys-Knight. They retained LeBaron as a custom body subsidiary and, more important, as a source of ideas for mass-produced cars. During its ten years of existence, LeBaron came up with some 1,800 design ideas, many of which found their way onto mass-produced cars.

An example was the pennant-shaped raised panel, usually finished in a different color from the rest of the body, which started at the radiator, then

△ The 452-cubic-inch V16 Cadillac engine designed by Owen Nacker has been described as the first automobile engine to bear the mark of a stylist. A magnificent creation of chrome, polished aluminum, porcelain and enamel, it has a minimum of untidy wires which disfigured lesser engines. The banks of cylinders were at an angle of 45° and each had its own fuel distribution and exhaust system. Hydraulic valve silencers were used, and valves were overhead, operated from a single centrally-mounted camshaft. Displacement was 452 cubic inches, the largest in the American industry until the appearance of the 491-cubic-inch Marmon 16 in November 1930.

◁ The Cadillac V16 was identified by a circular medallion at the center of a concave tie-bar. Huge bowl headlights were featured, with trumpet horns beneath each light.

▽ ▷ CADILLAC V16 TOWN CAR

The Town Car was one of 54 body styles offered by Fleetwood on the Cadillac V16 chassis. The roof covering the chauffeur's compartment could be opened. Fleetwood's official name for the style was Transformable Town Cabriolet; most had closed, leather-covered upper rear quarter panels, though an alternative style had small rear quarter windows. The price of a five-passenger model was $7,000, while a seven-passenger, with two folding opera seats, cost $7,150. Prices on other V16s ran from $5,350 for a two-passenger roadster to $9,700 for a seven-passenger Town Brougham. The V16's best sales were in its first year, 1930, with more than 2,800 finding customers, but sales declined as the Depression deepened — only 364 in 1931 and fewer than 300 in 1932. The quality of the car also acted against repeat sales; it was so good that cutomers saw no reason to buy a new one for at least five years.

OWNER: AUBURN-CORD-DUESENBERG MUSEUM

broadened to the full width of the body at the windshield, continuing to form the belt line of the body. Hugo Pfau modified this to sweep back into the front doors, resulting in what was known as the "LeBaron sweep panel."

This was copied by other coachbuilders including Weymann, who used it on Duesenberg Js and SJs, and Central Mfg. Co. of Connersville, Indiana, who used it on Clark Gable's Duesenberg SSJ. Central also made bodies for Auburn, and the LeBaron sweep was seen on its speedsters and even on the tiny American Austin roadster which was styled by Alexis de Sakhnoffsky. A variation, in which the panel swept low through the front door to the rear, was used on some Chryslers around 1930.

One of the first stylists to break from the anonymity of the early days was J. Frank de Causse (1879-1928). Born in France, he studied architecture and art history, and was apparently bitten by the horseless carriage bug early on. He combined

his interests by joining the prestigious Paris house of Kellner as an apprentice draftsman. In 1904, when he was 25, he became assistant manager, a post he held until he was lured from Kellner by Locomobile in the fall of 1914. The prestigious Bridgeport company had used outside coachbuilders up to this date, but then decided that an in-house design office would be advantageous. The company never actually built the bodies, which were made by such firms as Demarest, Healy, Holbrook and Locke to the designs of de Causse.

Within a few years, a distinct de Causse style began to appear; characteristics included flat panels for hood sides and doors, the horizontal proportions of the former becoming vertical in the latter, and a wide double parallel stripe on the sides of the hood and running along the tops of the doors through to the rear of the body. His designs encompassed most of the standard types fitted to expensive cars, limousines, landaulets and town cars, but it was

△ 1932 DV32 STUTZ MONTE CARLO
Stutz was a highly regarded name with many sporting achievements to its credit. From 1929 to the end of production in 1935, only two engine sizes were offered, a six and a 322-cubic-inch in-line eight. It was available in two forms, the SV16 and DV32, the letters standing for Single Valve and Dual Valve respectively, and the figures representing the number of valves. This 1932 DV32 was called the Monte Carlo sedan ("Strictly European in every detail," claimed Stutz advertising) and has a Weymann body. This used fabric paneling over a wooden frame, though from 1933 aluminum paneling was used. Production was very limited, about 125 in 1932, 110 in 1933, and six in 1934. Figures for 1935 are not known. Amazingly, 55 models were listed in 1933. The 1932 Monte Carlo sold for $4,895 (or $5,895 with the DV32 engine). Top of the range was the Transformable Town Car by Fleetwood, which sold for a whopping $7,495.
OWNER: GILMORE CAR MUSEUM, KALAMAZOO, MiCHIGAN

among his open cars that his originality really showed. These included canoe-type four-passenger roadsters with pointed tails, and a Type Sportif four-passenger with a separate tonneau cowl and windshield for the rear-seat passengers. This was built in 1916 for Rodman Wanamaker and was the first of the design which came to be known as the dual-cowl phaeton. It was very popular in the 1920s, and is often considered by collectors to be the most desirable style available.

Few people have given de Causse and Locomobile credit for this pioneering design. We do not know how much input came from Mr. Wanamaker, for customers often discussed the work with designers at every stage. Although his first designs for Locomobile had sidemounted spare wheels, de Causse soon moved these to the rear where they gave the cars a rakish appearance. Some of his designs had military-looking, flat-topped fenders, probably inspired by World War I. Among them were two actual military vehicles, the limousines built for General John Pershing for use in Europe. They had narrow bodies, dual rear tires and sloping windshields. Pershing liked to be driven fast and found that at 80mph the vertical windshield tended to crack, hence the sloping V-shaped design which was far in advance of its time.

△ This view of the Stutz Monte Carlo shows its low lines, characteristic of the make since the introduction of the Safety Stutz in 1926. This had an underslung worm drive which allowed for exceptionally low bodies.

▷ The Stutz mascot was the Egyptian Sun God, Ra.

ART OF THE AMERICAN AUTOMOBILE

△ The instrument panel and exterior styling details of the Stutz Monte Carlo have a European feel, with much more wood than that of the Duesenberg or Cadillac. Charles Weymann, whose entire American output of bodies was taken by Stutz in 1928-30, was a Frenchman, so the European feel is perhaps not surprising.

△ The Stutz's in-line eight engine was designed by Charles "Pop" Greuter, a Swiss-born engineer who had built his own car as early as 1896 and had subsequently worked for the Holyoke and Matheson companies in America. This is the twin-camshaft 32-valve DV32 model. Theoretically these engines were available in all models, at a cost of $1,000 over that of the SV16-powered chassis.

De Causse's Locomobiles were among the most expensive American cars of their day. With interior fittings designed by Tiffany and colors planned by the actress and interior decorator Elsie de Wolf, they cost up to $8,500. Customers were a cross-section of wealthy East Coast families and individuals: Vanderbilts, William Carnegie, Lolita Armour, Lawrence Copley Thaw, and two of the Wanamakers, Rodman and John. Locomobile sales were good in the years 1915 to 1920, but a lot of material was bought on credit, and when the banks began to call in their loans, the company got into difficulties. It went into receivership in March 1922, and though it was rescued by Emlen Hare and later, more successfully, by Billy Durant, the Custom Body Department was sacrificed.

Frank de Causse set up his own office as a consultant and obtained commissions from his old partners, Demarest, Healy and Locke. He also designed some open and closed bodies for German-made Benz chassis, which were built by the little-known Schildwachter Autobody Company. Four styles were proposed, but how many were actually built is not known. Another commission came from Durant, who asked him to style the Flint, a new medium-priced car he was planning to put on the market. Durant still regarded de Causse as his associate and was therefore highly incensed when

the designer was approached by H.H. Franklin to style a new line for his 1925 models. Franklin had admired de Causse's work on Locomobiles for several years, and rejected a Murphy design for the new Franklin in favor of de Causse's.

The 1925 Franklin was a radical change for the Syracuse company; previous models with their horse-collar shaped front ends were increasingly hard to sell, and a group of major dealers threatened to switch to other makes if something was not done. The new models had virtually nothing in common with their predecessors apart from their air-cooled engines and wooden frames. De Causse had been given carte blanche by Franklin to style the car from front to rear. A wide rectangular "radiator" gave the car the appearance of a water-cooled model; the body lines, though very far from streamlined, were much cleaner and lighter than most contemporary

designs. In particular, the framework surrounding the windshield and doors was lightened in appearance by the use of slim but strong metal pillars in place of wooden ones.

The prototypes were shown at the 1924 New York Salon at the Commodore Hotel, though not without some conniving on the part of de Causse. The Salon was a very exclusive affair, open only to invited guests and to prestige car makers and coach-builders. No Ford or Chevy ever entered its portals. The organizers were happy to welcome Frank de Causse when he had Locomobiles to display, but they had never admitted Franklins, and rejected them on the grounds that they must surely have cost less than $5,000. De Causse answered that they cost $10,000 each, whereupon they were admitted. It was true that the hand-built prototypes had cost at least $10,000, but the price tags on the

production models started at $2,700.

In fact, it was not even revealed that they were Franklins until the spring of 1925. De Causse worked mainly from his New York studio, though in close consultation with Franklin's Body Department chief, W. H. Emond. His designs were built for Franklin by Willoughby, a respected coachbuilder located conveniently at Utica, some 40 miles east of Syracuse.

Frank de Causse did not believe in annual face-lifts; in a rare public pronouncement, he said "The dictates of good taste in automobile design cannot be observed when frequent changes in body features occur." His designs for Franklin lasted longer than he did, for he succumbed to cancer in May 1928, at the age of 48. He was succeeded by Ray Dietrich, who continued many of de Causse's ideas up to 1933.

◁ △ PACKARD ELEVENTH SERIES SUPER EIGHT COUPE-ROADSTER

Although it was in the top league of American quality cars, Packard did not have a great deal to do with custom coachbuilders, as it had its own body department which produced excellent, if largely conservative, designs. However, with the arrival of the 12-cylinder Twelve in 1932, custom styles began to be offered in the range, by such firms as Dietrich and LeBaron. All 1934 models were known as the Eleventh Series, a sequence started in 1924 (First Series) and continuing to the 26th Series in 1953. This is an Eleventh Series Super Eight two/four passenger coupe-roadster, which sold for $3,070. Its styling combines modern features like fender skirts and a slanted windshield with Packard's traditional vertical radiator. In 1935 this gave way to a slanting radiator, except on the Twelve, and this followed the smaller cars for the 1936 season. The stylish mascot is a non-standard option.

OWNER: DOOR PRAIRIE MUSEUM

△ HARLEY EARL (1893-1969)
Founder of General Motors' Art & Colour department in 1928, which
has shaped the cars – and the stylists – ever since. Buicks, Cadillacs,
La Salles, Chevrolets, Oldsmobiles and Pontiacs all got the Earl treatment.
He is pictured here at the wheel of the 1951 Le Sabre.
PHOTO: GENERAL MOTORS

CHAPTER TWO

MORE THAN THE FROSTING ON THE ENGINEER'S CAKE

"Nobody could have put General Motors into the design
business like Harley did because Harley had the guts,
he had the size, he had the vision, he had the eyes,
he had everything to do it with."

Frank Hershey, designer at GM from 1928 until 1950

I N AN ACUTE observation on the great stylist Harley Earl (1893-1969), historian Michael Lamm said Earl's contribution to the American economy was to make styling "more than the frosting on the engineer's cake." Through his work at General Motors from 1927 to his retirement in 1959, he made styling and color essential ingredients of the annual model change; it was this annual change, more marked in the American industry than anywhere else in the world, that has kept the factories going. He shares the credit with the two men who recognized his potential and became his friends, GM president Alfred P. Sloan and Cadillac president Lawrence P. Fisher.

Harley J. Earl was born in Los Angeles in November 1893. By the age of 16 he was modeling cars out of clay which he dug from the ground on the family vacation ranch in the Tehachapi Mountains. His father, J.W. Earl, operated a carriage shop which built and repaired horse-drawn vehicles,

△ 1927 LA SALLE ROADSTER
Harley Earl stands next to a 1927 La Salle roadster, one of 11 styles available in the car's first year. His height of 6' 4" makes the car seem smaller than it was.

◁ 1927 LA SALLE SEDAN
On this four-door, five-passenger sedan, the artillery wheels were standard, but more handsome wire wheels, as on the roadster, were an option.
PHOTOS: GENERAL MOTORS

and all his four sons worked there, if only on a part-time basis after school. In 1908 the Earl Carriage Works became the Earl Automobile Works, making accessory windshields, wire- and wood-spoked wheels, tops, and seats. They began building complete bodies in 1911, and Harley doubtless had some say in their design. When he was 21, his father sent him to Stanford University to study law, but he became ill and did not complete the course. Once back in Hollywood, he soon became immersed in the family business, taking over from his father during the next few years.

When the Earls setttled in Hollywood in 1900, it was a small rural village without even one hotel. The first commercial building, the Hollywood Hotel, opened in 1903. It had 33 rooms and two baths. Ten years later, the infant movie industry had emerged, the hotel was upgraded to 100 rooms and 66 baths, and the Earl Automobile Works had a new kind of customer. Many of the early movies had period settings, and the Earls were commissioned to build Roman chariots, Napoleonic carriages, and royal coaches. By 1919, movie stars and producers were ordering custom bodies for their cars from the Earl works, and Harley was largely responsible for these. His customers chose makes like Cadillac and Pierce-Arrow for their quality, but they were not happy with the sober styling that was the norm east of the Rockies. Harley's first commissions, therefore, were not for complete bodies, but for dramatically reworked and embellished factory bodies. Disk or wire wheels replaced the sober

artilleries, spare tires were side-mounted rather than at the back, windshield angles were raked, fancy trunks or golf racks were added at the rear; above all, the bodies were painted in brighter colors. The flamboyance of the stars and the bright hues that were part of the California landscape led him to an uninhibited use of color not seen in previous auto bodies. A preoccupation with color was one of Harley Earl's characteristics in later life.

Earl's first customized cars to attract press attention were a Marmon phaeton and a Chandler town car, both of which were shown at the Los Angeles Auto Show in January 1919. "These cars are designed by Harley J. Earl," said the *Los Angeles Times*, "…who has sprung into prominence as a maker of motor fashions almost overnight." Much was made of the fact that the customer for the Marmon was a New York banker who had the cream of the traditional coachbuilders on his doorstep, yet chose to order his bodywork from California. The

car cost him $7,000, when a regular Marmon 34 four-passenger roadster could be had for $4,000. The *L.A. Times* pointed out that many of the Earl factory workforce of nearly 100 men came from eastern firms such as Fleetwood, Holbrook and Packard.

In July 1919 the Earl Automobile Works was bought by Cadillac dealer Don Lee, who immediately changed its name to the Don Lee Coach & Body Works. Harley Earl retained his position as chief designer and continued to produce

▽   1934 LA SALLE SERIES 350 CONVERTIBLE COUPE
In 1934 La Salle styling diverged from Cadillac's more noticeably than before. Styling was by Jules Agramonte, working under Harley Earl's direction. The Series 350 convertible coupe sold for $1,695.
OWNER: ROBERT LUTZ, CHRYSLER CORPORATION

innovative styling for stars such as Pauline Frederick, Anne May, Mary Miles Minter, Jack Pickford, and in particular Roscoe "Fatty" Arbuckle, who had at least three Earl-designed cars.

The last was the most flamboyant, and fortunately it still survives today. It was based on the massive Pierce-Arrow Model 66, already an obsolete model by 1919, with the largest displacement engine of any American car, at 824 cubic inches. The radiator was redesigned and only the "A" pierced by an arrow above the radiator cap gave a clue to the chassis' identity. The Pierce-Arrow frog headlights were replaced by huge drum-type lights, while the body was restyled completely. It flowed in a straight line from radiator to windshield, and the belt line from there to the rear was dipped, making the car seem lower than it was. The body cost has been estimated at $28,000, with the chassis adding another $6,000. This total of $34,000 is equivalent to around $700,000 today.

Over the next few years, the Don Lee Coach & Body Works began to make less flamboyant bodies in longer runs. In 1925 they placed an order for 100 Cadillac chassis which were then fitted with Don Lee custom bodies. This naturally drew the attention of Cadillac's new president, Lawrence P. Fisher, who soon struck a personal rapport with Harley Earl. As Michael Lamm observed, "While Earl wasn't in Fisher's league as a playboy, he could keep up with L.P. on a bar stool, on the fairway, as a clothes horse, and on the topics of cars, sports, money and people." At one Los Angeles party, Earl said to Fisher, "I can make a car for you, like your Chevrolet, to look like a Cadillac." "If you can do that," Fisher replied, "you've got yourself a job."

Fisher and GM president Alfred P. Sloan were in agreement on the need for styling as a positive ingredient in the popular car. In addition to the basic attraction of a better-looking product, styling was valuable commercially, as relatively small and inexpensive changes could be made annually. This was the concept of planned obsolescence, anathema to traditional designers like Frank de Causse, or manufacturers like Henry Ford. To Sloan, a primary function of a new model was to create a certain amount of dissatisfaction with the old one. To Henry, it seemed ridiculous that a 1923 model should be rejected because it did not look like a 1925. "We want the man who buys one of our

products never to have to buy another." His sales force may not have sympathized with this attitude, but we understand what he meant. However, the Sloan philosophy prevailed, and by the 1930s Fords were undergoing annual cosmetic changes just like all other cars.

One of Sloan's most important ideas was a multi-pronged attack on the market, "a car for every price and purpose." In 1926 he already had Chevrolet for the mass market, followed by Pontiac, new that year, Oldsmobile, Buick and Cadillac; but he saw the need for a car of Cadillac quality, but somewhat smaller in size and lower in price. Style would clearly be very important for such a car, and it was

with the specific purpose of designing it that he invited Harley Earl to Detroit. The car was to be called the La Salle, in honor of the French nobleman and explorer René Robert Cavalier de la Salle, who claimed Louisiana in 1682 for his king, Louis XIV.

Earl moved East in January 1926, and the design of the new car took about three months. Earl had only one assistant, a wood modeler named Ralph Pew, but his four full-size mock-ups were modeled in clay. Earl had used this medium in California, and his interest in it may have dated from his boyhood days, but it was new to Detroit. He made four models – a roadster, a convertible coupe, an open

tourer and a sedan. Earl openly admitted that he took his inspiration for the La Salle from the French-built Hispano-Suiza, a car he admired above all others. "When you are a designer, you kind of think, 'well, if I were building a car for myself from the chassis up, what would I do?' The Hispano was a car I was deeply in love with, from stem to stern. I didn't want to take too big a chance and do something that didn't look like anything." From the Hisso came the strong peaked radiator shape with its winged emblem, the big bowl headlights with badge tie-bar between them, and the graceful front fenders. The two-tone color schemes were Earl's own. The hood, fenders and top were in a darker color, which might be black, brown, dark blue, with the body panels in lighter tones. Only the top of the line semi-custom bodies by Fleetwood did not have dual-tone paintwork.

Sloan and Fisher approved the clay models as soon as they saw them, and although that particular commission was complete, Earl was invited to accompany Sloan to the Paris Salon in October 1926. There Sloan commissioned several designs from Hibbard & Darrin, a Paris-based firm operated by two Americans, Thomas Hibbard, who had been with LeBaron, and Howard "Dutch" Darrin.

The La Salle was launched to great acclaim in March 1927, winning several styling awards in the U.S. and in Europe. Sales in the 1927 and 1928 model years (1927 was less than half a year) were 26,807 cars, beating those of the parent Cadillac. In fact, apart from 1937, La Salle never sold so well again, and the line was dropped after 1940, but that was in no way Harley Earl's fault. The 1927 La Salle has its place in history as the first mass-produced car to be designed by a stylist.

Although Earl returned to California after completing his work on the La Salle, he was not to remain there for long. Alfred Sloan's own words (from his autobiography, *My Years with General Motors*), tell the story. "I was so impressed with Mr. Earl's work that I decided to obtain the advantages of his talents for other General Motors car divisions. On June 23, 1927, I took up with the executive committee a plan to establish a special department to study the question of art and color combinations in General Motors products. Fifty persons would make up the department, ten of them designers and the rest shop workers and clerical and

◁ △   1934 LA SALLE
The 1934 La Salle was the epitome of mid-'30s Harley Earl styling, with its fully skirted pontoon fenders curving over the front wheels and tall, narrow grille which completely disguised the practical function of a radiator. It was a radical change from the 1933 La Salles, yet the changes were acceptable to the public, unlike the more radical Chrysler Airflow. Also noteworthy are the "biplane" bumpers and chrome chevrons on the leading edge of the fenders.

▷   The 1934 La Salle's hood emblem.

△ The La Salle's black-faced dials with white numbering came, like the engines, from Oldsmobile. It was only by sourcing many components from other GM divisions that the La Salle's price could be kept low, at least $1,000 below equivalent Cadillacs.

△ The 1934 La Salle's engine was an in-line eight made by Oldsmobile. Dimensions were the same as those of the engines used on Olds cars, but output was 5hp greater.

▷ The porthole hood ventilators, five on each side, were another innovative feature on the 1934 La Salle. Portholes, which lasted only two seasons on La Salles, would become a Buick feature after World War II.

administrative assistants. I invited Mr. Earl to head this new department, which we called the Art & Colour Section. Mr. Earl's duties were to direct general production body design, and to conduct research and development programs in special car designs."

Harley Earl and his family moved to Detroit in the fall of 1927, and on January 1, 1928, the Art & Colour Section officially became a part of General Motors organization. The English spelling of colour was always used.

O UR FATHER WHO ART IN STYLING, HARLEY BE THY NAME ...
The American auto industry has never been more blessed with the right man at the right time than it was when Harley Earl moved to Detroit. His influence was incalculable, not just in the way he capitalized on the public's emerging demand for style in everyday objects, but also in the "nursery" his Art & Colour Section provided for stylists who went on to other companies. Almost all the great names in styling from the 1930s to the 1960s worked at some time in Art & Colour: Gene Bordinat (Ford), Gordon Buehrig (Auburn and Cord), Elwood Engel (Chrysler), Frank Hershey (Pontiac and Ford), Al Leamy (Auburn and Cord), Strother McMinn (Pasadena Art Center of Design), Richard Teague (Packard and AMC), John Tjaarda

(Lincoln Zephyr), and Alex Tremulis (Tucker) to mention only a few. Also there was Bill Mitchell, who took over from Earl in 1959, and headed GM styling until 1977.

Earl dominated his realm not only by his skills and personality, but by his sheer physical presence. At 6' 4" tall, and weighing around 220 pounds, he was literally looked up to by his staff. Added to this basic advantage were a very strong personality, boundless self-confidence, and it must be admitted, an understanding and close friendship with Alfred Sloan which, in the last resort, enabled him to get his own way. Bill Mitchell recalls, "In the summer he'd go on a cruise with Sloan on his yacht down in the Atlantic. We'd make up books on the new ideas he'd sell him."

That yacht figured large in people's awe of Earl; another designer, on the styling of the 1941 Cadillac Sixty Special said, "The executives were hemming and hawing, and they didn't know whether they were going to take it or not... He looked down on them, and finally he couldn't stand it any longer. He got red in the face and said 'Gentlemen, what am I going to tell Mr. Sloan when he asks me?' They approved the car in ten minutes... They knew he had Sloan's ear. He could talk Sloan into doing anything he wanted. How many guys spent a month or so on Sloan's yacht every year?"

Like most successful leaders, Earl inspired not only respect from his subordinates, but awe and fear as well. Gordon Buehrig said, "All of us designers were afraid of him; at least I was."

"He just scared the hell out of you," another recalled, "because he was a very tall, very imposing sort of guy. When he came back from vacation in Florida, he would come through the studios and everybody would know – almost like a magnetic presence – that he was around, somewhere. There was a hot line. 'God, Harley's on the first floor, he's on the second floor… he's in the Buick studio…' He really kind of terrified people." Not without reason was it said "Our father who art in styling, Harley be thy name."

Frank Hershey, who worked with Earl from 1928 to 1950, summed up his boss in these words: "Nobody could have put General Motors into the design business like Harley did because Harley had the guts, he had the size, he had the vision, he had the eyes, he had everything to do it with."

Surprisingly, Earl was no draftsman and he was a poor communicator. He had to tell others what he wanted drawn, and his vocabulary was limited and unique to himself. "I want that line to have a duflunky, to come across, have a little hook on it, and then do a little rashoom or a zong," was a typical instruction. Needless to say, his subordinates soon learned to interpret these cryptic requests. Thomas L. Hibbard, who left his Paris coachbuilding business Hibbard & Darrin to join GM in 1932, said, "I never saw Earl wield a pencil or make a design suggestion on paper."

Chevrolet designer Kenneth Coppock said of Earl that he was not a designer, but a superb critic of design. "He took an active part in all our designs; his system was mainly to let each studio come up with lots of its own ideas and sketches. Then he'd sit down and go over them as a critic. He'd pick out one or two concepts worth exploring, and we'd proceed from there. He frequently would come into Chevrolet with ideas from the other studios. We never knew that exactly, but I always suspected that was his technique. He'd sort of play one studio against the other. He was very good at that, too. 'Oh boy,' he'd say, 'They've got a design over in the Pontiac studios that's a good one. You guys aren't coming up with them like they are'." In fact, up to 1937, the GM studios were in one large room divided by huge blackboards; while the Pontiac stylists couldn't see what the Oldmobile boys were doing, they could certainly hear them. "Sometimes paper airplanes would sail over the blackboards from the next studio, as a kind of friendly harassment," recalled Strother McMinn. All this coziness came to an end in 1937 when a new building called Research Annex B was completed, with the top four floors given over to styling studios. Each marque now had its own room with clay modeling facilities, air-conditioning to keep clay models at a constant temperature, compressed air lines for airbrush illustrations, and locked doors. At the same time, the name Art & Colour Section gave way to Styling Section.

Harley Earl created little, but he had an unerring eye for the best ideas of others. "If you showed him ten drawings on the wall, he'd pick the best one every time." His eye was such that he could see a drawing from 40 feet away and call out, "I thought I told you to lower that line."

He would look at a vast number of designs before making a final choice; John Foster

▽ 1956 FIREBIRD II
The gas-turbine Firebird II of 1956 was one of Harley Earl's pet projects. Widely seen at Motoramas across the nation, the Firebird was the American industry's first gas-turbine passenger car suitable for highway use.
PHOTO: GENERAL MOTORS

(Oldsmobile studio, 1930s) said "My biggest recollection is of details, doing 1,800 tail lights and 400 hood ornaments and 300 side ornaments; hubcaps by the hundreds – there always seemed to be an indecisive area where nobody could decide what a thing should look like."

Contrary to some suggestions, Earl did not work directly in clay; even in his California days, he produced two-dimensional drawings, front, side and rear elevations, first. At GM he always insisted on the prime importance of drawings, even though he did not do them himself. Woe betide any designer who made a clay model without having drawings to show as well.

THE ART & COLOUR SECTION

The use of color in automobile bodies became much more significant after the introduction of quick-drying Duco Satin Finish paint. Harley Earl would not have had much to keep his section busy had it not been for the work of the Paint and Enamel Committee. Before 1924 the only rapid-drying paint was black enamel. Colors required multiple applications and took up to 14 days to dry, hence Henry Ford's remark that you could have a Model T in any color so long as it was black. Sloan assigned Charles Kettering, more famous for his integrated electric lighting and starting system on the 1912 Cadillac, to the development of a fast-drying color lacquer, which was first seen on the 1924 Oaklands. Essentially a nitro-cellulose lacquer solution, it had been developed originally by the DuPont laboratories and was perfected for automotive use by Kettering's team. Its use cut the time required to paint an Oakland body from 336 to 13 hours, and as a bonus, the material cost was lower, at $2.26 per car against $2.33 for the older paints. It would soon be available in all the colors of the rainbow, but the 1924 Oaklands came in blue only, earning that model the name "True Blue Oakland Six."

Duco paints were also adopted by Chevrolet in 1924, followed by other GM Divisions such as Buick and Oldsmobile. Ford reluctantly offered two colors (dark green and dark maroon) on the 1926 Model Ts, ending a 12-year reign of "Any Color so Long as it is Black." The final Model Ts of the 1927

season came in seven colors, though they were less striking than those on Chevrolets.

The first Chevrolets to show the influence of the Art & Colour Section were the International Model ACs of 1929, which were also the first to use the new "Stove Bolt Six" engine, which would remain without major change until 1955. Sheet-metal changes included a new cowl, hood, and fenders, and a more attractive radiator shell.

Another early design to issue from Art & Colour was less successful. Buick was celebrating its Silver Anniversary in 1929 and wanted a new model. The most distinctive feature of Earl's design was the elimination of the usual molding along the belt line, replaced by a slight bulge, running from the bottom of the windows forward into the radiator. Earl's intention was that the bulge would emphasize length in a more subtle way than conventional molding. Unfortunately, the engineers didn't follow his instructions when making the dies, and in the car itself, the bulge was much more pronounced.

△ 1938 BUICK Y-JOB
Earl's first concept car for GM. The grille was copied almost exactly on regular Buicks for 1942, but the concealed headlights never made it onto a production Buick.
PHOTO: GENERAL MOTORS

▷ 1959 FIREBIRD III
Harley Earl standing next to Firebird III which was developed by a "brains trust" under Earl's direction, and revealed in 1959, the year of his retirement. Airplane influence is very evident in the dual bubble canopies and fins. Two engines were used, a regenerative turbine and an auxiliary to power all the accessories, which included throttle and braking. Control was through a stick: forward for acceleration, back for braking, right for right turn and so on.
PHOTO: GENERAL MOTORS

▷ Harley Earl with four concept cars – the Buick Y-Job, Firebird I, Firebird II, and Le Sabre.
PHOTO: GENERAL MOTORS

ART OF THE AMERICAN AUTOMOBILE

Buick called it the Silver Anniversary Model, but the public soon dubbed it the Pregnant Buick. Magazines were usually very sparing in their criticism of new cars in those days, but the motoring editor of *Country Life* wrote "The appearance of this model... is not as fortunate as it might be. Too bad, for the model preceding it was such a swell looking turnout." The buyers stayed away in droves, Buick's market share fell to less than half what it had been the year before, and for 1930 straight lines were back again.

One can imagine that after this debacle Earl was more insistent that his designs were incorporated in the dies before production was authorized. He never had a comparable disaster and wisely avoided the way-out streamlining of Chrysler's Airflow. He distrusted the scientific evidence in favor of aerodynamics, instinctively knowing that the public was innately conservative. Instead, he concentrated on various parts of the car, which over four years led to an integrated design, less dramatic than the Airflow but much more saleable.

The first step was to integrate the trunk with the rear of the sedan body. Up to the 1933 season, luggage accommodation on standard cars was limited to a folding platform to which cases had to

be strapped. The few built-on trunks which had been seen were custom items and were more like boxes than integral parts of the bodywork. The integrated trunk was seen on some 1933 models, such as the Chevrolet Master Eagle town sedan and the Buick Victoria Coupe. Two other important steps in Chevrolet design were a swept rear to the sedan body, in which the back curved outwards at the bottom, instead of being tucked in as on the '32s, and the appearance of skirts on the front fenders. The swept tail, or beaver tail, was called the Airstream design, a name adopted by Chrysler for their less radical cars of 1935. Fender skirts, which became almost universal by 1934, had been pioneered by Amos Northup of the Murray Body Co., and first seen on the Graham Blue Streak Eight of 1932.

For 1934, Chevrolet sedans had either beaver tails and luggage racks, or integral trunks. The spare wheel was still external, behind the trunk, but from 1936 it was carried internally on the sedans, but still outside on coupes. Sloan approved of the built-in trunk as it altered the proportions of the car, making it longer and apparently lower, as well as offering practical protection from the weather.

Another important step toward integrated design was GM's introduction of the all-steel "turret top" on 1935 Cadillacs, La Salles, Oldsmobiles and Pontiacs, and 1936 Buicks and Chevrolets. The one-piece curved roofs were stamped out on huge 500-ton presses, the use of which dictated the form. U.S. Steel's high-speed strip mill provided sheet metal in 88-inch strips. It is said that Harley Earl favored big, swooping curves over angular lines, and it is fortunate that he did, for curves were inextricably linked with the new manufacturing process. As Bill Mitchell (who favored a more angular appearance) said, "When they went to steel bodies, they couldn't get those sharp lines, and thus the big radiuses came in... you had to make that to get the die out."

The curvilinear style also spread to fenders. For years, front fenders had been straight or slightly concave in shape, and this was continued after skirts

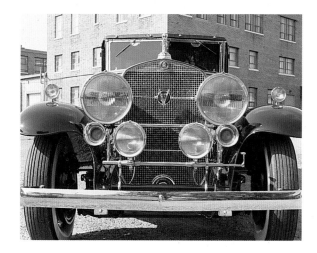

△ The 1931 Cadillac V16 shows no move towards the integated styling of the later 1930s. The wheels are exposed, and the headlights separate from the hood.

▽ The Duesenberg Model J has radiator shutters and more decorative bumpers than the Cadillac.

came in on the 1933 models. A more bulbous shape was first seen on the special Cadillac V16 coupe built for the 1933 Chicago Century of Progress Exposition. This was a very important car, the first of Earl's showcars which were to float ideas before the public. Later, equally significant cars were the Buick Y-Job of 1938 and Le Sabre of 1951. In addition to the bulbous, or pontoon, fenders, the Cadillac featured a V-windshield and fastback coupe styling. The latter was much admired by Gordon Buehrig who was working for GM at the time, and clearly inspired his Cord 810 of 1936.

Pontoon fenders were seen on the regular Cadillacs and La Salles for 1934, and for 1936 were adopted on Buicks, Chevrolets, Oldsmobiles and Pontiacs. The pontoon effect became even more pronounced in the years 1937 to 1941, and then the fenders on the 1942 models from all GM Divisions were tentatively extended into the front doors, starting the process which was to lead to total integration by 1949. However, the first GM car to have fenders extended into the front doors was not American at all; it came from the German Opel factory, where Frank Hershey and his assistant George Jergenson styled the advanced Kapitan sedan. Designed in 1936 and in production from December 1938 to October 1940, and again after the war, the Kapitan had rectangular headlights fully faired into the fenders as well as the extensions into the doors. These were features which Hershey would like to have included on American cars, but were prevented by the cost. From 1936 on, the rear fenders on GM cars mirrored those at the front in their shape.

△ The 1928 Auburn radiator is styled to the extent of a bar down the center but there is not a grille yet.

The expense of the heavy presses led to sharing of body styles between the different GM Divisons. Chevrolet had the largest output, so their bodies were engineered and styled by themselves, and the lower volume divisions like Buick, Olds and Pontiac had to share the Chevy's central body. Fenders, grille, hood and trunk were the responsibility of the individual division. This applied to the '36 models; by 1941 body sharing had become widespread. The 1939 Chevrolet B-body sedan was seen on the 1940 Buick Century, Oldsmobile Sixty and Pontiac DeLuxe. Also featured in 1940 was the C-body, a more modern style inspired by the 1938 Cadillac Sixty Special. A low and sleek-looking four-door, four-window sedan, the C-body was available on the Buick Series 50 Super and Series 70 Roadmaster, Cadillac Series 62, La Salle Special, Oldsmobile Ninety and Pontiac Torpedo Eight. For 1941 came a new B series of fastback sedans and coupes on Buick, Cadillac, Oldsmobile and Pontiac chassis.

If bodies were becoming more uniform, the different makes had to be distinguished by other means, and Harley Earl was aware of the supreme importance of the front end. In 1933, he said, "The most important part of the design of an automobile is the grille, the face of it. That is the whole design,

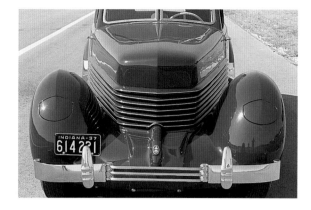

△ The Cord 810 was a dramatic styling breakthrough with its concealed headlights and wraparound grille.

▽ The 1934 La Salle was less striking than the Cord, but it was two years older. Harley Earl did not favor being too far ahead of public taste.

right there." In the 1920s the grille did not exist; the vertical honeycomb radiator fronted the hood, and any distinguishing features between different makes were provided by the shape of the radiator and its surrounds. Then radiator guards appeared, while some expensive cars such as Lincoln had thermostatic shutters. V-shaped grilles arrived on the 1932 Graham and 1933 GM cars, and from 1936 onwards, grilles broke out in a riot of fencers' masks (1936 Buick), ships' prows (1936 Lincoln Zephyr), waterfalls (1936 Pontiac, 1939 Chrysler), and butterflies (1941 Dodge). Naturally all manufacturers joined in the craze for highly decorated grilles, but the lead came from GM's Art & Colour Section.

Up to 1938, with the exception of Gordon Buehrig's radical Cord 810, all American cars had vertical grilles which, however ornate, filled the whole space from the bumper up to the top of the hood. For once, Earl's studios were not first in the field to break away from this, that honor going to Bob Gregorie's 1938 Lincoln Zephyr. For 1939, however, practically the whole industry turned to divided two- or three-piece grilles, or if single, as on the 1939 Buick, they were horizontal and occupied only the lower part of the front end. The only exceptions were Packard and the

▽ By 1941 nearly all American cars had abandoned the veritcal grille occupying the whole of the front end. This is a Lincoln Continental.

top models from Cadillac and Lincoln.

Headlights began to be mounted in the front fenders on the Cord 810 and Lincoln Zephyr, and this idea became standard practice by 1940. Significantly, the trend had been foretold as early as 1931, when no cars actually featured it. Writing in the *SAE* (Society of Automotive Engineers) *Journal* of January 7, 1931, L. Clayton Hill, chairman of the Body Section of the SAE, said "I think lamps are going to disappear as individual units out in front of the car; they will be built into the car. We shall gradually lead the public up to this by incorporating lamps into the radiator, then in the bonnet [hood], and finally the fenders into the hood and lamps. Almost before we are aware of it, the whole front end of the car will be made as one streamlined unit."

After World War II, other parts of the car became distinctive styling points. Portholes meant Buick, tailfins were Cadillac, rockets symbolized Oldsmobile, silver streaks were instant identification for Pontiac. These, too, were designs sanctioned by Harley Earl, but it was his work on the GM cars of the 1930s which made that decade the most important in American auto design. In no other decade were the cars at the end so different from those at the beginning.

△ BILL MITCHELL (b. 1912)

Mitchell was hired by Earl at GM's Art & Colour section in 1935 and the following year became head of the Cadillac studio. His first major achievement there was the 1938 Sixty Special. He is pictured here with his 1966 Mako Shark II.

PHOTO: GENERAL MOTORS

CHAPTER THREE

"GASOLINE IN YOUR VEINS" – THE INFLUENCE OF BILL MITCHELL

"If I hadn't gone to work for Barron Collier and been around the Collier boys' cars, I'd probably be a Buick dealer today."

Bill Mitchell

LTHOUGH HARLEY EARL remained at the head of GM's design studios until 1959, he was supported throughout by many talented designers who submitted ideas to him. Most prominent among these was Bill Mitchell, who took over as Vice President, Styling, in 1959. The title is slightly misleading – like Earl, he was not the vice-president of the styling division, but an executive vice-president of General Motors, alongside VPs of engineering, research, manufacturing, and finance.

Bill Mitchell was born in Cleveland, Ohio, in 1912 and raised in Pennsylvania, the son of a Buick dealer who took as trade-ins many exotic cars such as Mercers and Stutzes. These would be repainted and modified for re-sale, and to young Mitchell they were doubtless more exciting than his father's new Buicks. So he had "gasoline in his veins" from an early age, something he said was essential in order to become a real car designer. Although he was sent to the Carnegie Institute of Technology in Pittsburgh, he was more interested in drawing than

◁ Bill Mitchell at his drawing board at GM Design.
PHOTO: GENERAL MOTORS

◁ Mitchell with two of his favorite cars; behind him the Sting Ray racer of 1959, and in front the production Corvette Sting Ray coupe of 1963.
PHOTO: GENERAL MOTORS

△ Mitchell with the 1959 Sting Ray, and behind him some of the cars with which he was associated; the Buick Y-Job and Le Sabre in the far background, the 1963 Buick Riviera on the left, Corvette and Corvair prototypes in the center.
PHOTO: GENERAL MOTORS

engineering and soon moved to the Art Students' League in New York, where he studied nights while holding a day job as an illustrator at Barron Collier Advertising Agency. This was one of the leading agencies, famous for its creative staff, both writers and artists, which numbered Scott Fitzgerald among its copywriters. Bill Mitchell became friendly with Barron Collier's three sons, Barron, Jr., Sam, and Miles, and together the young men raced sports cars, MGs, Rileys and homemade jobs, around the driveways on the Collier estate, Overlook, in the Pocantico Hills up the Hudson River valley. Later, Mitchell would admit his debt to the Colliers, who showed his drawings to a friend of Harley Earl. "My working for the Colliers shaped my life… my father was a small-town Buick dealer in Pennsylvania. If I hadn't gone to work for Barron Collier and been around the Collier boys' cars, I'd probably be a Buick dealer today."

This is overly modest – his talent would have found an outlet somewhere, though he might never have gone to General Motors. As it was, the Colliers' friend, insurance exective Walter Carey, invited Mitchell to send some drawings to Harley Earl. The response (from Earl's assistant Howard O'Leary) was "These are real cars; now make up some designs." The made-up designs, which included a gorgeous swoopy-line convertible with front and rear wheels covered, in the manner of a Figoni et Falaschi body of four years later, so impressed Earl that young Mitchell, aged 23, was hired as a designer in the Art & Colour Section in December 1935. At that time, the intake of designers was very informal. A portfolio such as Mitchell submitted would earn a place for a trial period, so the studio consisted, as Strother McMinn recalled, of "a wild mix of seasoned professionals, mad illustrators, art moderne architects, highly skilled pattern makers, subtly sensitive sculptors and car-crazy kids."

PHOTO: GENERAL MOTORS

△ 1938 CADILLAC SIXTY SPECIAL

This was Bill Mitchell's first major work and it had several advanced features. It was the first GM car to dispense with running boards, which would disappear almost completely four years later. The V-grille was somewhat Cord-like, and on one prototype it was closer to the Cord as it ran right around the hood.

The frame was 3 inches lower than the regular Sixty, Cadillac built 3,703 Sixty Specials in the 1938 season, more than any other car in the line.

THE CADILLAC SIXTY SPECIAL

Earl quickly recognized Mitchell's creative talents and in 1936 made him head of the Cadillac studio, with responsibility for creating a new, more youthful model as a supplement to the Sixty line. Cadillac chief Nicholas Dreystadt had been impressed by Gordon Buehrig's Cord 810, as had the whole industry, and he saw that Cadillac had resources of men and manufacture denied to the small Cord organization. There was nothing wrong with the Cord's design, but production delays and teething troubles were fatal to the project (see Chapter 12). The Sixty Special was intended to appeal to the Cord market (at $2,090, it was $95 more expensive than the Cord Beverly sedan, but $5 cheaper than the better-trimmed Westchester), but it used a stock Cadillac engine and transmission and a lower chassis frame with a three-inch longer wheelbase. The appeal was to be in the body, which was down to Earl's department and his new pupil, Bill Mitchell. The design was originally intended to be badged as a La Salle, and Mitchell's first exercises featured that marque's tall narrow radiator grille. The decision to make it a Cadillac probably arose from Cadillac executives' reluctance to see the junior marque steal publicity and sales from them. La Salle had only three more seasons to run, anyway.

The original Cadillac design was more Cord-like than the production models, with grille bars running around the side of the hood, and headlights built into the fenders. On the final model these were abandoned so that the Sixty Special could share grille, hood and fenders with the other Cadillac Sixtys. As far back as the windshield, the Special was almost identical to the other cars, though the hood was lower, but from there on there were striking differences. The roof line, at 65 inches, was three inches lower; there were no running boards; the window area was 32 percent greater than on other Sixtys; and the trunk was longer and more completely faired into the bodywork. The overall effect was almost that of a four-door convertible with the top up. Perhaps because of this, no convertibles were offered in the Sixty Special line, though two examples were built, one of which was driven by Bill Mitchell. There was also a coupe for William Knudsen and at least one two-door convertible body by Brunn.

The Sixty Special was not only a sales success, beating the regular Sixty sedan by more than 200 units, but its influence was immense. The absence of running boards, seen on the Cord 810 but an innovation for a General Motors car, soon spread to other Cadillac models and to U.S. cars generally by 1941. The larger window areas were seen on the GM B-bodies for 1939, and the low, four-window sedans inspired the C-bodies on Buicks, Cadillacs, Oldsmobiles and Pontiacs in 1940-41.

The Sixty Special was littled changed for 1939 and 1940, though it gained the new split grille common to all V8 Cadillacs. Side-mounted spare wheels were optional, as they had been in 1938, but they gave the car a heavier appearance. There was a

◁ ▽ The Cadillac Sixty Special was a style leader and a very good looking car in its own right. It was selected by the book *Style in Industrial Products 1900-1960* as one of the greatest designs of the period.

▽ The grille shows the strong Cord influence. It was made of die-cast zinc alloy by GM's Ternstedt Division, and though brittle and given to pitting it was a prestige item and was said to exert a powerful positive influence on sales.

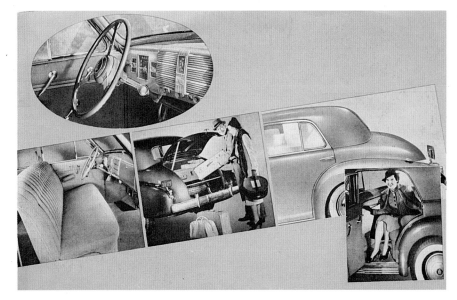

more widespread use of dual colors. For 1941 more drastic changes were made, with a new horizontal grille and a valance panel between the bottom of the grille and the front bumper. Headlights were now built into the front fenders, fulfilling Carlton Hill's prophecy made ten years before. Most important of all in the light of future design was the extension of the fenders into the front doors, the beginning of total integration, and, finally, the disappearance of the fender as an individual structure. Mitchell could have taken this step in 1941 or earlier, as designs for fully integrated fenders were already seen in the Styling Studio and were featured on Alex Tremulis' Thunderbolt designed for Chrysler in 1940. However, Harley Earl never believed in being too far ahead of public taste; one year was okay, but five or ten years a recipe for disaster, as the Chrysler Airflow had shown. Thus in 1941 fenders that extended halfway into the front doors were seen only on the Sixty Special; for 1942 the style was featured on all Cadillacs except the formal 75 sedans and limousines, and this feature continued for 1946 and

1947. On the '48 models, the fender line ran right through to the rear and even then the rear fender stood proud of the rear door in an echo of the old separate fender design. It was still there in vestigial form through the 1950s; only on the radical 1959 Cadillacs did it disappear completely, to give a flat panel from headlights to rear lights, something we take for granted today.

Bill Mitchell's star was rising in the years before World War II, and he took several trips with Harley

Earl which cemented the friendship in the same way that Earl's months on Alfred Sloan's yacht had done 12 years earlier. In many ways the two designers were similar – autocratic, accepting only the best – though Mitchell was more approachable and did not inspire the awe verging on terror that Earl did. From 1942 to 1945 Mitchell was in the U.S. Navy, and on his return to GM, he was promoted to general assistant to Earl. Although Harley still had 14 years to go before retirement, he

anticipated this by forming his own industrial design company, with his son William as director. He persuaded Mitchell to join this company as general manager. They were concerned with all kinds of product, from kitchen equipment to soap containers, and judging from remarks he made many years later, this cannot have been very congenial for Mitchell. When asked in an interview with C. Edson Armi in the 1980s what car designers knew about icebox design, he replied, "They don't want to know anything about it. They don't give a damn about it. They are different people entirely."

In 1950 Mitchell was back with GM, becoming assistant director of design to Earl, and taking over as Vice-President, Styling, in December 1959. Despite his talents, his appointment was not received with unalloyed enthusiasm. The new president of General Motors, Jack Gordon, said to him, "Harley just told me that you're going to take his job, and I don't like it one goddam bit. Now you're going to have to prove to me that you can do this." This was just the challenge that Mitchell needed: "Well, that's just the best thing he ever said to me. Boy, I just ran the hell out of the room."

◁ Artist's impression of the Sixty convertible. This was sometimes called the "forgotten Sixty" because so much attention was paid to the Special. The regular Sixty was made in four body styles: coupe and sedan, plus the corresponding convertibles.
ILLUSTRATION: GENERAL MOTORS

◁ The 1939 Sixty Special had a new grille and longer, torpedo-like headlights, but the body was unchanged.

△ ▷ The prototype Sixty Special photographed in April 1937. Few changes were made between this and the production car, though the latter would have fewer hood louvers and a more distinctive hood ornament.
PHOTOS: GENERAL MOTORS

△ HARLEY EARL (1893-1969)

It was time for new ideas and new investment. GM spent £150 million on new bodies in 1948-49. For Harley Earl, the first major post-war car was the 1948 Cadillac, which boasted the first pontoon fenders and the first tail fins.

CHAPTER FOUR

EARL'S POST-WAR DESIGNS

"The most important part of an automobile is the grille,
the face of it. That is the whole design right there."

Harley Earl

ART OF THE AMERICAN AUTOMOBILE

BEFORE LOOKING AT THE striking cars that Mitchell gave to GM in the '60s, we need to backtrack a bit and look at the very important designs developed under Harley Earl's direction in the previous decade. Foremost among these was the 1948 Cadillac, which introduced the full pontoon fender to GM cars and was the first to incorporate a tail fin, that icon of the 1950s which has been loved and hated ever since.

Earl was fascinated by the input that airplane design could make to cars, and in 1941 he took a group of his stylists, including Frank Hershey and Bill Mitchell, out to Selfridge Field military airbase near Detroit to view the Lockheed P-38 Lightning. "We had to stand 30 feet away," recalled Mitchell, "because it was still in security. We all admired the P-38's streamlining and individuality in design, with its twin fuselages and tail fins." They absorbed details and made sketches for several hours (Earl must have had a good contact with the Air Force, for the Lightning was still on the secret list), and when they returned to the studios the designers were put to work; small models of cars incorporating many of the P-38's features were made in all the studios. At least two running prototypes were made, but America's entry into World War II shut down development for several years.

The P-38-inspired fins were quite modest on the 1948 Cadillac — in Mitchell's words, "merely a humped-up taillight, really." Cadillac advertising simply called them "rudder-type styling." The left taillight hinged up to reveal the fuel tank opening; this had been a Cadillac feature since the 1941 models, but caused some anxiety to Jack Gordon who feared it was a fire hazard. However, general manager Nicholas Dreystadt observed that if Gordon could design engines for Sherman tanks, he could cope with a safe taillight over the gas cap. Earl was undecided about the fin at first. Designer Frank Hershey recalled, "One day Harley came running in, all excited. He said 'take that goddam fin off, nobody wants it.' I covered the fin with a big sheet, and he came in a week later with Nick Dreystadt and again told me to take it off, and threatened to fire me if I didn't. I thought it was a good feature and left it on, and just three or four days later he came in to tell me to leave it on, it was going over great. He even suggested increasing the size for 1949."

The other important legacy from the P-38 was the chrome slash on the front of the rear fenders, simulating an air intake. Inspired by the genuine air intakes on the P-38, this chrome slash had appeared on some models of the 1947 line; it is worth remembering that not all Cadillacs featured the new styling at first. The big, formal 75 sedans and limousines retained their upright appearance, which dated back to 1941, up to the 1950 season. The new lines were seen on the 60 Special, 61 and 62, the most attractive body being the fastback two-door sedanet. The fastback had been seen on other GM cars, but the Cadillac's longer rear fenders and kicked-up taillights made the body seen lower than, say, the Chevrolet Fleetline. The Caddy's lines were echoed in the famous R-type Continental Bentley of 1952. Some of the designs showed further P-38 influence in triple bullet forms, one on

◁ 1938 BUICK Y-JOB
The Buick Y-Job concept car was built on a 1938 Roadmaster chassis, and with successive updating was still touring the country at shows after the war. Among its features were concealed headlights, an electrically-operated top which folded into the forward part of the trunk, and a pointed boat-tail reminiscent of the West Coast hot rods which both Harley Earl and Bill Mitchell loved. The concealed lights were replaced by external ones when the car was shown after the war.
OWNER: BUICK MOTOR CORPORATION

△ BUICK Y-JOB
The profile of the Y-Job shows clearly the fenders faired into the doors, which were seen on production Buicks for the 1942 season. The chrome flashes on front and rear fenders add considerable distinction to the car.

each side below the headlights and one in the center, recalling the two engines and body nacelle of the airplane. These never saw production, although the bumper overriders became increasingly bullet-like over the next few years. The 1949 Oldsmobiles also showed P-38 influence in their front fenders, which took their shape from the Lockheed's engine shrouding, with a headlight in place of the propeller, and a similar-shaped air scoop underneath.

Another innovation on the '48 Cadillac was the curved windshield. Like the fins, it was the brainchild of Julio Andrade, and initially it found no favor with Harley Earl. "I got it because I kept crying about it," remembered Andrade. "Finally Harley Earl and Henry Louve and me went to see a glass specialist at Dartmouth University, and there we proved it could be used in production."

These styling changes did not come cheaply. The new bodies on all five lines cost GM $150 million during 1948-49; Ford and Chrysler spent about $90 million each, Packard $20 million, Hudson and Studebaker $16 million each, and Nash $15 million. For the Cadillac Division, the investment paid off; it was the only GM division to exceed its pre-war production peak, selling 66,209 compared with a combined 1941 total for Cadillac and La Salle of 59,572.

Earl's suggestion of bigger fins for 1949 didn't

happen then, but this hardly mattered, for the '49 Cadillacs were fitted with brand-new valve-in-head V8 engines which more than compensated for minimal styling changes. The first major change to the fins came on the 1957 models, when they became longer and more prominent. They became larger still in 1958 and reached their peak in 1959, when they were V-shaped in profile, with bullet-like protrusions in the base of the V.

H ARLEY EARL AND THE MOTORAMAS

In the 1950s, one of the greatest annual attractions for auto enthusiasts was the General Motors Motorama, a lavish display of new cars and styling exercises, supported by music and stage revues featuring leggy showgirls. Held intermittently from 1949 to 1961, these shows had their origin in the annual industrialists' luncheons hosted by Alfred Sloan at New York's Waldorf-Astoria Hotel from 1931 until after World War II. He used them for important new model and policy announcements, and invitations were eagerly sought by the elite of Wall Street. The luncheons were held at the same time as the auto salons, and after the war GM decided to expand them into shows of its own, and to admit the general public. The name Motorama was not used until the shows began traveling around the country in 1953; the first show held in January 1949 was called "Transportation Unlimited." Moving the cars to the Waldorf and then on to other destinations, such as Boston, Miami, Los Angeles, San Francisco, Dallas and Kansas City, was a major exercise involving more than 140 trucks. Crowds would assemble just to watch the unloading; among those who braved the cold of a New York January was the Duke of Windsor, who had an apartment in Waldorf Towers.

The importance of these shows from the styling point of view was that they let the public know what the styling studios were thinking about, opening the doors to what had been secret domains and whetting the appetite for features that might be on the showroom floor in two or three years' time. On top of that, the public got a first-rate show as good as any Broadway production, completely free of charge.

The first GM showcar, the 1933 Cadillac V16

▽ 1951 LE SABRE

Harley Earl at the wheel of Le Sabre, GM's first post-war concept car. Built in 1951, it had a specially-designed 215-cubic-inch aluminum V8 engine with a Roots-type supercharger. The fins were already familiar from current Cadillacs, and the kicked-up front bumpers were seen on 1954 Cadillacs. The wraparound windshield was widely adopted on cars worldwide from 1954.

PHOTO: GENERAL MOTORS

fastback coupe, predated the Motoramas by 16 years, but a later showcar, the 1938 Buick Y-Job, survived the war to appear at the Waldorf in 1949. When it appeared, it seemed very advanced, too way out to have popular appeal, perhaps, yet several of its features were soon seen on production Buicks. The low horizontal grille, revolutionary at a date when regular Buicks still had vertical grilles, was almost exactly replicated on the 1942 models, while the absence of running boards and extension of fenders into the doors was also seen on the '42 production cars. More radical were the concealed headlights (which Buicks never used, though they were seen on the 1942 De Sotos), the electric-powered top which folded into the forward part of the trunk, and the pointed boat tail, reminiscent of California hot rods. Earl and Mitchell were both enthusiastic about the California custom car scene. They much preferred the atmosphere there to that of Detroit which, Mitchell said "...had no

▽ 1953 LE SABRE

Show cars like Le Sabre were regularly updated as it was too expensive to build a new car each year. Differences between this 1953 version and the original car pictured on page 51 include disk wheels with imitation spokes, and grilles above the bumpers.

PHOTO: GENERAL MOTORS

ART OF THE AMERICAN AUTOMOBILE

△ GM engineers examine the engine of the Le Sabre. This gave 335hp, yet weighed only 550 pounds. The cylinder head and crankcase were made of aluminum, and the exhaust valves were sodium cooled. Le Sabre is preserved today by GM Design.

PHOTO: GENERAL MOTORS

automobile spirit, they're a bunch of fender makers; they didn't have any feeling for automobiles." Earl perhaps sensed that the public would not take to retractable headlights, for one of the modifications made to the Y-Job in 1949 was to install regular exposed lights. The first GM production car to have concealed lights was the Corvette Sting Ray of 1963, but that was a Mitchell design, launched four years after Earl's retirement.

The next Buick showcar, launched at the 1951 Chicago Show but seen at later Motoramas, was the

Le Sabre, which Earl named for the F-86 Sabre jet fighter. This was a more completely new car than the Y-Job, for while the latter had a standard Roadmaster 8 engine, the Le Sabre was powered by a 215-cubic-inch aluminum head and block V8 which anticipated the power unit of the 1962 Buick Special compact car. Not only was this very advanced for 1948, when the car was first planned, but it also featured a Roots-type supercharger. The body showed Earl's fascination with aircraft. In the post-war years, the jet-powered plane was becoming more widespread, and designs such as the Lockheed Shooting Star inspired stylists. Both the frontal air intake and the nozzle at the rear, together with the forms of the front and rear fenders, were clearly aircraft-inspired.

Le Sabre's body was very advanced; all major parts such as hood, rear deck, doors and front fender valances were magnesium castings. An electro-hydraulic pump generated pressure to work the convertible top and the built-in jacking system. The design was a mixture of far-out ideas which never saw production, such as the retractable headlights incorporated in the air-intake and the methanol fuel cell, and concepts which seemed equally bizarre but soon became commonplace. Chief among these was the wraparound windshield, which was standardized on GM cars for 1954 and became recognized wear on all U.S. cars, and many European ones, for about six years. This was also airplane-inspired, from the bubble cockpit canopy of the P-38. Producing the necessary curves for wraparound shields proved a major headache for the glass makers, Libby-Owens-Ford, but Earl was so insistent that they come up with an answer that eventually they did.

Le Sabre's kicked-up front bumpers and exhaust incorporated into the fins were put into production on the 1954 Cadillacs. A less obvious

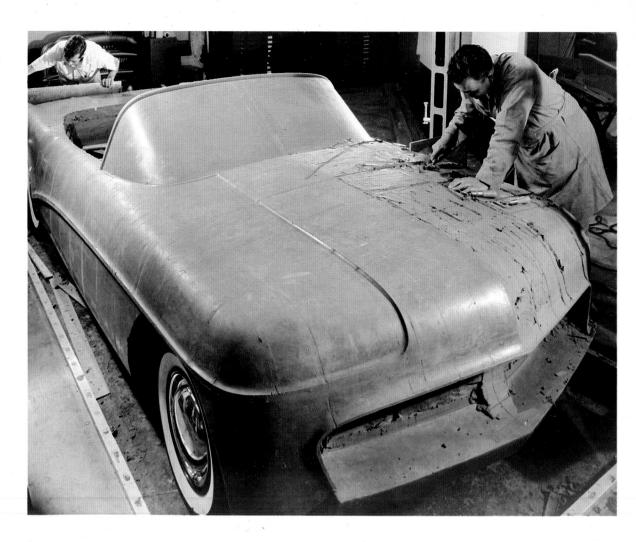

△ Staff at GM Technical Center work on the clay of the Buick showcar Wildcat III. The final version which appeared in 1959 did not have the concealed headlights of the clay.
PHOTO: GENERAL MOTORS

◁ ▷ The first Wildcat showcar was launched in 1953. It had a fiberglass body which was said to have been used for testing the viability of this material, though Chevrolet was already using it for the Corvette. The Wildcat was powered by a 188hp version of Buick's new V8 engine. An unusual feature was the use of air scoops built into the front wheel disks. The disks remained stationary while the wheels revolved around them.
OWNER: JOE BORTZ

feature which has become widespread was the electrically operated radio antenna, while the eye-level speedometer numerals, now generally called a head-up display, was hailed as a new safety development on some German cars in the 1980s.

Le Sabre was shown at numerous auto shows as well as at the Motoramas and traveled to Europe for the 1951 Paris Salon. Unlike many showcars, it was fully driveable and covered about 45,000 miles on the road, many of them with Harley Earl at the wheel. Like the Y-Job, it was modified over the years, gaining new wheel disks with imitation wire spokes in 1953, and losing the rear fender skirts. Unlike many other showcars which were scrapped, Le Sabre remains with GM Design today.

THE CORVETTE

Although often described as a Buick, Le Sabre was really a corporate GM car, but numerous other

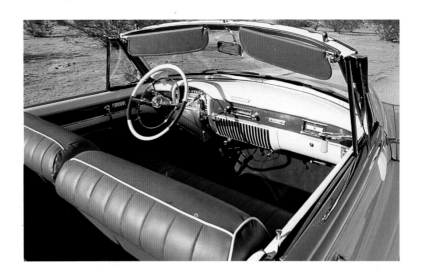

Motorama cars carried Buick, Cadillac, Chevrolet, Oldsmobile and Pontiac badges and provided styling ideas which were later seen on production cars. The Motoramas of 1949 and 1950 had not featured any Chevrolets, as the mass-production make did not seem very suitable for the Motorama glamour treatment. Chevrolet Division general manager T. H. Keating was not happy with that, and for the 1953 Motorama (the show wasn't held in '51 or '52), word went out that Chevrolet must have at least one showcar. They ended up with three, one of which became America's best-known sports car, the Corvette. It was the only Motorama car to reach the market with little modification.

ART OF THE AMERICAN AUTOMOBILE

◁ ▽ ▷ 1953 CADILLAC SERIES 62 CONVERTIBLE
This car was somewhat overshadowed by the Eldorado convertible, a limited production car which sold for $3,607 more than the Series 62. Nevertheless, the 62 was a glamorous car in its own right, with new interior choices in one- or two-tone colors, and optional chrome wire wheels. The external spare wheel cover is an extra not listed by the factory. Factory options did, however, include power steering at $177 and Autronic Eye automatic headlight beam control at $53.
OWNER: WALLY HERMAN

▷ 1953 CADILLAC SERIES 62 COUPE DE VILLE
The 1953s had new bumpers and grille with "bombs" which doubled as bumper guards. Parking or fog lights were located in the outer ends of the grille, below the headlights. This two-door hardtop cost $3,995.
OWNER: WALLY HERMAN

▽ 1954 CADILLAC ELDORADO
The Eldorado was a limited production Cadillac with its own body shell when introduced in 1953. The 1954 Eldorado shown here was less distinctive, and shared a body with the Series 62 convertible. Individual touches included broad chrome-ribbed panels on the lower rear fenders, Cadillac crests in gold on the door sills and rear fenders, and a lavishly equipped leather interior. For this the customer paid $1,300 more than for a Series 62, less than half the extra on the 1953 models.
OWNER: GILMORE CAR MUSEUM, KALAMAZOO, MICHIGAN

▷ 1954 CHEVROLET CORVETTE
This all-new line (facing page) was in complete contrast to the Cadillacs but still a Harley Earl design.
OWNER: GILMORE CAR MUSEUM, KALAMAZOO, MICHIGAN

ART OF THE AMERICAN AUTOMOBILE

The concept of the Corvette, and its styling, were due to Harley Earl, with the mechanical elements coming from Chevrolet chief engineer Ed Cole. Earl was interested in the European sports cars which were coming into the U.S., particularly the Jaguar XK120, and was fired by the idea of a reasonable-priced roadster suitable for youngsters such as his son who was just entering college in 1950. At $4,745 the Jag was only for rich kids, but Earl dreamed of a car selling for around $1,000. It wasn't necessarily going to be a Chevy; indeed, Earl planned a V8 engine for it, which Chevy did not have until 1955. His ideas were set down in full-size drawings by a young designer/engineer named Bob McLean. Because the Jaguar had an in-line six engine, McLean incorporated this in his drawings, and Earl apparently did not object. It was set back in the frame just as the Chevrolet unit was in the final design. The next step was a full-size clay mock-up, in which form it was first seen by Ed Cole, T. H. Keating and GM president Harlow Curtice. The body was quite different from any other Chevrolet, lower and with a simple horizontal grille with vertical bars, fencing-mask mesh over the headlights and a wraparound windshield.

Once the decision was taken for it to become a Chevrolet Motorama car, Cole began work on the mechanical side. The readily available engine was the familiar Chevrolet "Stove Bolt" six, and the chassis was a stock Chevrolet shortened by 13 inches

1954 CORVETTE

△ This car was very similar to the first model of 1953, which only entered production in mid-season, on June 30. The 1954s were available in Pennant Blue and Sportsman Red, in addition to the Polo White which was the only color available in 1953.

▷ The protruding, fender-integrated taillights were a feature of the Corvette from 1953 through 1955.

to give a wheelbase of 102 inches, the same as the Jaguar's. This meant that the driver could put his hand on the rear wheel. The engine was souped up to give 150bhp compared with 108 from the standard unit, but a two-speed Powerglide automatic transmission robbed the original Corvette of any pretence of high performance.

To avoid expensive tooling when it was not certain if the car would ever see production, the body was made of fiberglass, unknown on a production car then, though a few makers of bodies for kit cars, like the Devin and Woodill Wildfire, were already using the material. When it went on show at the Waldorf Astoria in January 1953, the

new car did not even carry the name Corvette; it was simply badged Chevrolet on its front fenders. However, the public did not need a snappy name to be persuaded that here was an exciting new car. They flocked around the GM display asking when they could get their hands on one, and this was one factor that led GM to put the car in production. The other was that they knew Ford had a two-seater in preparation (Ford engineers and stylists were among the most eager students of the Chevrolet) and did not want to be caught on the hop. The Corvette, as it was quickly named, went into production in September 1953, while Ford's Thunderbird was not revealed until October 1954, as a 1955 model.

Harley Earl and Ed Cole must have been very pleased with their dream car which became reality, though Harley's dream price of $1,000 had soared to $3,513. By then, Jaguar had reduced its price for the XK120 to $3,345. The 1954 Motorama saw three Corvette derivatives – a hardtop, a fastback coupe called the Corvair, and a two-door station wagon, the Nomad. It is not certain if Earl expected these to see production as well as the roadster, or if they were in the more usual Motorama role of ideas cars. The coupe was a very attractive-looking car, but the Nomad was more significant as some of its features found their way into a production Chevy wagon, also called Nomad, which was made from 1955 to 1957.

1955 CHEVROLET BEL AIR SPORTS COUPE
△ ▷ The 1955 Chevrolet was completely restyled as well as receiving a new V8 engine. The advertising, "New Look, New Life, New Everything" was justified. Styling was by Clare MacKichan, Chuck Stebbins, Bob Veryzer and Carl Renner under Harley Earl's direction. This hardtop, officially called the Sports Coupe, was part of the top Bel Air line, and sold for $2,166. Production in the 1955 season was 185,562, second highest of the Bel Airs.

OWNER: WARD GAPPER

Earl appointed as designer of the "Waldorf Nomad" Carl Renner, who came up with a stylish design, certainly the sleekest station wagon ever built. Because it had a Corvette front end, some people think it was built on a Corvette chassis, but in fact it used the standard 115-inch wheelbase of the regular Chevrolets. Among its features were a ribbed roof, which was carried onto the production Nomad, and a rear window which disappeared electrically into the tailgate, an idea which found its way onto production Chevy wagons in 1959. The roof was a telescopic steel construction, which was the reason for the flutes, but this was rejected for the production Nomad on grounds of cost and the

risk of rain leaks. In 1962 Brooks Stevens designed a sliding roof station wagon for Studebaker, and sure enough, it did leak.

The move from 1954 Waldorf Nomad to 1955 production Nomad shows how styling ideas are translated. In charge of styling the 1955 Chevys, which marked a significant break from their predecessors, was Clare MacKichan. The ribbed roof and tailgate were retained, as were the side windows with their angled division parallel to the C-pillar. In fact, Carl Renner remembered cutting and splicing the Waldorf Nomad blackboard drawing itself, with the result that car's upper body was attached to the higher belt line of the

△ Badge from the Bel Air featuring the Chevrolet "bow-tie" trademark. Used since 1914, it reportedly came from the wallpaper in a Paris hotel that GM's founder Billy Durant once stayed in.

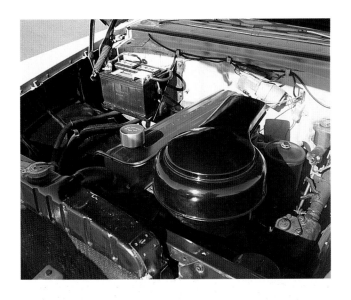

1955 CHEVROLET BEL AIR FOUR-DOOR SEDAN
This was the most popular of the Bel Air line, and 345,372 cars were made. The wraparound windshield and belt-line dip had been seen on limited production cars such as Buick's Skylark and Cadillac's Eldorado two years before.

◁ This car has the 235½-cubic-inch six-cylinder engine with cast-iron block that dated back in basic design to the late 1920s.
OWNER: DAN ROWE

▽ 1955 CHEVROLET
The egg-crate grille on this1955 Chevrolet was a favorite of Harley Earl and was clearly inspired by Ferrari. However, the public did not view it favorably and for 1956 the grille was lower and more conventional.
OWNER: DAN ROWE

regular Chevrolet. A significant difference was the retention of the showcar's fully exposed rear wheels. Standard models, including the Two-Ten Handyman wagon, had partial wheel covers. The windshield came from the 1955 hardtop, and the floor from the two-door wagon.

The Nomads of 1955 to 1957 were specialty cars and accounted for only 3.1 percent of total Chevy wagon production. They cost $393 more than the Handyman, but their prices on the collector market today are much higher, more than double that of the regular wagon.

The Corvette was by far the most important Motorama car, spawning as it did a whole new line for Chevrolet, which is still in production today. The only other car to have a major influence on a production model was the 1954 Cadillac Park Avenue luxury sedan, which developed into the Eldorado Brougham of 1957-58. Three inches longer than the regular Fleetwood Sixty Special, it had a four-door hardtop body style and large front wheel cutouts which became standard on the next major Cadillac restyle in 1957. The 1955 Motorama car was the first to bear the name Eldorado

△ 1955 CHEVROLET BEL AIR AND 1959 CHEVROLET
BISCAYNE
These two cars show the rapid progress made in GM
styling in the 1950s. Modern though the '55 car was, it
seems old fashioned beside the '69 Biscayne with its
wide, wing-shaped rear deck.
OWNER: DAN ROWE

▷ The '55 Bel Air's speedometer read to 110mph,
though top speed was around 95mph.

◁ 1956 BUICK CENTURION SHOWCAR
Buick's showcar in 1956 was the Centurion four-passenger coupe which used a fiberglass body, the upper part painted red and the lower having a brushed metallic finish. The stop and back-up lights were located in a "bomb" in the center of the rear end. The twin pods at the lower end of the rear fenders carried the taillights. At the front, the fenders projected several inches ahead of the grille, a styling feature not used on any production Buicks. The Centurion's most unusual feature was the closed-circuit TV system which replaced the rearview mirror.

ILLUSTRATION: GENERAL MOTORS

Brougham and was closer still to the production model, with four headlights. For the 1956 show, Cadillac built two Eldorado Broughams, a pre-production four-door hardtop and a town car, with open chauffeur's compartment harking back to the early 1930s. Both featured the very low hood and rear deck, actually lower than the fenders. The hardtop's roof was of brushed stainless steel, and a line led from the fenders to a vertical molding in the center of the sculptured rear door. Both these features were carried on in the production Eldorado Brougham. The fins of the 1954-56 showcars were more massive than those on production Cadillacs, but by 1957, they had caught up, so in that respect if in no other, the Eldorado Broughams were no different from lesser Cadillacs.

◁ △ 1959 CADILLAC SERIES 62
In 1959 the Harley Earl era reached its peak and appropriately, it was in the Cadillac line, the top models of GM, that the most lavish styling excesses were seen. This fine example is wearing a lot better than many of the more recent autos seen in the background at the Self-Service Salvage scrapyard in Phoenix, Arizona.
OWNER: JIM POWELL

The Eldo Brougham was an exceedingly complex and expensive car, with a price tag of $13,074, more than $3,000 above that of the rival Continental Mark II, and $5,508 more than the next most expensive Cadillac. Only 704 were made in two seasons, and it is unlikely that Cadillac made a profit on any of them.

Harley Earl was not idle in retirement. Since 1945 he had operated his own design consultancy, Harley Earl Associates, and for the last ten years of his life he concentrated on this. His contract with GM understandably forbade him to design anything which would compete with their products, so he turned his attention to a plumber's showroom, carpet sweepers (for Bissell), aircraft interiors (for Convair and Alcoa), and cookies (for Nabisco).

△ ▷ 1959 CADILLAC

The Cadillac line was completely restyled for 1959, with a new grille described as a "glittering cliff of chrome," distinctive roof lines, and of course, those fins. They have been described as a response to Virgil Exner's finned 1957 Chryslers, but with a three-year lag between design and production, they would have been dreamed up in 1956 at the latest, when Chrysler fins were still quite modest. One of Earl's dictums was "Go all the way, then back off," but there wasn't much backing off with the '59 Caddy — as if a frontal grille wasn't enough, there was another across the lower rear deck. The taillights were in the horizontal pods springing from the center of the fins; back-up lights were recessed in the outer pods of the rear bumpers.

OWNER: JIM POWELL

△ 1959 CHEVROLET BISCAYNE SEDAN

"All New, All Over Again" went the Chevrolet slogan for 1959, and it was no exageration. Bodies were wider and roomier, glass area was increased, there was a new grille, and above all, the bat-wing rear deck, described by writer Tom McCahill as "big enough to land a Piper Cub." The cavernous trunk had a capacity of 32 cubic feet. As with the contemporary Cadillacs, the styling team was given a very free hand by Earl. "We were encouraged to do the wildest things," said Clare MacKichan. "One design had the headlights one above the other in the center."

OWNER: DAN ROWE

▽ Like other 1959 Chevrolets, the Biscayne line could be had with six-cylinder or V8 engines. This is the 235½-cubic-inch six with cast-iron block which developed 135hp. A very long-lived design, it dated back to 1929, and would survive in Chevrolets until 1963 when it was replaced by an over-square six.

△ The rear lights of the '59 Chevrolet were completely new, and complemented the wide bat-wing rear deck. Sometimes called cat's eye lights, they incorporated stop and back-up lights.

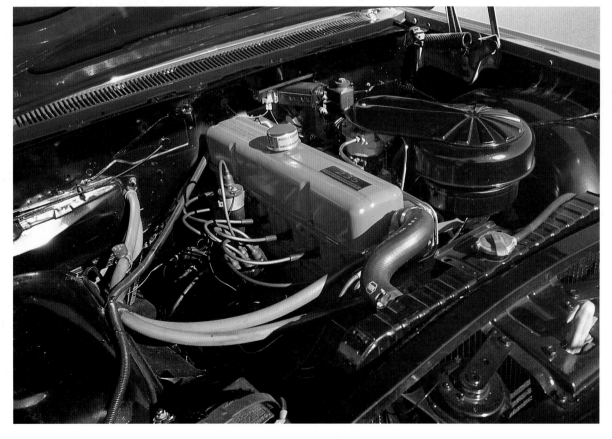

1959 CHEVROLET BISCAYNE

It is hard to believe that this opulent-looking car was, in fact, one of the lowest priced of the '59 Chevys. This Biscayne was the base line, with the Bel Air and Impala higher up the range. Biscaynes started at $2,160 for a two-door utility sedan. Other styles in the Biscayne line included a four-door sedan, a six-passenger two-door sedan, and the two models of station wagon.

The body shell was shared with Pontiac, as had been the custom for some time, but for 1959 some models of Buick and Oldsmobile also used this body. The decoration, including the bat-wing rear deck, was necessary to distinguish between the different makes. So, paradoxically, the flamboyance of design was part of an economy drive.

OWNER: DAN ROWE

△ BILL MITCHELL (b. 1912)
Mitchell succeeded Harley Earl as Vice-President, Styling at GM in 1959.
He shaped motoring in the Sixties with cars like the Riviera, Thunderbird,
Corvette and Toronado. After bearing the brunt of changes brought
about by fuel restrictions and new safety regulations, he retired in 1977.
PHOTO: GENERAL MOTORS

CHAPTER FIVE

BILL MITCHELL TAKES OVER

"Mitchell's philosophy of operation was different from Earl's
– just like day and night… he generally unreined the horses
and let people do their thing."

GM designer

O N NOVEMBER 22, 1959, Harley Earl celebrated his 66th birthday, and eight days later General Motors announced his retirement. Despite Jack Gordon's already quoted reservations about Bill Mitchell, he was really the only man to step into the shoes of "Mistearl." Ever since he had been picked by Earl to oversee the styling of the 1938 Cadillac Sixty Special, Mitchell had worked closely with the head of styling and enjoyed a personal rapport denied to other stylists. The two men were alike in many ways – self-confident, extrovert, domineering and flamboyant in dress and manner, yet Mitchell was less intimidating. Earl terrified his juniors, so much so that in 1951 Alexander Kostelow, the director of the Pratt Institute, was hired to advise about halting the rapid turnover of demoralized artists.

With Mitchell, there was less confrontation and more communication. As Vincent Kaptur, Jr., recalls, "I think Mitchell, in contrast to Earl, tried to avoid that mad, direct confrontation. When Earl walked in the door, everyone would say, 'Oh, Jesus Christ,' and they were ready for all hell and brimstone to come down on you. But with Mitchell, it wasn't that way. I am sure there were outbursts under Mitchell, but I can't recall any."

Earl undoubtedly suffered from his inability to draw and to put ideas into words, what were politely called "communication difficulties." Mitchell was a good draftsman and fluent in communicating ideas, though part of his style was to give designers a relatively free rein. As one explained, "Mitchell's philosophy of operation was different from Earl's – just like day and night. To put it as simply as I know how, in the Earl philosophy, people were just pencils in his hands, 'Do what I tell you,' with all the communications problems. 'Don't you understand what I want? Use this sweep!' Whereas with Mitchell, it was 'I want to see what you can do.' And he never criticized anyone for doing something. If it ended up god-awful, he might be critical about wasting time, and how you let a dumb-assed thing like that get this far. But he generally unreined the horses and let people do their thing."

Among Mitchell's many changes was a revolution in the making of initial sketches. Traditionally this had been done with colored pencils, tempera and washes, but Mitchell's preferred method was to use taped silhouettes, the basic car being blocked out or extended by half-inch black tape. This allowed changes to be made much more quickly than with drawings, and fulfilled Mitchell's desire for a rapid turnover of ideas. Within five years of his taking over, the Chevrolet studio alone produced as many designs in a year as the entire GM studios had created annually under Earl.

Mitchell also reversed the priority between the body room and the production studios. Under Earl, the bodyroom was the main design area where the vice-president spent most of his time. The various parts of the body, front end, hood, roof, doors, etc., were sculpted in clay, amalgamated, and then re-created in each divisional studio where the finishing touches, hood ornaments, grilles, door moldings and lights would be added. Earl did not rate the production studios very highly. "You designers are nothing but a bunch of dressmakers," he would say.

Mitchell promoted the importance of the studios, moving all designers from the body room to the production studios, where all aspects of design would be worked on. The body room became a receiving center where designs were assessed and argued over, rather than an innovating area. And he stressed the importance of the designers, whether they were doing a main body line or a filler cap. "You are not dress designers," he would say, in

▽ 1956 CHEVROLET IMPALA SHOWCAR
This showcar used a name later given to top-line Chevrolets from 1959. The coupe body was fiberglass trimmed with stainless steel. Powered by a 225hp Super Turbo-Fire V8, it had a speedometer with a red light which got brighter and brighter as speed increased.
ILLUSTRATION: GENERAL MOTORS

ART OF THE AMERICAN AUTOMOBILE

direct contradition of his former boss. He also planned farther ahead, by means of an advanced planning studio located next to the production studio. Here designers worked on the next generation of cars, perhaps four or five years ahead, while the production studio looked after the current model under development. The advance designers could check the progress of their ideas and maybe complain if the main theme they had established was not being followed through. Nevertheless, the production studio man was the senior, and designers in the advanced planning studio hoped for promotion before long.

Apart from all these studios, Mitchell had his own basement where he worked on his own projects. Not all of these saw the light of day, but one that did was the Corvette Sting Ray. When Dave Holls went to him with an idea for a new Corvette, he was told, "Aw, don't fool around. Don't flatter yourself, kid – I am the one who does the Corvettes around here."

Bill Porter, who worked in the GM studios from

◁ △ 1962 CHEVROLET CORVAIR MONZA SPYDER
Although planning began in the Earl era, the Corvair was very much a product of the Mitchell school of styling, with crisp, strongly contoured lines and little decoration. With its rear-mounted flat six engine, the Corvair bore no resemblance to any previous Chevrolet. Named for Italy's Grand Prix race venue, the Monza was a top model of Corvair with bucket seats, front arm rests, carpeting, and many other features only available in lesser Corvairs at extra cost.
PHOTOS: NATIONAL MOTOR MUSEUM, BEAULIEU

the 1960s onward, has some interesting insights into the differences between Earl and Mitchell. "Earl was a kind of form man – very aware of three dimensional forms, to the extent that he even set up headlight rules, having to do with the reflections of the forms. Sculptors and modelers who worked with him said he was often worried about the intersection of forms; that was his design preoccupation. Obviously he was interested in proportions because he wanted everything to be lower, longer and wider, which he believed was the way cars should go.

△ 1964 BUICK RIVIERA

In its second year the Riviera underwent only minimal changes, restricted to a new optional 360hp V8 engine and minor trim variations. A rival to the four-passenger Ford Thunderbird, the Riviera was 3 inches longer than the Ford, but 9 inches shorter than the Buick Electra. Mitchell envisaged it as "something between a Ferrari and a Rolls," the grille based on the Ferrari 250GT, and the sharp body lines from the custom-bodied Rolls-Royces which abounded in London at that time.

OWNER: DAN BRASCH

"However, Bill Mitchell was not interested in forms in that sense at all, but in contours and lines and overall patterns. If the pattern of a car made up of lines or forms was strong and had a neat personality, that would cause Mitchell to react very quickly – that was what he went for, that was his true zone of consciousness. He saw cars in those terms of strong patterns. Not that forms could not be part of it, but he liked, really above all, lines and edges." (Interview with Nicky Wright, 1994)

THE KIND OF CAR YOU WEAR — THE 1963 RIVIERA

Throughout his working life, Bill Mitchell never forgot the glamorous, long-hooded luxury cars which he admired on the New York streets of his boyhood, the Rolls-Royces, Hispano-Suizas and Isotta-Fraschinis. From them he also gained an admiration for lean, sculptured lines which were directly opposed to the bulbous, rounded shapes favored by Earl. Mitchell contrived to achieve his leaner look with the '38 Cadillac Sixty Special, and his ideas found their greatest expression in the '63 Buick Riviera.

Buick first used the Riviera name on a two-door model in the 1949 Roadmaster series. It was called the Riviera Hardtop Coupe and was a trend-setter in that it had the appearance of a convertible with the top up, giving it all the connotations of luxury and sexiness that the convertible had gathered around it, but with a permanent roof. Buick claimed it was the first hardtop; Chrysler disputed the claim, recalling the similar designs in their 1946 Town & Country series. However, Chrysler made only seven of their hardtops, while Buick made 4,343 in the first season alone. From 1949 to 1958, all Buick's two-door hardtops were called Riviera and made in the cheaper Super line as well as the Roadmaster from 1950. Confusingly, the name was also used for some four-doors, but Rivieras were always above-average cars with some distinction in style or trim, even when, as from 1959 to 1962, the name was carried only by one four-door hardtop. Thus it was very appropriate that the name should become prominent again with the new "personal" coupe launched for 1963.

▽ 1964 BUICK RIVIERA
The Riviera's body was built by Fisher in its Cleveland, Ohio, plant and shipped to Flint for final assembly. Fisher developed a technique for incorporating the frameless glass that Mitchell wanted — the door had a detachable outer panel which could be bolted on after the door had been hung, glass fitted against the seals and locks and strikers adjusted. Buick built 37,658 of these in 1964.

The spur to produce this new model was undoubtedly the success of Ford's four-passenger Thunderbird. The two-door model of 1955 had been successful enough, its 195hp V8 engine outperforming the Corvette's 150hp six, but four seats attracted many more customers. Admittedly, the four-passenger T-Bird of 1958 was no longer a sports car, but it outsold both its predecessor and the still sporty (and now more powerful) Corvette. By 1962 the T-Bird was America's leading four-passenger luxury car. Mitchell found it galling to see Ford designers studying General Motors' Motorama cars and incorporating their ideas on production models, while all his company had to show were beautiful dreams.

Plans for GM's answer were laid in 1960, and Mitchell says that the idea for the new Riviera's crisp lines came from a Rolls-Royce that he found parked outside his London hotel on a foggy night in 1959. Although the body was too high for a modern car (he was probably looking at a custom-bodied Silver Wraith of the 1950s, perhaps by Hooper or H. J. Mulliner), the sheer lines and sharp angles seemed just right.

By August 1960, Mitchell's dream had been built as a full-size clay, the work largely that of Buick's Ned Nickles. It was not necessarily going to be a Buick, though, and at first it bore the name La Salle II. Mitchell had a great fondness for the La Salle concept of a smaller luxury car and particularly admired the long hood and narrow grille of the 1934 models. There were plans to give the 1960 car a single narrow grille, but it was too soon after the Edsel debacle for any such design to be taken seriously. Instead, Nickles used two vertical grilles, one on each side, ahead of the fenders, with a conventional horizontal grille in between. This grille was inspired by the Ferrari 250GT, and indeed Mitchell had envisaged the car as "something between a Ferrari and a Rolls." On one design, the headlights were incorporated in these grilles, but they ended up closer to the center, in the main grille. Parking lights were at the sides, however, and the headlights found their way there on the '65 Riviera.

If the car was going to carry a La Salle badge, it would have to be made by Cadillac, but this division was not interested in the concept, being very successful with their existing models. The same answer came from Chevrolet, and perhaps the concept was too upscale for Chevrolet anyway.

ART OF THE AMERICAN AUTOMOBILE

◁ △ The standard engine in the '64 Riviera was a 425-cubic-inch V8 developing 340hp, but a 360hp option was available with twin four-barrel Carter carburetors and finned aluminum rocker covers. The twin Carters cost $190 extra, on top of the $4,385 price of a Riviera. This engine was also available in Buick's Wildcat and Electra lines.

This left Buick, Oldsmobile or Pontiac, and in an unprecedented move, GM management staged a contest between the three divisions, each to make a presentation showing why they needed, and would make a success of, the car.

Buick took the unusual step of hiring their ad agency, McCann Erickson, to make the presentation, and it paid off. Mitchell was pleased with the result because Buick did not plan to change his baby.

"At first, I didn't care who got it as long as they would promise not to change it. Jack Wolfram at Oldsmobile wanted to change it, make it more sports-orientated, maybe with a blower." (Olds had a turbocharger on their 1962-63 F85 Jetfire). "Pontiac's de Lorean also wanted to touch it. Buick's new general manager Ed Rollert agreed not to touch it. That's why I am glad Buick won the competition. This is the way a design ought to be done. The designer should build a car and the manufacturers, the agents, come in and bid for it."

At 117 inches of wheelbase, the Riviera was nine inches shorter than the standard Buick Electra, yet was three inches longer than the Thunderbird. The body had been designed with little thought for mechanical elements, understandably as no one knew who would build it, yet it sat very well on the standard Electra chassis and suspension design. The engine was again a regular Buick unit, the

△ The '64 Riviera had many features limited to that model, including a glare-proof inside mirror, padded instrument panel and deep pile carpet. The leather interior on the '63 Riviera was not continued for '64.

325hp 402-cubic-inch V8, with an optional 425 giving 340bhp.

To provide some degree of exclusivity, Buick promised to make no more than 40,000 Rivieras per year. In the 1963, season they achieved this easily, but figures dropped slightly for 1964 and 1965, to 37,658 and 34,586 respectively.

Up to 1971, the Riviera design evolved gradually, gaining a gently sloping fastback for 1966 and at the same time losing the side vent window, which Mitchell never liked. He said his wife complained that all she could hear at speed was the awful noise caused by the old-fashioned vent windows. "This wasn't well accepted by the engineers at first. I remember a meeting about this, and all the cigar smokers objected to taking out the vents. Hell, this was the same kind of thinking that said we shouldn't have eliminated running boards."

For 1971 the Riviera was completely restyled, with a forward thrusting, pointed grille and a boat-tail rear end with a downward curved window

△ 1963 CHEVROLET CORVETTE STING RAY
The first Corvette to bear Bill Mitchell's distinctive imprint, the Sting Ray was also the first production GM car to have concealed headlights. The wraparound split rear window was controversial; many people found it gave poor visibility, but to Mitchell, it was an essential part of the design. Even so, he was forced to abandon it on the 1964 Sting Ray.

PHOTO: NATIONAL MOTOR MUSEUM, BEAULIEU

ART OF THE AMERICAN AUTOMOBILE

△ 1963 CORVETTE STING RAY CONVERTIBLE
The convertible Sting Ray was less of an individual car than the coupe, though it sold better. In the 1963 season the two models were neck and neck, 10,594 coupes and 10,919 convertibles, but in 1964 the figures were 8,304 and 14,925, and this proportion lasted for the next four years. Corvettes had all-independent suspension – coil springs in front, transverse leaf springs and lower wishbones at the rear.

PHOTO: NATIONAL MOTOR MUSEUM, BEAULIEU

reminiscent of Mitchell's 1963 Corvette Sting Ray and also Earl's Buick Y-Job. Unlike the Corvette, though, the rear window was undivided. The wheelbase was increased to 122 inches, which combined with the fastback to give a much longer, lower appearance than previous Rivieras. The trouble was that the body had been styled originally for a smaller car, based on the intermediate A-body. The Riviera was a full-size B-body. Reactions were mixed; *Motor Trend* said "Either it's beautiful or it's the 1971 Kaiser Darrin." Even its creator, Mitchell, had his reservations: "We went for a speedboat and ended up with a tugboat. It was just too big, too wide."

The boat-tail Riviera lasted for only three seasons, and for 1974 the Riviera was a much more conventional car, more like a two-door sedan than a coupe, with a straightforward rear window and large B-pillars, behind which the same side windows had almost the appearance of opera windows on a pseudo-formal town sedan. This car was forced on GM Styling by Buick general manager Lee Mays, and Mitchell was not happy either with Mays or his car. This theme lasted for five years, then for 1979 came a downsized Riviera with front drive and a body and mechanical units shared with Cadillac's Eldorado and Olds' Toronado.

GOING LIKE HELL JUST SITTING STILL – 1963 CORVETTE STING RAY

The Corvette as made from 1953 to 1962 was essentially Harley Earl's car; the concept was his, and its growth in power and decoration were consistent with the Earl philosophy. Fins apart, it could be said that the 1959-62 Corvette was the '59 Cadillac on a short wheelbase and with only two seats. While it lasted into the Mitchell era, it was always a carry-over design. When Bill snarled at Dave Holls, "Don't flatter yourself, kid – I am the one who does the Corvettes around here," he was doubtless referring to his new baby, which emerged for the 1963 season as the Sting Ray.

Code-numbered XP-720, the Sting Ray design began in the fall of 1959, when the old style still had three years to run. According to Mitchell, it embodied his love for the knife-edged, fleet-looking appearance better than any other car he did. "I like to have them look like they are going like hell just sitting still," and he certainly succeeded with the Sting Ray. It had its origins in two one-off designs; one was the first to bear the name Sting Ray, a fiberglass shell on the Sr-2 racing chassis. GM had given up racing after 1957 as a gesture to the safety lobby (President Jack Gordon was on the National Safety Council), and the chassis was headed for storage when Mitchell managed to buy it. With former California hot-rodder Larry Shinoda,

Bill designed a sleek body best described by Strother McMinn as "an aerodynamically curved shingle barely passing over the wheels, with tapered 'blips' for clearance." Driven by Dick Thompson, the car had a successful racing career in 1959-60.

The Sting Ray's other ancestor was the Mako Shark, a showcar of 1960 which shared the Sting Ray's triple "blips," one over each front wheel and one down the center of the hood, and also its

exhaust emerging just behind the front wheel. However, while the Sting Ray had a single functional pipe, one on each side for each bank of cylinders, the Mako Shark had four on each side, feeding into a muffler below the doors. The Shark was directly inspired by its counterparts in nature. "You go look at sharks," said Mitchell. "I've been down to Bimini and seen them. Jesus, they are exciting to look at."

◁ 1965 CORVETTE CONVERTIBLE
△ 1967 CORVETTE COUPE

Corvettes underwent only minor external changes from 1964 to 1968. Under the hood, however, there were increasingly powerful V8 engine options. While the original 1963 engine gave 250hp from 327 cubic inches, in 1965 you could have a 396-cubic-inch giving 425hp; in 1966 displacement was up to 427 cubic inches. Standard transmission was a three-speed manual, but in 1965 only 1.2 percent of buyers went for it; 89.6 percent chose the four-speed manual, and less than 10 percent took the automatic.

PHOTOS: NATIONAL MOTOR MUSEUM, BEAULIEU

The Mako Shark was said to be Bill Mitchell's favorite of all his designs, and the production Sting Ray his favorite car that made it to the market place. Its front end was very close to the Shark's, very smooth with no visible radiator or headlights (these were retractable) and the three blips. The wheel blips were necessitated by the low hood line, while the center blip was purely decorative. Back of the scuttle, the Sting Ray did not follow the Shark so closely; the latter's wraparound windshield was not used, and most important, the 'Ray was a closed coupe with a tapered fastback and a controversial wraparound split rear window. On this window the controversy seemed to be between Mitchell and the rest. To Bill it was an essential part of the car; "If you take that thing off, you might as well forget the whole thing." The man in charge of engineering the Sting Ray, Zora Arkus-Duntov, thought that the purpose of a rear window was to see out of, something not easy to do on the coupe. (There was also a convertible, but it was a less distinctive car.) The magazines shared Duntov's view, or lack of view, as it happened:

"… all we could see in the rear view mirror was that silly bar splitting the rear window down the middle." *Road & Track*

"The bar down the center of the rear window makes it all but impossible to see out via the rear view mirror." *Car Life*

"The rear window on the coupe is designed more for looks than practicality." *Motor Trend*

Mitchell was forced to abandon the split window on the '64 Sting Ray, though, as often happens, because of its originality, the split window model is the most collectible today.

Even more than previous Corvettes, the Sting Ray was promoted as a personal dream car: "The American everyman driving it felt it was designed solely to allow him to win his personal race against fate." (Mike Major in *Special Interest Autos*, February 1987). Advertising stressed the impulsive, irrational nature of Sting Ray purchase: "Only a man with a heart of stone could withstand temptation like this. You can wear a blindfold, have your wife tie you to the old family sedan, lock up the checkbook, anything of the kind; but Mister, if you ever hankered to buy a sports car, you're about to become the owner of a new Corvette Sting Ray. Sensible talk about the family budget, the good years left in your present car, any kind of rational thought, forget it!"

The next major restyling of the Corvette came for the 1968 season, when the fastback was replaced by a tunnel-roof coupe. This featured a removable rear window and a two-piece detachable roof section. The Sting Ray name disappeared on this model, only to be back for '69 as a single word, Stingray.

WE'VE GOT A CAR LIKE NOBODY ELSE – THE OLDS TORONADO

We have seen that once a man became Vice-President, Styling, he had less direct input into the design of cars and more of a watching brief over the work of his subordinates. This was true of Bill Mitchell as the '60s progressed. Probably no post-war car was so much his own as the 1938 Cadillac Sixty Special, designed when he was working under Harley Earl, though the Sting Ray was a pet project

◁ ▷ 1966 Oldsmobile Toronado could be viewed as Oldsmobile's Riviera, and was styled by David North. Although the basic shell had to be shared with the Riviera and Cadillac's Eldorado, North gave it a distinctive appearance. The unusual name came from a 1963 Chevrolet showcar. It has no known meaning.
PHOTO (LEFT): NATIONAL MOTOR MUSEUM, BEAULIEU
△ The 1968 model had a heavier and less attractive front end.
PHOTO: NICK GEORGANO

of his. One of GM's most distinctive cars of the 1960s, the Oldsmobile Toronado, was a product of the Mitchell era and received his sanction, but its design was mainly down to David R. North.

It had its origin in a free expression competition organized by Olds' studio chief Stanley Wilen in 1962. Finding his staff bogged down by everyday routine and lacking enthusiasm, he encouraged them to design their own dream car. "I let them blow steam at the board, just design things that meant something to them. I'd felt them tightening up so I asked them to do something wild and

exciting just to relieve the tension – but something meaningful, with real potential for Oldsmobile. The designers went crazy… I can't remember all of them, but one I do remember was Dave North's red rendering, a red car on a black background. The thing just sang. It stood there in the room, and as people walked by it, they stopped and sat down and just studied it."

The Flame Red Car might have remained a drawing on the wall, had not the GM hierarchy decided to let Oldsmobile do its own Riviera. Economics dictated that it had to share a basic body shell with other GM cars, the Riviera and the forthcoming Cadillac Eldorado, but there was plenty of scope for Dave North's individual design to be grafted onto the shell to make a truly distinctive car.

The front end in particular was very smooth, with retractable headlights and a narrow grille. Bill Mitchell had to fight to preserve that simplicity (and lost out on the '68 model, which had a heavier, rectangular grille). Oldsmobile's chief engineer and then general manager, John Beltz, argued in favor of opening up the grille, but Mitchell eventually prevailed; and when he saw the finished product, Beltz was gracious enough to say, "Bill, I'm so glad you had the guts to do it, because we have a car like nobody else."

Even more important than its styling was the Toronado's drive system which was via a three-speed Hydramatic to the front wheels. As America's first production front-drive car since the 1936-37 Cord 810, it provoked comparison with Gordon Buehrig's creation. How much did Dave North think about the Cord when he designed the Toronado? He admits that the wide grille owed something to the Cord, though of course he could not wrap it around the hood, inside the fenders, as hood and fenders were an integral unit by the '60s. However, he did have photos of the Cord on his desk…

The Toronado did not sell too well at first, being easily beaten by the more conventional Riviera for the first five years. Then the controversial '71 Riviera hit Buick sales badly, and the Toro outsold Riviera well into the 1970s. Interestingly, by the mid-70s, the more expensive Cadillac Eldorado, also with front drive, was outselling both the Riviera and the Toronado.

DESIGNED IN WASHINGTON?

Since the early 1970s, a new and very powerful factor has entered car design: the effect of government-mandated standards on two fronts, safety and fuel economy. The former hit first, with the bumper regulations of 1972 and 1974. The 1972 law (for '73 models, though most manufacturers included it on their '72s) required nil deformation in an impact up to 2mph, and the later one stipulated a bumper height of between 16 and 20 inches. Suddenly the stylists had to take on board alien rules, and they came first. Only after you had designed a bumper of the right strength and height could you start to think about style. GM chief designer Ron Hill observed, "All of a sudden, social consciousness took hold. There was a push for

safety... The bumper laws became paramount. You had to design your cars around bumpers."

Today's stylists also feel strongly about bumpers. "Cars lacked character largely from bumper standards (no more plan view shape) and down-sizing for gas mileage demands," says ex-Chrysler stylist Fred Schimmel. Another Chrysler man, Dave Cummins, remarked, "A creative industry was hit for the first time with lots of legislation affecting the appearance of bumpers, lighting and structure."

The next blow fell in 1975 with the Energy Conservation and Oil Policy Act. The shortage of gasoline prompted by the Arab limits on sales to the U.S. (because she had supported Israel in the 1973 war), and a 70 percent price hike led the government to take serious steps to curb consumption. They imposed Corporate Average Fuel

Economy limits on all manufacturers for the 1978 model year. The initial level was 18 miles per gallon over the whole lines, so obviously a smaller output of thirsty full-size cars helps the average. (The 1995 level is 27½ mpg.)

Fuel economy meant smaller engines, which in turn dictated smaller cars, and all American models were downsized between 1977 and 1980. The Cadillac De Ville sedan of 1977 was 8½ inches shorter in wheelbase than the '76, and 900 pounds lighter. By 1981 it had lost a further 200 pounds, and the 1985 models were shorter by another 10½ inches. To stylists used to the long look, it was an almost impossible challenge to make an attractive car on such a short wheelbase. Blandness ruled, and few inspired designs emerged. GM chief designer Dave Holls was horrified at the scene: "The era I hated the worst was the first size-down, '77, '78, '79. Those cars I hated with a passion. They were awful; it was a horrible era. When I came back from Europe and saw those cars – I had been working on the Opel Senator. I came back and saw those Malibus, the '77 B-cars, and even the Citation. Everyone else was just as bad then. The Chrysler K-car was even more square, Ford was terrible then, too. What did they have, a Fairmont? They had nothing. Thunderbirds had disintegrated into the worst; the model before this (the 1983 car) was an incredibly awful car. They were still worse than us." (Interview with C. Edson Armi, 1983)

Poor Bill Mitchell has borne the brunt of the criticism of this era's GM cars, because he was Vice President, Styling, up to his retirement in 1977. But there was little he could do, given the constraints of size, particularly before all-new designs could appear. When they did, with such cars as GM's 1982 J-cars, which used the same body pressings for all five divisions (and Brazil's Chevrolets, Britain's Vauxhalls, and Germany's Opels), he was not happy with the blandness which resulted. "They all look alike. I have to read the emblems to know what the hell they are." However, Dave Cummins thinks that the industry overcame these problems in the

'80s. "We decided to work together instead of each guy for himself, and we now have some of the most imaginative and desirable products out there. Bill's words might have been largely correct when he said them, but they can't hold up in today's environment."

Retirement from GM did not mean the end of Mitchell's working life, for, like Earl, he set up a consultancy doing work for, among others, Goodyear and Yamaha. Well into his seventies, he still enjoyed his Yamaha 1000 cafe racer and a much modified Pontiac Firebird Trans-Am powered by a Ferrari Daytona engine.

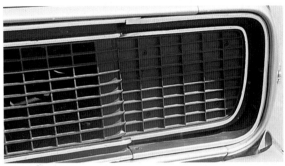

◁ 1967 CHEVROLET CAMARO SS
GM's answer to the Ford Mustang, the Camaro was also a four-passenger car made in coupe and convertible forms. Fastback and station wagon versions reached the clay stage but got no further. There was a great variety of engine and convenience options. This SS 350 has the 295hp 350-cubic-inch engine with individual grille, fender and gas-cap emblems.
△ Only the SS and RS (Rally Sport) versions had electrically-powered headlight covers. They opened sideways toward the center, and were hidden behind the grille when the lights were turned off.

△ HENRY FORD (1863-1947) AND EDSEL (1893-1943)
Whereas Henry was largely indifferent to the finer points of styling, for
his son Edsel it was of vital importance. Edsel provided the impetus for
the development of new lines and the establishment of design studios.

CHAPTER SIX

STYLING AT FORD

"My father made the most popular car in the world;
I want to make the best."

Edsel Ford

BEFORE 1932 THERE was no styling department at Ford. The notion of annual face-lifts aimed at producing customer dissatisfaction with last year's model was anathema to Henry Ford. Even offering different colors on the Model T came late (1926), and the variety was not as great as at Chevrolet. However, if Henry was largely indifferent to styling, his son Edsel was a complete contrast.

Like so many sons of thrusting, self-made men, Edsel Ford was less assertive but much more sensitive than his father, and had a marked aesthetic sense. This he shared with his wife, the former Eleanor Lowthian Clay, whom he married in 1916, and who may well have influenced him in his artistic appreciation. Unlike the Fords, the Clays filled their house with art: "Eleanor, as a little girl, became quite used to paintings bearing funny French names hanging on the wall, and to the idea that old furniture could actually be more valuable than new." (*Ford* by Robert Lacey)

By the mid-1920s, the young Fords were among the leading patrons of art in the United States, and it was Edsel who commissioned the Mexican artist Diego Rivera to paint the famous frescoes on the walls of the Detroit Institute of Arts. These survive today, despite the initial hostility of the Detroit elite who considered them ugly, factory-orientated and communistic in tone. For one thing, the frescoes showed with equal dignity black, American Indian, and Asian faces, as well as white.

Edsel's first involvement with car styling came in 1923 when he began consultations with the coachbuilders who were working on the recently acquired Lincoln. There was nothing wrong with the Lincoln's engineering, but the early bodies, designed when the Lelands owned the firm, were uninspired and did much to bring about Lincoln's receivership, from which Henry Ford rescued it for a bargain $8 million.

Edsel saw his opportunity to make his mark on the Ford automotive scene. "My father made the most popular car in the world; I want to make the best," he said. He engaged Hermann Brunn of the Buffalo coachbuilding firm to design a new line of bodies for the 1923 Lincolns, and was also involved in discussions with Judkins of Merrimac, Massachusetts, who built a custom sedan for him in 1923. Brunn continued to supply custom and semi-custom bodies to Lincoln until the Buffalo house closed its doors in 1941. While he did not actually design any bodies, Edsel became increasingly involved with Lincoln during the 1920s and set up his own studio in the plant. His father accepted that this was his son's role in the company ("We've got a pretty good man in my son. He knows style, how a car ought to look"), but Edsel still needed physical expression of his freedom from his father. Though he was much less deeply involved, Edsel's role at Lincoln was similar to Harley Earl's at General Motors, not designing but approving everything that went on. In 1925 he commissioned from Gorham, the silversmiths, the greyhound hood mascot which became a recognized accessory from 1926. He was also responsible for luring Ray Dietrich from LeBaron to set up Dietrich Inc. as the custom body arm of the Murray Corporation. They built many beautiful custom bodies for Lincoln and also developed designs for standard bodies.

▷ 1931 FORD MODEL A
CONVERTIBLE SEDAN
Thanks to Edsel's influence, Model As looked more expensive than they were, especially this top-of-the-range model priced at only $640. A mid-season model was introduced in June, its top folded away neatly in the trunk. Just 4,864 were made.
OWNER: GILMORE CAR MUSEUM, KALAMAZOO, MICHIGAN

ART OF THE AMERICAN AUTOMOBILE

The distinction between full custom and semi-custom bodies was hard to define at this period. Full customs, or one-offs designed and built to the order of a single customer, were rare, and it was Edsel who made the best custom designs available in small series to a wider variety of client. If a particular body appealed to him, he would commission perhaps ten or twenty to become part of the Lincoln catalog and therefore considerably cheaper than a true custom. Or he would buy the design to be made in series by Murray or in Lincoln's own body shops.

H ENRY'S MADE A LADY OUT OF LIZZIE: THE MODEL A

The arrival of the Ford Model A on December 2, 1927, was a landmark in automotive history. Not only did it mean that the vast Ford plants, silent for six months, could roll again, but the antiquated Model T was replaced by an up-to-date car with which Ford could look rivals in the face. Country

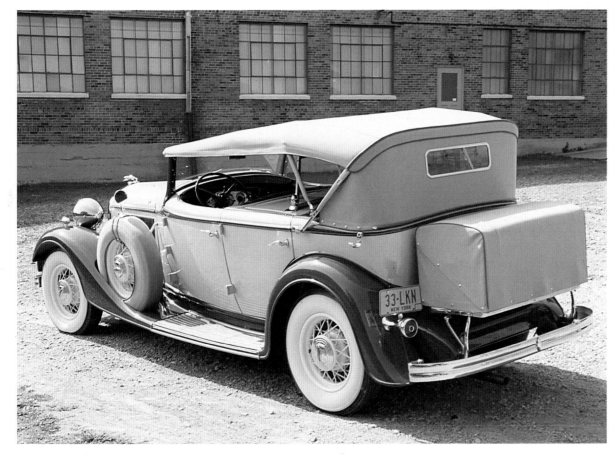

◁ △ 1933 LINCOLN KA DUAL-COWL PHAETON
The 125hp KA could be distinguished from the 150hp KB by its use of forward-hinged doors at front and rear. With a 136-inch wheelbase, it was also shorter by 9 inches. The dual-cowl style had been pioneered by Frank de Causse on a Locomobile in 1916. Rear-seat passengers rode in great comfort, but were a long way from the driver.
OWNER: AUBURN-CORD-DUESENBERG MUSEUM

cousin became country club. Edsel was closely involved with the new car, not only in styling but in such decisive matters as the replacement of Henry's beloved two-speed planetary transmission by a conventional sliding gear three-speeder. He insisted that the chassis be lower than the T's, to give a longer appearance, though the wheelbase was only 3½ inches longer. Edsel's exact involvement in the appearance of the Model A is uncertain, but as it was in many ways a miniature Lincoln, his influence was probably substantial. The radiator

shape was pure Lincoln, and the bodies, particularly the closed models, were as close to the larger car as one could hope for in a chassis shorter by 32½ inches. "Henry's made a lady out of Lizzie," went the song, but the credit should really be Edsel's.

F ORD
DESIGN STUDIO

February 1932 saw the introduction of the Ford V8, the first low-priced, mass-production car with an eight-cylinder engine. Its lines were a more rounded version of the Model A, nothing out of the ordinary, so perhaps it was no coincidence that before the year was out, Edsel Ford had hired

his company's first design consultant.

Eugene Turrenne Gregorie, always known as Bob, was born in 1909 and trained as a naval architect with Cox & Stevens before joining the Brewster body company (then owned by Rolls-Royce) from 1929 to 1931, followed by a brief stint under Harley Earl at GM's Art & Colour. He then went to Lincoln where Edsel first met him, asking him to style a small four-cylinder Ford for the British Ford company to build. Known as the Model Y, it was was highly successful and gave Ford its dominant position in Europe (the car was also made in France and Germany). Edsel asked Gregorie to style the 1933 Ford V8 on the same lines, and, indeed, it was more successful aesthetically because

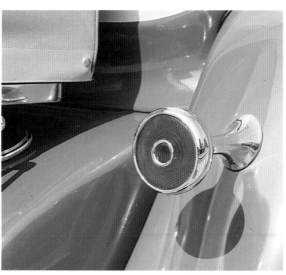

ART OF THE AMERICAN AUTOMOBILE

◁ △ The Lincoln's radiator was slanted for 1933 and mounted farther forward, part of the general trend among all car makers for moving radiator and engine forward. The thermostatic shutters were hidden behind a grille, which also concealed the dual horns. The hood still carried Lincoln's leaping greyhound mascot.

◁ Detail of the rear light.

OWNER: AUBURN-CORD-DUESENBERG MUSEUM

it had a longer wheelbase. Gregorie said that his feel for car design emerged during his boat period; certainly his love of boats made him sympathetic to Edsel. "Mr. Ford always liked the way I referred to the aft end of a car – like a boat. Designing boats

△ 1933 was the first year that all Lincolns had V12 engines, a 125hp 381.7-cubic-inch for the KA and a 447.9 cubic-inch unit which gave 150hp for the KB. No Lincoln would have fewer than 12 cylinders until 1949. Though less powerful than the KB, the KA was a smoother unit through all speed ranges.

△ The instrument panel was redesigned for 1933, with gages clustered in three circular groups.

gives you a great feeling of proportion and a sense for a beautiful line."

Up to 1935 Gregorie was a consultant to Ford rather than a full-time employee, but then Edsel set up the company's first styling studio, headed by Gregorie and with a small staff. It was a much more intimate set-up than GM's Art & Colour; there were only about ten staff, seven apprentices and three "untitled workers" (1938 figures), and, of course, there were no separate studios for different divisions like Buick, Pontiac and the like. Gregorie was in charge of all Ford and Lincoln design – trucks, buses and tractors as well as cars – and the studio was one big room. He had none of the hierarchical problems associated with GM, the stylist trying to please Harley Earl, Earl trying to please Sloan, and so on. "The elder Mr. Ford took virtually no interest in design or styling activities, leaving this phase of operations to Mr. Edsel Ford

and myself. There were no committees, etc., as is the usual practice. Decisions were quick and simple, which possibly accounts for some of the cleaner, simpler, straightforward styling we were able to accomplish. Mr. Edsel Ford and I were usually pretty much in agreement on clean, simple forms and designs." He led a pretty independent existence, never bothering to punch a timeclock, although he incurred the hostility of Henry's henchman Harry Bennett and Ford chief engineer Larry Sheldrick, both of whom would have been happy to see Gregorie fired.

While Bob Gregorie was responsible for all Fords between 1933 and 1948 (and the '49 Mercury which was designed before he left), three landmarks stand out – the 1936 Lincoln Zephyr, 1939 Mercury and 1940 Lincoln Continental.

The Zephyr was a joint effort with John Tjaarda, who was working for Briggs Motor Bodies. The story is a complex one. Dutch-born Tjaarda (d. 1962) arrived in America in 1923 and worked for coachbuilders Locke & Co. and for Duesenberg before becoming one of Harley Earl's acolytes at the GM Art & Colour Section in 1930. There Tjaarda submitted a radical rear-engined design as his contribution to one of Earl's competitions. He didn't win (that honor went to the coupe on the V16 Cadillac for the 1933 Chicago World's Fair), but his design was eventually productionized, as was

Gordon Buehrig's (as the Cord 810) and Phil Wright's (as the Pierce-Arrow Silver Arrow, though few were made).

Tjaarda's radical car featured a rear-mounted valve-in-head V8 engine. Although it was a five-passenger, four-door sedan, its engine was mounted ahead of the rear axle, making it a mid-engined design in the manner of 1960s sports cars like the Ferrari Dino and Lamborghini Miura. Tjaarda favored rear engines, but hated the power unit "hanging out over the rear axle" as in the later Tatra and Volkswagen. He knew (without testing it in practice) that a heavy weight at the very end of the chassis would cause severe handling problems, as it proved in the Tatras, though less so with the shorter and less powerful Volkswagen. Thus his design, named Sterkenburg after his full family name, Tjaarda van Sterkenburg, was a pioneer mid-

A clay model (left, top) of the Tjaarda design which became the Lincoln Zephyr. Dated October 1934, this is quite close to the final product and, unlike earlier designs, is clearly intended for a front-mounted engine. Fenders running into the front doors were not adopted on the production Zephyr.

PHOTO: THE COLLECTIONS OF HENRY FORD MUSEUM & GREENFIELD VILLAGE

◁ 1937 LINCOLN ZEPHYR SEDAN
The short hood and long body with full doors front and rear were clearly inherited from the original Sterkenburg design. The car was named for the *Burlington Zephyr*, a streamlined diesel-powered train that debuted in 1934 and set a new record for the Denver-Chicago run. The original Zephyrus was the god of the west wind in Greek mythology.

PHOTO: NATIONAL MOTOR MUSEUM, BEAULIEU

△ 1940 LINCOLN ZEPHYR SEDAN.
Priced at $1,400, the six-passenger sedan was the most popular Zephyr body style in 1940. This car is something of a hybrid, for while the grille indicates a date in 1940, the parking lights above the headlights were only introduced on the 1941 model.

PHOTO: NATIONAL MOTOR MUSEUM, BEAULIEU

engined car which also incorporated integral construction, independent suspension by parallel arms and rubber in torsion, and a combined engine, transaxle and suspension which could be detached in a single unit. The first Sterkenburg design of 1930 had a conventional radiator flanked by separate headlights, but a year or two later it had a rounded front like a Volkswagen Beetle, semi-faired-in headlights and a rounded tail with a fin running down the center.

These were no more than drawings and models, as Tjaarda could not obtain backing to build even a prototype. In 1932 he took a job with the Briggs Body Co. in Detroit as a designer/engineer, and it was here, or possibly even before he joined Briggs, that Edsel Ford first came across the Sterkenburg. He was fascinated by Tjaarda's far-sighted thinking and independence of mind, and set up a special department at Briggs where he could work unhindered. Edsel also had his own studio, and when Diego Rivera visited him there in 1932, he found him at work on an aerodynamic Lincoln coupe, possibly inspired by Tjaarda's car.

With Edsel's backing, Tjaarda was able to get a prototype built at Briggs, which was tested in 1934. Its lines were similar to those of the more streamlined Sterkenburg, though the fin had disappeared, and anticipated those of the Lincoln Zephyr. The rear-mounted engine was an aluminum block Ford V8 which weighed only 300 pounds and gave 85bhp. Air was supplied to the engine by two scoops just behind the rear door. The car weighed 3,200 pounds, exactly what its designer had forecast. This was fortunate since he had to rely on what he called "guessomatics" as there were no computers to calculate stress distribution.

The prototype was exhaustively tested at Ford's River Rouge track, reaching speeds claimed to be up to 110mph and proving stronger than conventional body/chassis cars. The speed seems on the high side, bearing in mind that the production Zephyr, with a more powerful V12 engine, could only reach 90mph. The stage was set for manufacture of the new design by Ford, though several important changes were to be made before its launch on November 2, 1935. The decision to market it under the Lincoln name was taken because the expensive V12 Lincolns were selling poorly in the Depression years, only 1400 in 1935, compared with 52,256 Packards and 23,559 Cadillacs and La Salles, and there were plans to close down Lincoln completely. The new car would have its own name, Lincoln Zephyr, and its own production lines. In fact, the bodies were were painted and trimmed in the Briggs factory, which also made the hood and fenders, and readied the body shell for engine installation. Edsel Ford told Tjaarda that he might almost send the mechanical parts to Briggs and have them complete the assembly and market the car, as there wasn't much left for Lincoln to do when Briggs was through.

Several of the radical features of the Tjaarda design were lost in the path to production, notably the rear engine and torsion bar suspension. Had the decisions been entirely up to Edsel, these might have been incorporated in the Zephyr, but he was walking a shaky tightrope between Tjaarda on one hand and his father and Charlie Sorensen on the

▷ 1940 LINCOLN CONTINENTAL CABRIOLET
Using mechanical components from the regular Zephyrs, the Continental carried a striking body which accounted for a price 60 percent above that of the Zephyr convertible, but assured it classic status in later years.

other. The elder Ford was wedded to his transverse leaf spring suspension, inherited from Model T days and used on all Fords up to 1948, the year after his death. "We use transverse springs for the same reason we use round wheels, because we have found nothing better for the purpose." The rear engine was voted down by public reaction at prototype viewings; only 50 percent favored it, too low a figure to be considered commercially safe.

The other big change was Edsel's decision; he felt that a standard V8 engine was unsuited to a car bearing the Lincoln name, and as the big cars had V12s, he ordered a smaller V12 from chief engineer Frank Johnson. It was a 267-cubic-inch unit with aluminum alloy heads and cast steel pistons. Output was 110hp, giving a top speed of over 90mph. The front engine dictated a longer hood, and restyling of the front end. This brought Bob Gregorie into the picture; he spent ten days at Briggs and came up with the distinctive V-shaped prow with matching headlights faired into the fenders. He used a similar

shape on the 1937 Fords, though this family likeness was not continued in later years. The Zephyr's body and rear end were pretty close to the Sterkenburg's.

Although the engine proved troublesome, the Zephyr was well received. Tjaarda reported that several eminent European designers including Ferdinand Porsche, Emile Mathis and Jorgen Rasmussen of Auto Union called it the only car coming out of America to command their interest. The British magazine *The Autocar*, in a pompously cautious phraseology, said "A certain amount of adjustment is needed as regards the unusual appearance, but from all points of view, a remarkable car has been produced." After World War II, the Museum of Modern Art in New York called the Zephyr "the first successfully designed streamlined car in America."

The first major change in Zephyr styling came on the 1938 models. It was very significant, as it represented a breakaway from the vertical grille

filling the whole of the front end of the car. Imitated in various forms by practically all American designers from 1939 on, it had a purely practical origin. The first Zephyrs did not cool well, particularly in the intense heat of Arizona and Texas, as the radiator core was tall and narrow and not well exposed to the fan which was mounted on the end of the crankshaft. Gregorie decided to install the radiator horizontally, in which case there was no need for a tall grille, only one sufficient to admit air to the low radiator. He chose two small intakes, one on each side of the pointed prow. As he said later, "That was the style leader of that year, but no one realized why we did it... So after that Buick and all the rest of them – all of General Motors – they started these low, horizontal grilles. That was the beginning of the horizontal grille thing, but they never knew why we had to do this. What it did, it created a whole styling change in the American car." (Interview with C. Edson Armi, January 1984)

◁ △ The Lincoln Continental was born of a discussion between Edsel Ford and Bob Gregorie about how the Zephyr engine could be used with more striking bodywork. The engine was barely changed apart from a side-mounted air cleaner necessitated by the lower hood line, and polished aluminum cylinder heads and manifolds. Sales of the 1940 model cabriolet were 350 and of the coupe, 54.

△ Compared with the regular Zephyr, the Continental's hood was 3 inches lower and 7 inches longer. Cowl and belt line were lower, too. The doors had no flare at the bottom.

For 1939 the horizontal grille bars were replaced by vertical ones, giving a waterfall effect, and this was continued through the 1941 season. Then came another grille change, which most connoisseurs today regard as unfortunate. Instead of leading fashion, Gregorie was obliged to follow it, in this case, Cadillac. In his own words, "The '41 Cadillac had a big, hefty, husky, bold appearance, you know. It had a great big front end, which I referred to as an architectural front end. It looked like the front of the public library in Washington, with pillars. I wanted flow lines, motion lines, clean flow, graceful shapes... Edsel liked the slender, delicate effect... But we needed a huskier-looking front end."

The bolder front end was a response to customer demand. "That is what people wanted. That is what they were paying more money for, heavier cars." It is not true that the '42 design was forced on Gregorie by the sales department; he definitely favored the style. Edsel probably didn't, but he was already a sick man, and as Gregorie said, he finally came around.

The 1942 Lincoln front end was certainly husky, with a more complex, split-level horizontal grille, heavier bumpers, "suitcase-style" front fenders and little wings on each side of the headlights. After the war, the grille became even heavier, with thicker bars, and this was continued until the arrival of all-new Lincolns in the spring of 1948.

THE CONTINENTAL

If the Zephyr was a Tjaarda design refined by Bob Gregorie, the Continental was a joint Gregorie/ Edsel Ford production, its timeless lines a tribute to the innate artistic sense of both men. It was not their first joint production, though it was the only one to sell to the public. The close rapport

◁ 1949 FORD CUSTOM CONVERTIBLE
The 1949 Ford was styled by a team led by George Walker, an outside consultant hired by Ford to design an all-new post-war car. His design was chosen instead of the one by Ford's own stylist, Bob Gregorie.
OWNER: JOHN BUCHANAN

between Ford and Gregorie led to customized roadsters and phaetons from 1932 on. Some were made in the Ford airplane plant where the Trimotor had been made, and where there were a number of skilled sheet metal workers. The 1934 phaeton was built on a lengthened V8 chassis, underslung at the rear, which was used on the Ford-powered Jensen sports cars. It had cutaway doors, no running boards, and a very European look about it. There were plans for more sophisticated bodies to be built on this chassis by the great coachbuilding houses who worked on the Lincoln V12 chassis, Brewster, Brunn, Derham and Judkins. However, nothing came of this, and the next Gregorie/Ford joint effort was an all-Lincoln product. As Bob Gregorie recalled, "In November 1938, Mr. Edsel Ford and I had a conversation... and talked about some car we might build in the future. I figured, 'Well, we've got the Zephyr, with a 12-cylinder engine, and we've got a whole bay empty in the Lincoln plant.' The

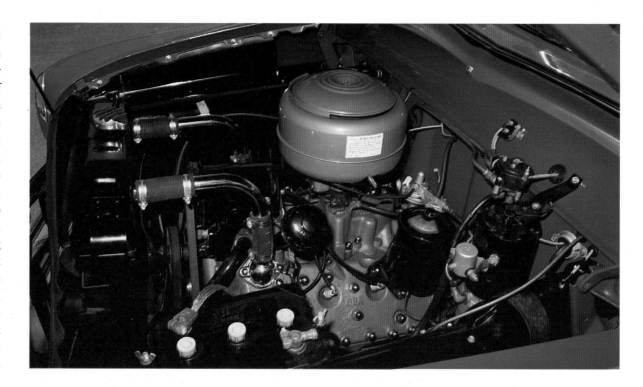

ART OF THE AMERICAN AUTOMOBILE

◁ The engine of the '49 Ford (top) was the major component to be unchanged from earlier cars. It was still the familiar flathead V8 whose origins dated back to 1932, though displacement was increased from 221 to 239 cubic inches in 1946. A 226-cubic-inch six was also offered.

◁ △ The '49 Ford had very clean, straight-through lines. This convertible cost $1,886 with the six-cylinder engine, and $1,949 with the V8.

△ A distinctive styling feature of the '49 Ford was the "spinner" in place of the usual grille. Above it were four block letters reading "FORD"; these tended to fall off, so for 1950 they were replaced by a crest.

bay had been used for finishing up the Model K custom bodies as they came in. Also, we had a nucleus of very fine body people at Lincoln, left over from the K, who could do beautiful custom painting and trim work." (Interview with Michael Lamm, 1989)

Gregorie came up with the basic lines of the Continental convertible in about an hour. He put a piece of vellum over a 1/10th scale blueprint of the current (1939 model) Zephyr sedan and sketched in the changes that he favored: a longer, lower hood; extended front fenders; dropped steering column. The most noticeable changes, at the rear end, were the shorter, bulkier trunk and outside mounted spare wheel cover. When Edsel saw the sketch, he

▷ 1950 MERCURY SEDAN
Very similar to the first new post-war Mercury of 1949, this car was one of Bob Gregorie's favorites. It was planned as a post-war Ford, but Ernest Breech thought it too large, so it became a Mercury instead. The harmonica-like horizontal grille gave the front end a character different from any contemporary American car.

OWNERS: DALE AND LINDA DEVINE

said "Don't change a line on it. How soon can we build it?"

Encouraged by this reaction, but still not thinking that it would be a production car, Gregorie went to work on a one tenth scale clay model, painted in Edsel's favorite gunmetal gray with white sidewall tires. Edsel's reaction was the same as before: "Let's not change a thing. I wouldn't change a line on it."

This was still November 1938, and Edsel wanted a complete car for his winter vacation in Florida in March 1939. Gregorie asked his chief draftsman Martin Regitko to prepare a full-size paper draft which was sent to the Lincoln plant. There, in the unused bays which had seen work on Model K custom bodies, panel beaters hammered out the shape by hand. "They didn't have any hammer forms or anything; just did it all by eye."

The car was not yet called a Continental; just "the Special Lincoln Zephyr for Edsel Ford." As such it was shipped to Florida, and within two weeks Edsel cabled enthusiastically that he could sell a thousand of them. Virtually no changes were made on the first production cars, 25 of which were sold as 1939 models. The trunk was a little deeper. There were no real body dies until 1941, so all 350 convertibles and 54 coupes in the 1940 series were handmade. Despite rumors, there were no exact replicas of the cars Edsel Ford built for his sons Henry and Benson, or anyone else. Considering the classic aura which has gathered around the Continental in recent years, its launch was a low-

key affair; as Lincoln historian James K. Wagner observed, "The casual manner in which the Zephyr Continental cabriolet was announced suggests that the Lincoln marketing people of 1939-40 knew not what they had."

The Continental name was used for the 1940 and subsequent production cars, chosen by Edsel because he thought the lines resembled those of continental designs. Interestingly, Bob Gregorie was never entirely happy with the Continental. He told C. Edson Armi, "I thought it was kind of weak in the rear end. I didn't care too much for the pinched-in rear end. It reminded me a little bit of a dog with his tail between his legs. But Mr. Ford liked it…that delicate bumper is what Mr. Ford liked, and, after all, I built it for him." Gregorie

favored a bulkier look, which he obtained on the front end of all 1942 Lincolns, including the Continental. There was even more chrome on the 1946-48 models, and it is one of these which Gregorie drives in his retirement.

Drawings exist showing Gregorie's plans for a second generation Continental. Dating from December 1945, they show a bulky car similar to the 1949 V8 Lincoln, with some Continental touches such as the exposed spare wheel. But with Edsel dead, there was little enthusiasm for the concept at Ford. Both Gregorie and Thomas Hibbard (design director 1947-48) agree that the

◁ The rear view of the 1950 Mercury shows a few styling changes from the '49s, in particular a new single-piece back light and cockleshell-shaped decklid handle and ornament. Surprisingly this four-door Sport Sedan was outsold by the two-door six-passenger coupe.

Conti never earned a cent of profit, and several key men at Ford such as Charles Sorensen and the Henrys, father and grandson, never had any love for the car. Hibbard admitted that the cars were cobbled up. "I remember distinctly going into the Lincoln plant and seeing the bodies assembled, the fenders and body panels and all, and the stuff was really very crudely built. The bodies had to have a lot of handwork to make them acceptable. Of course, when they got through with them, the Continentals looked good, but underneath they were still pretty bad." (Interview with Michael Lamm, 1973)

The Continental disappeared along with the V12 engine in 1948, and by the time the theme was

▽ ▷ 1956 MERCURY MONTEREY
Promoted as "The Big M," the 1956 Mercury line was made in three series: the low-priced Medalist, mid-range Monterey, and top model Montclair. Styling was not greatly changed from 1955, but the hood now carried a big "M" above the grille. Coupes such as this Monterey were 2 inches lower than sedans at 58.6 inches. This car sold for $2,630. With sales of 42,863, it was the most popular of the 1956 Monterey line.
OWNERS: DALE AND LINDA DEVINE

▷ 1951 FORD CONVERTIBLE
Details such as the back lights were particularly stylish on this car (facing page).

revived with the Continental Mark II of 1955, Bob Gregorie was no longer with Ford.

THE MERCURY

In the early 1930s, Ford was at a disadvantage compared to its rivals because there was a great gap between the top V8 at $750 and the Lincoln V12 whose prices ran from $4,200 up to $6,800. The gap was bridged to some extent by the $1,275 Lincoln Zephyr in 1936, but Ford still had nothing for the upwardly mobile owner to trade up to. Consequently they tended to turn to a Pontiac De Luxe Eight or a Dodge Deluxe, and probably ceased to be Ford customers forever. Edsel had been pressing his father for an upscale Ford, but while the old man recognized his son's styling talent, he was not willing to give him the independence to promote what was essentially a marketing exercise.

The choice of name was Edsel's, and he is said to have considered more than 100 names before choosing Mercury, the Roman messenger god.

There had already been five makes of car called Mercury, three in the U.S. and two in Britain, but they were all pretty obscure, and Edsel had probably never heard of any of them. At first, he favored the name Ford-Mercury, and it was shown as such at the 1938 New York Show. However, sales people found resistance to the idea of "just another Ford," and against Edsel's wishes ("What's wrong with the name Ford – it's been good for 40 years, hasn't it?"), production cars were just Mercurys.

For a new car to claim a significant segment of a market its makers had not competed in before, it needed to be distinctive yet recognizable as a Ford product. This was Ford's brief to Gregorie and the engineers. In fact, the car was very close in general lines to the Ford V8, yet there was not a single interchangeable panel between the two bodies on the 1939 and 1940 models; for 1941 they were identical except for trim and grille. The 1939 Mercury was four inches longer in wheelbase, the additional length being taken up by a longer hood. Body styles were two- and four-door sedans, convertible and sedan-coupe. This was the most

△ 1951 FORD CUSTOM DE LUXE CONVERTIBLE
Ford abandoned the central spinner grille for 1951 in
favor of a less striking twin spinner theme. The Custom
De Luxe was the top line which included a convertible
and a hardtop coupe.
OWNER: CHARLES SAATHOFF

▷ For 1951 Ford continued to offer two engines, a
226-cubic-inch six and this V8 (top) of 239 cubic inches
which developed 100hp. Both engines were available in
De Luxe and Custom De Luxe lines, but the Crestliner
two-door sedan, Victoria hardtop and convertible came
only with the V8.

▷ The rear view shows the taillight lenses and the
licence plate cover which were redesigned for 1951.

ART OF THE AMERICAN AUTOMOBILE

distinctive body, having no equivalent in the Ford stable. It used the same doors and body shell as the convertible, but had a hard top, with very thin B-pillars and chrome surrounds to the windows. These pillars were similar to those used on the Continental coupe. The Mercury's grille was the same shape as the Ford's, but it had horizontal bars in place of vertical ones.

Despite accusations of being a "pumped-up Ford," the Mercury sold well in its first season, totaling 60,214 for the '39 models. As one would expect, the four-door sedan was the most popular, at 33,140 units, but the sedan-coupe sold 7,664. Prices were $894 to $994, compared with $700 to $790 for the equivalent Fords. There were no major styling changes for 1940, though an additional style was the four-door convertible sedan at $1,272. From 1941

through 1948, the Mercury shared sheet metal with the Ford, but for 1949, an all-new body was used. This, and the contemporary Lincolns, had its origin in a series of design studies made during World War II, and is thus a Gregorie car, though he had left Ford more than two years before the cars were launched.

When the U.S. entered the war in December 1941, there was an immediate switch of priorities from auto manufacture to production for the military. All passenger car output ceased by early February 1942, and the styling departments turned to projects like camouflage for B-24 bombers. However, they realized that the war would end sooner or later, and that new cars would be needed when it did, so from around 1943 sketches and clay models again appeared on the agenda of the Ford

styling department. They had the all-enveloping slab-sided look which characterized production cars from 1948 on, and several of the Lincoln and Mercury designs had fastbacks, which both Edsel and Gregorie liked. This was carried through to production on one model of the 1948-49 Lincoln line, the Cosmopolitan Town Sedan which, though much bulkier, had vestiges of the Zephyr in its appearance. Interestingly, it did not sell as well as the notchback Sport Sedan and was dropped in January 1949.

A look at the wartime designs for Ford, Mercury and Lincoln quickly reveals that Mercurys were closer to Lincolns than to Fords, in a reversal of the make's styling up to that time. The Mercury styles were clearly junior Lincolns rather than upscale Fords, a distinction which was reinforced when the Lincoln-Mercury Division was set up in October 1945. One of the results was to form an independent dealer network for Lincoln-Mercury, whereas previously even the big Lincolns had been sold mainly by selected Ford dealers. The 1946-48 Mercurys, of course, were still basically Fords, as they were carry-overs from before the war.

▷   1955 FORD SUNLINER TWO-DOOR TOWN SEDAN
▽   1955 FORD SUNLINER CONVERTIBLE

Fords were given a completely new look for 1955 by Frank Hershey. He had to use the basic 1952-54 body shell but, with a wraparound windshield, hooded headlights, wider grille and a characteristic dip in the belt line, he contrived to make the cars seem all new. The Fairlane, named for the Ford family estate, was a new top line replacing the Crestliner. The convertible sold for $2,324 and the sedan for $2,060, with V8 engines. Six-cylinder prices were $100 less.

PHOTOS: NATIONAL MOTOR MUSEUM, BEAULIEU

LET'S JUST DELUXE-Y THE HELL OUT OF THESE CARS

Bob Gregorie called the 1949 Mercury one of his favorite designs. There is no doubt that while he had a strong personal empathy with Edsel Ford, he favored a bulkier style of body and did not share Edsel's fondness for delicacy in bumpers and grilles. Thus, Ford's death on May 26, 1943, released Gregorie to indulge his own ideas. The car that emerged as the '49 Mercury was originally intended to be a big Ford, and to understand this situation, you need to understand company policy at the end of the war. Edsel's death just five months

short of his 50th birthday left the styling department without a guru and the company without a leader. Old Henry, already 80 years old and past his best, was so devastated by his son's death, for which he felt partly responsible, that he became unable to give the company any leadership. Ford was a major contributor to the war effort, yet in the summer of 1943 it was lurching from crisis to crisis like a ship bereft of power and steering. President Roosevelt was seriously worried and asked Navy Secretary Frank Knox to release from the service Edsel's son, 25-year-old Henry II.

The post-war plan, worked out by Henry II, his

right-hand man Ernest Breech, and a group of young men who came to be known as the Whiz Kids, was for four lines of car: a small compact Ford (c.98-inch wheelbase), a standard-sized Ford (118-inch wheelbase), Mercurys on two wheelbases (120 and 123 inches), and Lincolns on three wheelbases (125, 128 and 132 inches). The compact Ford was tested with four-, five- and six-cylinder engines, and its body proposals were from the Edsel era of delicate lines and minimal chrome. Once GM abandoned its plan for a small car, Ford did the same, though the compact's body style became the French Ford Vedette, with a small-block V8 engine.

The standard Ford was the car on which Gregorie worked in 1944-45. After Edsel's death, he was responsible to Charlie Sorensen, who was number two in the company, and who had no time for delicacy of line. "Bob," he said, "let's just deluxe-y the hell out of these cars." This encouraged Gregorie to indulge himself in filling out the body compared with previous designs. The new Ford had a wider trunk with "a little more beef, with full round shapes, just like those big Italian gals." Like all the wartime designs, it was a full-width car, but the slab-sided effect was modified by a surface relief line, a boat designer's trick, starting as a simple line behind the rear wheel, running forward and then stepped up in the door. (front door

in the production car, but the clay models were two-door coupes), and expanding into the hood. The grille was a rolled horizontal design resembling a harmonica in surface, with (on the production car) a vertical chrome bar about the same size in the center, and the bumper overriders.

When Ernest Breech saw and drove the car in 1946, he felt it was too large to be a standard Ford and suggested that instead it should be the new Mercury, and that Gregorie's Mercury should become a Lincoln. This is how it turned out. The Mercury was very close to the 1944 Ford design; it rode on an all-new X-frame chassis of 118-inches wheelbase with coil spring independent front suspension shared with other Fords.

△ 1961 LINCOLN CONTINENTAL CONVERTIBLE
The Continental was completely restyled for 1961, reflecting a new philosophy that big was not necessarily better. With the enormous 1960 Continental, Lincoln had tried to out-do Harley Earl, but the 1961 was described by Lincoln historian James Wagner as using the Mercedes-Benz approach rather than that of General Motors. Its wheelbase was 8 inches shorter than the 1960 model, the overall length was reduced by 15 inches. However, it still seated six passengers in great comfort. Lincoln was the only company in America at this time to make a four-door convertible.

ART OF THE AMERICAN AUTOMOBILE

GEORGE WALKER AND THE 1949 FORD

Having promoted the Ford to a Mercury, there remained the problem of finding a design for the 1949 Ford. Breech decided on an all-new package (apart from the engine which was the familiar flathead V8, though slightly enlarged in displacement from the pre-war unit). Rather than relying on in-house talent, he invited an outside consultant and close personal friend, George Walker, to submit a design in addition to Gregorie. Walker ran an industrial design studio which had been responsible for Nash styling since 1937. The staff was aided by two very talented men, Elwood P. Engel, later VP of styling at Chrysler, and Joseph Oros, who was to become VP of design for Ford of Europe. Walker's role was not unlike that of Harley Earl; his designers did the drawing and he then selected the design which he wanted to use. According to Frank Hershey, he had no talent as a designer, but he was a good salesman of his ideas and those which were suggested to him. Several designs were submitted to Walker, and the one he chose as a starting point for the new Ford was made by Richard Caleal, aided by Bob Bourke and Holden Koto, all three ex-Loewy studio men. The scale clay was baked in Caleal's kitchen oven, "seriously affecting the quality of cuisine in the Caleal household for months," said Bourke.

Several important changes were made on the full-size clay. In particular, the roof line was raised to give better access and headroom, and this

▽ George Walker with a 1959 Thunderbird and, in the background, a 1908 Ford Model T. The four-passenger T-bird, sometimes called the Big Bird, sold much better than the two-passenger model of 1955-57.

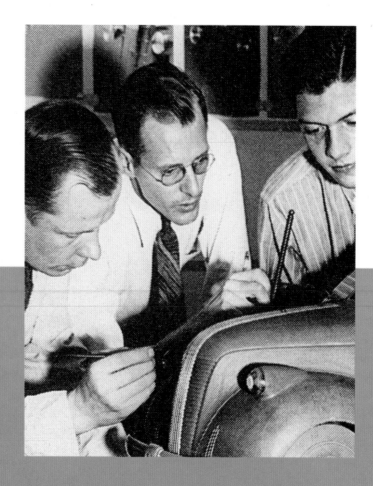

△ FRANK HERSHEY (b.1905)
Frank Hershey working on the clay of the 1935 Pontiac Silver
Streak for GM. His other very famous car was the first
Thunderbird for Ford.

CHAPTER SEVEN

FRANK HERSHEY: FROM GM TO FORD

"Our philosophy was to make a car that, while it was a sports car, a banker, for instance, could drive it up to his bank in the morning with a certain amount of dignity."

Frank Hershey on the Thunderbird

ONE OF THE most talented of the many stylists who worked for Harley Earl was Franklin Quick Hershey, best known for two very different cars from different companies, the Pontiac Silver Streak of 1935, and the first Ford Thunderbird of 1955. He was born in Detroit in 1905 into a motor-minded family who were personally acquainted with Henry Ford, the

Dodge brothers and the Lelands. His mother was the first woman to drive a car in Detroit (a 1903 single-cylinder Cadillac), and the family bought a new Cadillac each year from 1903 to 1920. After that, so much money was put into a ranch at La Puente, California, that there was not much left over for new cars.

Like his mentor Harley Earl, Frank grew up loving automobiles more than anything else in the

world. He joined the Walter Murphy coachbuilding company in November 1928, working under Frank Spring, who was later chief designer for Hudson (see Chapter 16). He moved briefly to the GM Art & Colour Section, then back to Murphy, where he stayed until it closed down at the end of 1931. During this period he designed the only 8-liter Bentley to be bodied by the Pasadena firm. The convertible sedan was very much in the Murphy

ART OF THE AMERICAN AUTOMOBILE

1934 PONTIAC EIGHT SEDAN
Frank Hershey gave the new 1933 Pontiac an up-to-date body to go with its new in-line eight engine. Chevrolet Master body stampings were wedded to a longer frame, the space being taken up by the longer hood over the straight-eight engine. The radiator grille was slanted and also given a V. Horizontal flashes on the fender skirts gave an impression of speed. This 1934 car has different hood louvers from the '33, these being "borrowed" by Harley Earl from the contemporary Cadillac. This is the Touring Sedan, the first Pontiac to have a built-in trunk. It sold for $805. The two-door version cost $745.

PHOTOS: NATIONAL MOTOR MUSEUM, BEAULIEU

idiom and could easily have been on a Duesenberg chassis, but the pointed Bentley radiator was retained, and it is said that this was the inspiration for the 1933 Pontiac, which was Hershey's first major work.

After Murphy folded, Hershey spent a few months back with Frank Spring, who was now with Hudson. Then he returned to the GM fold just as Harley Earl was setting up individual studios for each division. He was assigned to the Pontiac studio, which was about to launch an all-new low-price straight-eight. This was to be a make-or-break car for Pontiac, which was struggling with the out-of-date Oakland V8 and an uninspired six. Sales had dropped from 224,784 in 1928 to 51,621 in 1932, and there was serious talk of closing Pontiac down, only six years after it had appeared as a make. The 223-cubic-inch straight-eight was a response to Ford's

V8, for the Oakland unit was too expensive to make and did not run smoothly. Unfortunately Pontiac had produced a fine engine, but no one had bothered much with styling. When Hershey saw the mock-up for the new car, he exclaimed, "Here, they've got this brand new eight-cylinder car, and it doesn't look a bit different from the old one."

Earl agreed that something needed to be done, but they were only a few weeks from the launch date. He gave Hershey two weeks to come up with a more attractive design, with the obvious restriction that the body shell, shared with Chevrolet, could not be changed.

The hood and radiator were redesigned, given a sloping grille with a slight V to it, inspired by the Bentley, and a tapered curve at the bottom which was similar to that on the 1932 Packard Light Eight. The hood louvers were given a slight rearward slant,

◁ △　1956 FORD THUNDERBIRD
The detachable hardtop with its porthole windows could be had together with a soft top for $290; the soft top alone cost $75. Portholes were new in 1956, and 80 percent of buyers preferred them to the plain hardtop. Among the "convenience options" were the windshield washer and power-operated windows.

△　The regular engine was a 292-cubic-inch V8, giving 193 or 198hp, but for 1956 a Special V8 giving 215hp from 321 cubic inches was available at a cost of $123 more than the basic price of $3,151.

OWNERS: BUD AND BONITA LILLY

parallel to that of the grille, creating an impression of speed. An important improvement was the fender skirt, which had been pioneered by Graham's stylist Amos Northup on the 1932 models. All GM divisions had skirts for 1933, as did Ford, Packard and several other makes (though not Chrysler), but Pontiac's were particularly attractive, with three horizontal flashes, or speed streaks, on both front and rear skirts.

Hershey's redesign worked wonders for Pontiac, whose sales for 1933 nearly doubled, when the industry was still languishing from the effects of the Depression. Only small changes were made for 1934, but these included an extra seven inches on the hood length, new horizontal hood louvers, and longer, bullet-shaped headlight buckets. The hood louvers were taken from those of Cadillac by Earl himself; this was a small example of his borrowing of ideas from one studio to use in another.

The next major change came for Pontiac on the 1935 models, known as the Silver Streaks. It originated in an entry for Earl's 1933 styling competition (another entry in this competition was Gordon Buehrig's design which eventually became the Cord 810). As first visualized by Hershey, it had a narrow grille wrapped around the bumper and

running up the front of the car and along the hood to the windshield. It also had headlights built into the side of the hood close to the grille, no running boards, and a fastback body. This was too much for Earl and the production people. He told Hershey to make it more "production possible." When the stylist hesitated, Earl said, "Look, you want your job? You've wasted too much time doing nothing. You are to go down there and take that car and make it work. Make it like it is supposed to be – more like our present direction – and you've got to use the Chevrolet body."

So out went the faired-in headlights and the fastback, and the streak did not extend to the bumpers. The production car was very striking, nevertheless, and gave Pontiac an identity which lasted up to 1956. Two explanations have been given for the origin of the silver streak. Hershey says that he was inspired by a photo of a pre-World War I racing Napier, which had a wide oil cooler with aluminum fins. "I fell in love with that thing," he says. "The oil cooler was about eight inches wide with just these lovely aluminum fins showing, and what I did was simply to continue it along the top of the hood and down over the grille."

Clay modeler Clark Whitcombe says that he

brought some molding strips into the studio, but as it was late, there was no one there to hand the strips to. He just draped them over the hood of a clay model and went home. Next morning, someone saw the strips on the hood and exclaimed, "That's it!" Perhaps both explanations are true; the draped strips coincided with Hershey's inspiration from the Napier.

The 1935 Silver Streak was continued for 1936 with little change. It was also used in modified form on 1936 GMC trucks, and there was hint of it on the front of the GMC-built Greyhound buses. Frank Hershey's last design for Pontiac was the 1937 line, which used a modified silver streak with a wider grille surrounding it, though the streak was continued along the hood top to the windshield as on the original design. The bodies were no longer those of the A-body Chevrolet, but were the B-bodies used on Oldsmobiles, La Salles and the small Buicks. For 1938 Virgil Exner took over at Pontiac; Hershey went to the Buick studio, but did not stay there long as he was given responsibility for GM's German operation, Opel, at Russelsheim.

The 1938 Opel Kapitan is an interesting design as it incorporated a number of features not seen on American GM cars for several years. These included rectangular headlights mounted in the front of the fenders, and fenders that extended halfway into the front doors. Hershey says that they were allowed a great deal of latitude at Opel because of a smaller production run, and so he could put on several ideas that the Detroit studios were prevented by cost from using. Chevrolet lights were not fully integrated into the fenders until 1942, and fenders that extended into the doors arrived the same year. The Opel's grille resembled that of the 1938 Cadillac Sixty Special to some extent, while the upper part of the grille ran around the hood to the scuttle, in the manner of the Cord 810.

Although his influence was seen most strongly at Opel, Frank Hershey's field included GM's operations in Britain (Vauxhall) and Australia

△ ▷ 1956 FORD THUNDERBIRD
Frank Hershey aimed to make this a sports car with "banker appeal," a car sufficiently dignified for the professional man to drive to work in. It was felt that Chevrolet's Corvette did not meet this requirement. As the T-bird was a better performer and cost $496 less, no wonder it sold better. In fact, the the sales figure for the first model (1954 and 1955) was 16,155 – nearly four times that of the Corvette.
OWNERS: BUD AND BONITA LILLY

ART OF THE AMERICAN AUTOMOBILE

(Holden). Although he has not been directly credited with the design, it seems possible that he influenced the fastback coupes, known as "slopers," that Holden built on Buick, Chevrolet, Oldsmobile, Pontiac and Vauxhall chassis between 1935 and 1940. While he was with the Pontiac studio of Art & Colour, Clare Hodgman, working under his direction, produced a drawing of a fastback coupe which was startlingly similar to the production bodies which emerged from Holden's Fisherman's Bend factory. (Holden did not make complete cars until after World War II.) On the other hand, perhaps it was a case of different minds working in the same direction. The slopers were quite similar to the Cadillac V16 coupe built for the 1933 Chicago Century of Progress Exposition.

Norm Darwin, the Holden historian, says that Holden stylists cannot have been influenced by the Cadillac as they were unaware of its existence, but surely *someone* at Holden would have seen a photo of this widely publicized car. Whatever their origin, the slopers were advanced cars for their day, and anticipated Chevrolet's 1946 Fleetline coupe by 11 years.

△ 1958 FORD THUNDERBIRD

The two-passenger T-bird was replaced for 1958 by a four-passenger car of greater size and much bulkier appearance. The Big Bird, or Square Bird, was 11 inches longer in wheelbase, 20 inches longer overall, and 815 pounds heavier. The engine was a new 352-cubic-inch V8 giving 300hp. Made in hardtop and convertible forms, the Big Bird sold nearly 38,000 units in its first year, getting on for double that of the 1957 Little Bird.

OWNERS: BOB AND COLLEEN MASON

△ The 1958 Big Bird had its spare wheel mounted
externally, adding 10 inches to the overall length.
However, this was considered necessary because
mounting it inside the trunk, as on the '57 Little Bird,
greatly reduced the luggage capacity.

◁ The Big Bird used the larger of Ford's new engines for 1958, the "big block" V8s in 332- and 352-cubic-inch sizes. Designed by Robert Stevenson, they were planned to be capable of enlargement up to 425 cubic inches if necessary. In fact, a 427 was launched in 1963, which powered the Cobra and was the largest engine option in the Mustang, as well as going into other Fords.

▽ The Big Bird had much more embellishment than its predecessor, or than the regular 1958 Fords. This door molding was only seen on the Thunderbird.
OWNERS: BOB AND COLLEEN MASON

ART OF THE AMERICAN AUTOMOBILE

▽ In contrast to the lavish exterior, the Thunderbird's dashboard was relatively simple. A vinyl-covered console and bucket seats were seen for the first time on a Thunderbird. Standard transmission was a three-speed manual, but an automatic was optional.

F ROM GM TO FORD

During World War II, Frank Hershey served as a lieutenant in the U.S. Navy. Earl did not want him to go, but Hershey had seen enough of Nazism during his years at Opel to feel strongly that he was not going to be kept out of the war. He was already head of GM's Advanced Design Studio, which worked on the more experimental designs. These were made to scale clay models, but not to full size. The only exceptions were two advanced Cadillacs which were not only made in full-size form, but were fitted with engines and ran at the proving grounds. They were very curvaceous, with semi-covered front and rear wheels, and proved too way-out for GM executives. "They just scared the hell out of them. They were too advanced," recalls Hershey. Like so many designs which never made it to production, the Cadillacs were scrapped.

△ The Big Bird's bold frontal styling with its combined bumper/grille inspired the whole Ford line for 1958.

▷ △ THUNDERBIRDS OF 1959 (FRONT) AND 1958
Basically similar in styling, the 1959 car had a number
of cosmetic changes. These included a horizontal bar
grille replacing the honeycomb, and a chrome arrow
instead of the rather heavy-looking four side stripes on
the door. For the first time a fully power-operated top
was provided for the T-bird convertible.

OWNERS: BOB AND COLLEEN MASON

At the same time that the advanced studio was working on the prototypes, work was going ahead on the car which would become the 1948 Cadillac. Much of the design work was done at Hershey's Winkler Mill farm north of Detroit because there was a four-month strike at the GM plants, from November 21, 1945, to March 13, 1946. The team consisted of Frank Hershey as chief designer, two other designers, three modelers and a sculptor. They produced a quarter-scale model, and Harley Earl visited from time to time to make his usual assessment of the ideas put forward. He favored a very simple, light grille, a "Tiffany front end" Hershey called it, yet within a year it was replaced by a heavier design to go with the new

valve-in-head V8 engine.

In 1950 Hershey left GM and joined Packard, but he soon "saw the handwriting on the wall," realizing that it was not a company with a long-term future, and moved on to Ford. Here he was his own man, director of styling and no longer under the shadow of Harley Earl. His most enduring legacy was the original Thunderbird, seen as a response to Chevrolet's Corvette, though the idea for a two-seater sports car had been around Ford management for some time.

In 1951 general manager Lewis D. Crusoe visited the Paris Salon with George Walker, who was still an outside consultant. Crusoe was very taken with the abundance of sports cars at the show –

Ferraris, the exotic new Spanish Pegaso, the Jaguar XK120 – and reportedly asked Walker, "Why don't we have something like that?" Walker replied, "Oh, but we do," and hastily phoned his studio to tell them to get a sports car going. Hershey says that he and his assistant Bill Boyer had been planning a two-seater for some time before Walker's call came through, and already had a clay model in a room off the main studio. A chassis engineer was sufficiently impressed with the clay to design a chassis for it. All this was happening in 1951 before anyone in senior management found out about it. One who was not pleased, because he had not been consulted, was Earl S. MacPherson of MacPherson strut suspension fame. He nearly torpedoed the project, but was dissuaded by the head of corporate planning, Chase Morsey. All this happened before George Walker's call came through, but the project did not get a firm go-ahead until after the Corvette appeared in early

1953. The Hershey/Boyer car was a remarkably clean, uncluttered design, angular and flat, in great contrast to the swooping curves of Earl's Corvette. Frank Hershey himself gave credit to Bill Boyer, though others who have been credited with important input into the final design were Bob Maguire (Ford passenger car studio head under Hershey) and Damon Woods.

The final design was simpler than early clays which featured canted fins and taillights, a wide egg-crate grille, and a sweepspear fender molding similar to that on the Fairlane sedans and convertibles. This feature appeared on a running Thunderbird prototype which became Ford Division General Manager Lewis Crusoe's personal car. It also had a bolt-on hardtop, and an external spare wheel mounted at the rear above extended and heavily chromed bumpers. The main decorative feature that survived to the production car was

▷ 1955 FORD FAIRLANE CROWN VICTORIA
One of the most striking of Frank Hershey's 1955 Ford Fairlanes was the Crown Victoria. Like all '55 Fords it featured a wraparound windshield, but it also had a two-tone paint job, and a chrome band over the roof which concealed the B-pillar of what was basically a 1954 two-door sedan body. Some cars had the optional Plexiglas roof in place of a steel top. Although it cost only $70 more, it was not a popular option, mainly because without air conditioning the interior became intolerably hot in sunshine.

▽ 1958 and 1959 THUNDERBIRDS
Sales rose steadily during the life of this model: 37,892 of the 1958s, 67,446 of the '59s and 92,798 in the 1960 season.

a highlight molding which ran forward from the taillight assembly through the door to the hood, ending below a row of diagonal louvers.

Hershey was determined that the Thunderbird (named for a figure in Native American mythology symbolizing power, swiftness and prosperity) should have dignity as well as sporting appeal. "Our philosophy was to make a car that, while it was a sports car, a banker, for instance, could drive it up to his bank in the morning with a certain amount of dignity." This is why the Thunderbird had less chrome and side decoration than the regular Ford Fairlanes, which were aimed at a mass market. The "banker appeal" also explained the civilized features which distinguished the T-bird from the Corvette, such as proper wind-up windows in place

of side curtains. The engine was a 292-cubic-inch V8 which gave 193 or 198hp, according to whether a manual or automatic transmission was used. Compared with the Corvette's 150hp six, this gave the T-bird better performance, and at $2,944 it cost $496 less than its GM rival. Sales of the first model (1954 and 1955) were 16,155, nearly four times those of the Corvette.

Hershey was also responsible for the regular 1955 Ford Fairlanes, which were a triumph of styling over engineering. The basic body shell was that of the 1952-54 models, but the '55s looked all new, thanks to a wraparound windshield, hooded headlights, wider grille and a distinctive dip in the belt line which showed off the two-tone color schemes to full advantage. It was continued without

major change for 1956; then all-new Fords appeared for 1957, though the dipped belt line was still there, moved to the rear of the door. Although Hershey and Damon Woods worked on the '57 Fords, Hershey left before the cars were launched. They were the most popular Fords for many years, selling only 130 less than Chevrolet, which on sales of more than 1.5 million, was a tiny margin. The 1959 Fords outsold Chevy by nearly 100,000, the first time they had toppled Chevy from the top spot since 1945.

In 1956 George Walker left his consultancy firm to become vice-president of styling at Ford, and Hershey found it impossible to work under him. He subsequently worked for Kaiser Aluminum on boat and office furniture design, and then for a Los Angeles firm. He retired in 1978.

△ John Najjar, executive stylist at Ford, in 1956 – before he had ever thought of the Mustang, which became one of the most important of all post-war cars.

CHAPTER EIGHT

LATER DESIGN AT FORD

"When I looked at the guys praising it – the off-beat crowd,
the real buffs – I said, 'that's sure not the car we want to build,
because it can't be a volume car. It's too far out!'"

Lee Iacocca on Mustang I

△ ▷ 1958 EDSEL RANGER AND CITATION
The Ranger (in the foreground above, and on the facing page) was one of the lower-priced Edsel lines, using a Ford Fairlane body including the roof stamping and front-door outers. Unique to the Edsel were the fenders, rear deck and quarter panels, and, of course, the front end. The concave scalloped sides of the rear quarter panels were similar to those on the 1958 Mercury but deeper and more arresting as they were in a different color from the rest of the car. The Citation two-door hardtop was a top model, using a Mercury body shell on a 124-inch wheelbase exclusive to Edsel. It sold for $3,535. Edsels did not have a factory of their own – the Ford-based EF cars were made in Kentucky, New Jersey, California and Massachusetts. The Mercury-based EMs came from Mercury's plant at Wayne, Michigan.

OWNERS: GLEN LUEDES (CITATION), CARROL W. CLARK (RANGER)

ART OF THE AMERICAN AUTOMOBILE

HERSHEY'S DEPARTURE IN 1956 meant that he had little, if any influence, on Ford's greatest post-war disaster, the Edsel. So much has been written about the front end of this unhappy car that many people blame its appearance for its failure in the marketplace, but this is probably less than half true.

The project which was to bear the name of Henry Ford's son was started in the early 1950s under the name E-car (for Experimental). It was a marketing exercise to extend Ford's share of the middle ground, in which GM had three makes, Pontiac, Oldsmobile and Buick, and Ford only one, Mercury. The idea was to offer a wide choice of engines and bodies bracketing Mercury at each end, so the cheaper ones would be cut-price Mercurys, and the most expensive, somewhere between the

Mercury and Lincoln lines. As originally conceived, the E-car was to have its own engines and body shells, but this was found to be too expensive, so existing Ford and Mercury components were to be used. This was the first step toward failure; the car was not distinctive enough to live up to its advertising hype.

Four lines of Edsel were offered for the 1958 season – Ranger and Pacer using Ford bodies, Corsair and Citation being Mercury based. There were also two- and four-door station wagons for six or nine passengers on the 116-inch wheelbase Ford wagon chassis. Prices ran from $2,519 for a Ranger two-door sedan to $3,801 for a Citation convertible. Comparable Mercury prices were $2,547 (Medallist two-door) and $4,118 (Park Lane convertible), so the Edsel did not, in fact, bracket Mercury, as had been the original intention.

Although Edsels were most readily identified by their grilles, there were individual features in the rest of the car. The upper surface of the rear deck was finned, and the side panels were distinctively scalloped to give an appearance different from either Ford or Mercury. Nevertheless, the main feature, on which Edsel styling succeeded or failed, was the vertical centerpiece to the grille, often likened to a horse collar. It was certainly distinctive; no other Amercian car since the pre-war Packard had used a vertical grille, though the idea came back in the following decade on the Lincoln Continental Mark III. The horse collar was flanked by horizontal grilles which, with the turn-signal lights, wrapped around the front end beneath the dual headlights. The Edsel was designed by Roy A. Brown, chief stylist for the George Walker Studios. His executive stylist was James Sipple.

▽ The galloping wild pony which gave Mustang its name, as envisaged by John Najjar. It was intended to face right, as here, but, somewhere along the line between the drawing board and production, its direction was reversed.

▽ Rear end of the first production Mustang.

▽ John Najjar's proposal for the interior of the Mach I Mustang which debuted in 1969.

DRAWINGS: COURTESY OF JOHN NAJJAR

important cars of the post-war era, the Mustang, appeared. Ever since the two-passenger Thunderbird went out of production in 1957, dealers and buyers had been asking for another two-passenger sporty car from Ford. The idea of a compact small car with appeal to a wide spectrum of buyers, but particularly to the young, was favored by Lee Iacocca, head of car and truck marketing at Ford since 1960. Vice President Robert McNamara put profits before pizzazz, and his darling was the Falcon; he was also considering an even smaller car to be made in Germany and using a V4 engine driving the front wheels. Named the Cardinal, it was never sold in the U.S. market, though a modified version was built for many years at Ford's Cologne plant under the Taunus name. In 1961 McNamara left Ford to become John F. Kennedy's Secretary of Defense; product decisions passed to Iacocca, who became general manager.

No less interested in profits, Iacocca was also a car lover and wanted to make cars which would appeal to like-minded people. Aged only 36 when he became Ford general manager, he wanted to sell to the growing youth market, the baby boomers who were ready to become drivers. Among his first steps in this direction were to give the full-size Galaxie a two-door fastback model, and to drop a V8 into the Falcon, to make the Falcon Futura Sprint.

Next he authorized research into a new model, a sporty car to appeal to the youth market.

This was largely the work of executive stylist John Najjar. In his own words, "Among the proposals I created was a full-size drawing for the Mustang I in January-February 1962. It was drawn in profile on white paper; it had the engine placed 'midship,' just ahead of the rear axle. The hood was tapered towards the front end. It had a roll-over bar for the driver and passenger. I had remembered that the Cardinal program featured a front-wheel-drive engine mounted transversely; the program was to be built in Germany but had died an early death. I contacted the engineering department in Germany to obtain drawings of the engine. The studio was working on an alternative clay model of a sport car at the time, which was being readied for a show. As Lee Iacocca and Dan Gurney were reviewing the models in each of the studios, I requested Robert Maguire, my boss, that the blackboard drawing be shown. All the models shown that day were received with a rather cool reception, but when Dan Gurney spotted the blackboard drawing, the response was immediate. We were told to start a full-size clay model immediately. In April 1962 we started the model and by October 1962 the Ford Design Office, in cooperation with engineering, had an operable vehicle for Dan Gurney to drive at

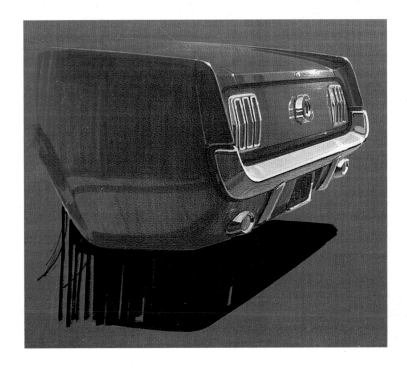

△ One of the earliest surviving Mustangs, this hardtop was completed on April 4, 1964, 13 days before the model's launch. It has the 260-cubic-inch V8, which was replaced in September 1964 by the 289.

Watkins Glen." (In fact, the work was contracted out to the California specialists Troutman & Barnes, with the necessary components, including the clay, being shipped out.)

"The Mustang showcar was a full overtime project from the day go. My exterior studio consisted of head stylist James Darden, four designers – Phil Clark and three others. Studio engineering consisted of three men and Ray Smith, and the clay modelers – eight men lead by Joe Siebold. The interior was created by James Sipple in the Ford Interior Studio. While the armature was being fabricated, we reviewed many sketches and had the shape of the vehicle pretty well established by the time we got the armature. Ray Smith had turned out volumes of feature ideas, such as the retractable licence plate and the adjustable steering wheel with the foot pedal assembly. I had obtained the drawings of the engine which we mounted amidships and this dictated the location of the air scoops. I had long dreamed about a vehicle which would carry the name Mustang. The half-wild hardy horse of the Western Plains and the famous World War II fighter airplane, the P-51. I had a tough time convincing Robert Maguire that the name would stir everyone's imagination. I made a sketch of the Mustang running horse and Phil Clark added the vertical three bars for the emblem.

Suffice it to say that everyone went all out, they put their hearts into the little vehicle. When we rolled it into the showroom for final approval by Herb Misch (engineer) and Gene Bordinat, it was an exciting time. They couldn't do anything but like the car. Soon they had Lee Iacocca rushing an immediate

build, and endorsing the showing of it at Watkins Glen."

The Mustang I was ready in time for the Grand Prix and earned glowing reports from journalists and race drivers, including Dan Gurney and Stirling Moss. *Car & Driver* thought the Mustang handled better than the first two-passenger Cooper. Not so enthusiastic was Lee Iacocca; car buff he may have been, but not to the exclusion of common sense. "When I looked at the guys praising it – the off-beat crowd, the real buffs – I said, 'that's sure not the car we want to build, because it can't be a volume car. It's too far out!'"

According to John Najjar, the Mustang II showcar was an invention of Gene Bordinat when the production Mustang was approved. "He

recognized that it would be a long time between the Watkins Glen introduction of the Mustang I and the introduction date of the production Mustang. So he proposed that a transition car be built which would show some of the features of the Mustang I and blended them into the look of the production Mustang. He set up a studio where this work on the car could be completed. Not being satisfied with the results in the studio, he suggested to me that I take a crack at it. By this time, I had been transferred to the Ford Interior Studio and really didn't have any time for it. I had James Sherborne make two sets of renderings showing how the transitory vehicle could look and made a presentation to Mr. Bordinat. He didn't like what he saw in the amount of change we had put into the

△ An early production Mustang convertible, dubbed the 1964½ Mustang as it appeared halfway through the 1964 season. It was priced at $2,624 – $246 more than the coupe.

OWNERS: RON AND KIA COLUMBO

ART OF THE AMERICAN AUTOMOBILE

◁ 1970 MUSTANG BOSS 429 COUPE
Named for its displacement of 429 cubic inches, the engine gave 375hp. It was only available for 1969 and 1970. The Boss models had sporty features of the Mach I – bucket seats, competition suspension and so on – plus quick ratio steering and a large hood scoop.

▽ 1970 MUSTANG CONVERTIBLE
This car has the 351 engine, which was descended from the 1962 302 engine, and was used in Mustangs from 1969 to 1973.

design and orally described the vehicle as he visualized it. That evening, I went home and after dinner cleared the dining room table and made four 18-inch by 24-inch sketches. The next day I showed the sketches to Gene and he liked them. He personally delivered them to Don De La Rossa, saying this is what the look of Mustang II should be. Later on, I had a hard time collecting my original sketches. The vehicle was subsequently completed and shown at the 1963 Watkins Glen Sports Car meet in the fall.

◁ 1973 MUSTANG 351 RAM AIR CONVERTIBLE
Mustangs were completely restyled for 1971, and the 1973s were similar. They were lower, wider and heavier than any previous models.

▷ 1974 MUSTANG II
Advertised as "The Right Car at the Right Time," this was a new – and smaller – car. The reduction in size and power reflected the general down-sizing brought about by the world oil crisis. The 1974 Mustang II was 13 inches shorter than the 1973, and 7 inches shorter even than the original 1964 car. The engine was a puny 140-cubic-inch four, giving 85hp, though a 169-cubic-inch V6 (105hp) was also available.

▽ 1973 MUSTANG CONVERTIBLE
The last convertible model to be made for a decade.

ART OF THE AMERICAN AUTOMOBILE

"A small presentation model, one-tenth scale, was built for showing to various colleges and advanced showings where the actual vehicle was not available. The model was in perfect detail with full suspension, painted white and mounted on a mirrored base which was carried in a mahogany box. I received this model from William Clay Ford's office upon my retirement. I later found out that a second model was built for Gene Bordinat.

"During the period I was assigned to the Advanced Studio, I had an idea which I thought would save the Design Center a lot of time. It was the requirement for 'in progress' photography of the full-size clay models. So I had a 16mm camera mounted on a wall of the studio and had a modeler take time-lapse photography as the model pro-gressed. When the film was ready to show, I had envisioned showing one or two shots at a time. It didn't turn out that way; we let the projector run at normal speed! The film was hilarious – everything was presented at accelerated speed!"

Apart from its complex technology, the Mustang I's biggest drawback was that it had only two seats. This seems paradoxical since it was dealer demand

△ 1978 MUSTANG KING COBRA
This was a special edition Mustang, only listed for one year. It sported "go faster" stripes with a snake motif on the hood, an echo of Pontiac's Firebird. Under the hood was a 302-cubic-inch V8.

for a successor to the two-passenger T-bird which had sparked off the whole Mustang project, but Iacocca wanted to reach an even wider market than the T-bird had done. The four-passenger "Big Bird" had always outsold the two-passenger model, and the new youth market was essentially a sociable one. So the specification for the new car included four seats, a stick shift, an overall length of 180 inches and maximum weight of 2,500 pounds. Also it had to use existing Ford components, including engines, as many as possible from the Falcon. In Harley Earl style, Gene Bordinat held a competition between four styling teams to come up with a car to meet Iacocca's specifications. They were all attractive, but the winner was by Joe Oros' studio, designed by his assistant David Ash. It was 186 inches long, just six inches over Iacocca's limit, and had a long hood and short passenger compartment, though it was, of course, a four-seater. It was christened the Cougar, a name later used for a Mercury derivative of the Mustang. The name was later changed to Torino, and then Mustang II, though this was not finally chosen until some time later.

There were few changes in the body design between Ash's prototype and the production car which debuted on April 17, 1964. The nose was firmed up, made more vertical and shortened, so that overall length came to down to 181½ inches. The tail was made neater, with smaller lights, and the bumpers were more substantial. But the overall proportions and the sculpted sides were unaltered. In addition to the convertible, a hardtop of similar proportions was offered, joined for 1965 by a fastback coupe.

△ 1987 MUSTANG COUPE
◁ 1988 MUSTANG COUPE
The 1987 model was a restyled version of the third generation Mustang, with the aerostyling seen on other Fords, including the European-type flush headlights. The V6 engine option was canceled, so there was nothing between the old 140-cubic-inch four and the 302-cubic-inch V8, now giving 225hp. As well as the coupes shown, a convertible was available at about 50 percent extra cost.

△ This sleek yellow car (top) was one of two Limited Edition Mustang convertibles made in 1993, in White (1,460 built) and in Yellow (1,419 built). With these, Ford said goodbye to the third generation Mustang.
△ ▷ The Mustang III showcar of 1993 was a really neat two-passenger sports car with its interior styled by Emeline King.

Apart from its attractive appearance, the secret of the Mustang's success was its variety; it was a car for all seasons, with engine options from a tame 101hp 170-cubic-inch six to a 271hp 289-cubic-inch V8. Prices ran from $2,368 to $3,850 for a V8 with four-speed transmission and all performance and handling options. Later, power went as high as 375hp from the 429-cubic-inch S-Boss engine.

Mustang sales exceeded Iacocca'a wildest dreams; he hoped for at least 100,000 in the first year, but when these were sold in four months, he was encouraged to aim higher, perhaps to rival the Falcon's 417,424. In fact, when April 16, 1965, arrived, the last customer bought Mustang number 418,812. The first model year was a long one, 16 months from the mid-1964 introduction to the end of August 1965, but even so, sales of 680,989 was a record for a new model. Even more remarkable, it was not a mainstream sedan like the Falcon.

The Mustang came to be known as the first of the pony cars, a breed of two-door personal coupes and convertibles. The name was doubtless an association with the wild pony which galloped across the grille, although it was also appropriate to the cars' size and nimble performance. Competitors soon appeared in the shape of Chevrolet's Camaro, Pontiac's Firebird, Plymouth's Barracuda, and American Motors' Javelin.

▽ The fourth generation Mustang of 1994 with all-new styling does not seem to have impressed its namesake in the background! For the first time since 1974 there was not a four-cylinder engine option. Power came from a 145hp V6 of 232 cubic inches used in the Taurus and Continental, or a 302-cubic-inch V8. The 1994 Mustang had a shorter-than-usual gestation period, 37 months compared with 48 to 54 months average, thanks to World Class Timing (WCT), a new system developed by Ford's North American Automotive Operations.

△ Virgil Exner (1909-1973)
In 1955 Exner's Forward Look, with its longer, lower lines and the
appearance of straining at the leash, transformed Chrysler's cars.
And for the rest of the Fifties, fins reigned supreme.
PHOTO: CHRYSLER CORPORATION

CHAPTER NINE

DESIGN AT CHRYSLER

A man "who loved cars and hated administration."

Bill Brownlie on Virgil Exner

CHRYSLER WAS SLOWER than GM or Ford in setting up a specific styling section. There was an Art & Colour Section (using, curiously, the same name and spelling as GM) in the early 1930s, but it was part of Engineering, and no one carried the title of stylist until 1935 when Ray Dietrich came in, working under Oliver H. Clark. Art & Colour was part of Clark's responsibility, but he was an engineer, not a stylist. There were not any separate studios for Dodge, De Soto or Plymouth, in contrast to Harley Earl's studios, and clays for all four Chrysler Corporation lines were sculpted alongside each other.

It is therefore all the more remarkable that Chrysler built some of the most beautiful cars in the early 1930s, and the most advanced and innovative design of the decade, the Airflow. The turning point in Chrysler styling came in 1931, when they replaced the flat, vertical radiator with a pointed one that sloped slightly rearward. Clearly modeled on the Cord L-29, it was the work of Herb Weissinger, who was an important figure in Chrysler's Art & Colour Section until he left for Kaiser-Frazer after World War II. It was the first V radiator grille to be adopted by a major U.S. car maker, and was closely copied by Renault in France on its 1932 models. The V was adopted right across

the Chrysler range, from the modestly priced $865 new Six to the Series CG Imperial with 384-cubic-inch straight-eight engine, and costing up to $3,575. The more expensive Imperials carried custom bodies by LeBaron, Waterhouse and other custom houses, but without Weissinger's grille, they would have lacked a great deal of their elegance.

The V radiator was continued without major change through the 1934 models and was also adopted on Plymouths. Chrysler cars received skirted fenders in 1934, later than most of the rest of the industry, but all these developments were overshadowed by the Airflow, the world's first attempt at streamlining a mass-production car.

THE AIRFLOW

The origins of the Airflow date back to 1927 when Chrysler's chief of research Carl Breer was driving from Highland Park, Michigan, to Gratiot Beach. In his own words (told to a reporter in 1964), "One late evening as dusk closed in, I noticed what I thought was a flock of a dozen or so geese flying across the road in the distance. To my surprise, this flock was really a group of airplanes heading for the Air Force's nearby Selfridge Field."

The similarity of airplanes to birds made him reflect on the slowness of automobile design to follow nature. In 1927, cars were basically big boxes with smaller boxes up front. It was obvious to anyone that they must be wasting some of their power simply in pushing air ahead of their vertical surfaces. This could be demonstrated in the simplest way by putting a hand out of the window of a moving car; if the hand was held vertically, the pressure was painful to the wrist; if the hand was turned flat, the pressure was eased. This is the feathering used by oarsmen when they move their oars through the air between strokes. The air resistance posed by vertical surfaces was already known to car designers; in Germany Paul Jaray had

◁ ▽ 1932 CHRYSLER CUSTOM IMPERIAL CL CONVERTIBLE COUPE BY LEBARON
The CL was the top model of Chrysler, with a 384.8-cubic-inch straight-eight engine. The 146-inch wheelbase allowed for very handsome bodies, not only formal sedans and limousines but coupes like this one by LeBaron. They built 28 of this style in 1932, selling for $3,295 each. The V radiator grille was designed by Herb Weissinger.
OWNER: DUKE DAVENPORT

◁ 1934 CUSTOM IMPERIAL CX AIRFLOW SEDAN
Airflows carried the top-line Imperial name. Hood
louvers date this car to 1934 but the grille is 1935.
▽ 1935 CHRYSLER C-1 AIRFLOW SEDAN
This six-passenger sedan sold 4,617 priced at $1,245.
PHOTOS: NATIONAL MOTOR MUSEUM, BEAULIEU

wrong direction all this time.' " The lesson was that resistance came from the rear of a square box as well as the front; if the rear could be sloped, resistance would be lower; therefore if the engine were at the rear, the bulk of the body could be at the front, giving a teardrop shape. At least one rear-engined prototype was made, but it was hopelessly tail heavy. Many clay models were made with varying degrees of streamlining, and in December 1932 a full-size running car began tests. Named the Trifon Special, for Demetrion Trifon, a Chrysler mechanic/driver who worked on the car, it was tested in great secrecy, taken out in a closed van to isolated farmland near West Branch, Michigan. Chrysler engineers followed the van in old, well-used cars rather than their limousines, to attract less attention.

been making streamlined bodies on various chassis, but they were only prototypes, and though they were slippery in shape, they were curiously high and not at all attractive.

Breer asked Dayton engineer Bill Earnshaw to check pressures on various shaped blocks of wood. Earnshaw happened to be a friend of pioneer aviator Orville Wright, who helped him design and build a small wind tunnel, the first of its kind used for automotive research. Breer then ordered a larger tunnel to be built at Chrysler's research center in Highland Park; in this he had the full backing of Walter Chrysler. "In those days, if we needed something we just went ahead and built it. Walter Chrysler never questioned us about what we were doing. We pioneered by not wasting time."

Using linseed oil and lampblack, and later strings, they traced air currents, and among their findings was the unexpected one that the conventional boxy shape gave less resistance when running backward. "I remember looking out on a parking lot from the fourth floor," said Breer, "and thinking 'Just imagine all those cars running in the

ART OF THE AMERICAN AUTOMOBILE

◁ 1936 AIRSTREAM DE LUXE EIGHT
Chrysler backed up its radical Airflows with the more conventional Airstream line. This five-passenger convertible sedan sold for $1,265.
ILLUSTRATION: CHRYSLER CORPORATION

Airflows, while the one-piece side panels exclusive of doors were common between the De Soto and the smaller Chryslers. The Imperials used two-piece side panels. Doors were more or less interchangeable, the right front door being similar to the left rear, with slight differences in the lower sheet metal. This contributed to cost cutting and meant that the Airflow's failure in the marketplace was less of a disaster to Chrysler than it might otherwise have been.

The Airflow was launched at the New York Automobile Show in January 1934. Reaction seems to have been mixed. While it was certainly no Model A or Mustang, it did attract several thousand orders immediately; the problem was that very few cars were available for immediate delivery, and by the time they came on stream, in March for the De Sotos and April for the Chryslers, the opposition had plenty of time to rubbish the car. As Carl Breer said, "There were a lot of rumors by the competition about the car. We had a lot of fallacies to combat and no cars to combat them with. If the show could have been in April, when our production began, it might have been different."

Not all the criticisms were fallacies; build quality was poor on the early Airflows, and problems such as an engine breaking loose at 80mph did not help their reputation. Something like the first 3,000 Airflows suffered from construction problems, and out of 11,292 delivered in 1934, that was quite a large number. And as Errett Lobban Cord found out two years later, to launch a radical car and not deliver for several months results in a lot of cancelled orders and a loss of confidence which never returns.

There remains the question of how much the Airflow's styling worked against it. Several so-called experts were enthusiastic; Professor Alexander Klemin, director of the Daniel Guggenheim School of Aeronautics, thought the car "splendid, just from

Walter Chrysler rode in the Trifon before the year was out and was very impressed. This encouraged Breer and his team, which included Oliver Clark, and his partners, Owen Skelton and Fred Zeder, in the design of the first Chrysler.

Though its appearance was somewhat ungainly, the Trifon contained all the elements of the production Airflow. This was a remarkably innovative car in many ways, and though its styling was, and is, the most obvious thing about it, its appearance was a response to practical engineering considerations. It was much less a styled car than its contemporaries from General Motors, perhaps because Oliver Clark was first and foremost an engineer rather than an artist. Indeed, in Chrysler's list of design goals, streamlining came second after improved weight distribution for ride, and was followed by structural strength, better mounting of bumpers and more room inside.

To get away from the vertical back which hampered aerodynamics, the Airflow was given a sloping tail. For rear-seat passengers to have enough headroom, the seats had to be moved farther forward than normal, which also had the advantage of positioning them ahead of the axle. However, if the rear seats went forward, so did the front seats and so did the engine, which had nowhere to go except over the front axle. This was a revolutionary move, which caused experimental engineer A. G. Herreschoff many headaches. He eventually placed the block one-third ahead of the axle and two-thirds behind it, tilting it 5° to the rear to keep the transmission tunnel low, and incorporating a special oil pan to accommodate axle travel. Weight distribution was greater on the front axle than was usual; instead of 40/60 percent between front and rear, it was 55/45 percent.

The body structure was unusual, too, being all steel at a time when most American cars were still using some wood in the frames, and having a light, cage-like frame that ran over the engine and along the roof line, as well as in the usual position. The body panels were carried on this frame, which was a step toward integral construction.

Airflows were sold with Chrysler and De Soto badges, in three different body styles, and with four different sizes of engine and on five wheelbases. Given this variety, it is remarkable that practically all body panels were interchangeable. The Budd-built one-piece back panels were common to all

AIRFLOW IMPERIAL
6-Passenger Coupe

△ A new Airflow model for 1935 was the Imperial Series C-2 six-passenger coupe (left). Really a two-door sedan, it rode on a 128-inch wheelbase and used a 323½ cubic-inch straight-eight engine. Production was exactly 200.
PICTURE: BRYAN K. GOODMAN COLLECTION

△ The 1936 Chrysler Imperial Airflow (above) was the most popular of the 1936 Airflows, with 4,259 delivered.
PHOTO: CHRYSLER CORPORATION

◁ 1937 was the last year for the Airflow. Only 4,600 were made in two series, the two-door coupe and four-door sedan, such as this fine example.
PHOTO: NATIONAL MOTOR MUSEUM, BEAULIEU

its appearance," while Carolyn Edmondson, a fashion artist on *Harper's Bazaar* found the Airflow "breathtakingly different." A De Soto Airflow coupe won the Grand Prix for aerodynamic styling in Monte Carlo.

Initially, orders made at the show were good, but this was a sophisticated buying public; doubtless buyers across the whole country were harder to convince. Long hoods were a sign of power and elegance, particularly important with upscale cars, and the Airflow had proportionally the shortest hood of any American car. As De Soto historian Don Butler wrote, "Prospective buyers had little understanding of styling, but they had personal tastes and definite preferences. They were accustomed to more prominent front-end features, and the Airflow

ART OF THE AMERICAN AUTOMOBILE

was just too different in that respect." Paul C. Wilson (*Chrome Dreams*) went further: "For most people it had a rhinocerine ungainliness which automatically consigned it to the outer darkness of motordom."

The claim has often been made that the Airflow failed to appeal because it was ahead of its time. Gordon Buehrig remembered hearing one salesman saying that the car was ten years ahead of its time and that the public was not ready for it. "That was back in 1934. I made a point of looking at some of these cars in 1944, and asking people about them. They looked just as bad in 1944 as they did in 1934."

Chrysler had hedged its bets with its 1934 program, offering the conventionally styled Six in two wheelbases, which easily outsold the Airflow. De Soto had no alternative to the Airflow and fared very badly, with a 47 percent drop in sales compared with 1933. For 1935 Chrysler hired Ray Dietrich to restyle the Airflow and design a new conventional model, called the Airstream. The Airflow's rear end was unchanged, as were the sides apart from a trivial rearrangement of the louvers, but at the front a pointed prow replaced the smooth waterfall of 1934. *Automotive Industries* (December 29, 1934) claimed that this change "…materially improved the appearance of these cars," but it did not improve sales, which were only 7,751 out of a Chrysler total of 38,533.

Chrysler kept the Airflow going until the end of the 1937 season, changing the prow along with

Airstream styling each year. Though the forward engine position became increasingly popular over the next few years, the Airflow's styling had no immediate impact on other American cars. The Lincoln Zephyr shared some of its features, such as a short hood and sloping back, but it evolved quite independently.

Abroad, a number of imitation Airflows appeared, but only one won wide acceptance. This was the Peugeot 402, which had a more sloping grille with headlights behind the grille bars. The body was quite similar to the Airflow, complete with winged motif on the rear wheel covers. Peugeot sold 58,748 402s, and 25,083 of the similar-styled 302. In Sweden the Volvo PV36 was an Airflow-like four-window sedan, but it only lasted one season, with 501 being made. In England, Singer offered its Airstream sedan on the Eleven chassis, with a waterfall front directly copied from the 1934 Airflow, though the body was less attractive due to the shorter wheelbase. It did not appeal to the British public. Of a planned 750, fewer than half were completed as Airstreams, the others receiving conventional bodies. The first Toyotas were quite Airflow-like in appearance, though they had free-standing headlights.

F | ALLOW YEARS AT CHRYSLER

For nearly 20 years after the Airflow, Chrysler styling was quiet, with no dominant stylists and

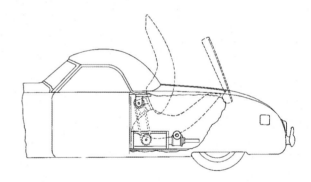

▽ 1940 CHRYSLER THUNDERBOLT CONVERTIBLE
This was one of two Chrysler showcars, the other being the six-passenger dual-cowl phaeton called the Newport. The Thunderbolt had very advanced styling, with concealed headlights and a straight-through slab-side body without separate fenders. The body was aluminum with a stainless-steel strip running around the lower edge. The metal top disappeared into the trunk, an idea not put into production until the Ford Skyliner of 1957.

PHOTOS: CHRYSLER CORPORATION

little in the way of innovation. The Airflow debacle inhibited flights of fancy, and Walter Chrysler's replacement as Corporation President by Kaufman T. Keller in 1934 did nothing to encourage experimentation. Keller was described as "... like Chrysler, an erstwhile railroad man, and a hearty two-fisted and go-getting an automotive executive as well." But he was conservative, and under his direction no one was encouraged to step out of line. Ray Dietrich stayed as head of the exterior design staff at Art & Colour until the end of 1938. There is no direct evidence that he and Keller disagreed, but Chrysler in the late 1930s cannot have been an ideal place for an innovative stylist. Oliver Clark remained in overall charge of styling, and one of his assistants was his son, Dean. For 1939 Dean designed an alternative to the regular business coupe. Called the Victoria Coupe, it was lighter and more airy, with a thinner B-pillar, longer cabin with proportionally shorter trunk, and a wider, split rear window. There were 16 more inches of interior room than in the standard coupe. Manufacture was entrusted to the Hayes Body Co. of Grand Rapids, Michigan, and only 1,000 Victoria Coupes were made, divided between three Chrysler lines, New Yorker, Windsor, and Imperial, and also one line each of De Soto and Dodge. The biggest number was made by Dodge, with 363 examples.

Dean Clark was responsible only for the upper body of the Hayes coupes; the rest of the 1939 styling was still the preserve of Ray Dietrich, and a very good job he made of it. The headlights were fully integrated into the fenders, and the grille was split into three components, two horizontal flashes near the top of the hood, and a waterfall below them. The Dodge shared the upper flashes, but there was a horizontal grille below them, while De Soto had a more integrated horizontal theme. Bodies were as streamlined as any in the industry, with fastback sedans which had wide split rear windows, in contrast to the thin, mailbox shapes of the coupe windows.

N EWPORT AND THUNDERBOLT

Two of the most striking Chryslers appeared just before the United States entered World War II. Christened Newport and Thunderbolt, they were

commissioned from the coachbuilders LeBaron, not production cars but as styling exercises for publicity, to remove the stigma of the Airflow and show that the Chrysler name could be associated with beautiful cars. Also, 1938 saw the appearance of Harley Earl's Buick Y-Job, and Kaufman Keller did not want to be left out. Of the Big Three, only Ford produced no "ideas cars" before the war.

By 1939 LeBaron had lost its two founders, Tom Hibbard and Ray Dietrich, and was guided by Ralph Roberts. There were close ties between LeBaron and Briggs, the mass producers, and as there was very little custom work coming LeBaron's way, Roberts was working for Briggs at the time the Chrysler cars were commissioned. Though he was not a trained designer, he had a very good eye, like Harley Earl, and it seems that the Newport was largely his work. Designed at Briggs and built by LeBaron, it was a six-passenger dual-cowl phaeton with dual windshields, push-button door handles, concealed headlights, and a flowing fender line from front to rear. The body was of aluminum,

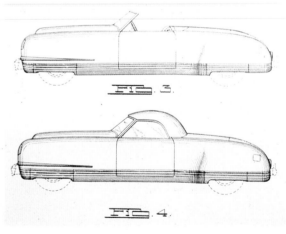

△ Ralph Roberts with his family and a Chrysler Thunderbolt (top). Though this car and the Newport were built by LeBaron, they were not styled by them, but by Alex Tremulis, who worked for Briggs, and Roberts.
△ Ralph Roberts' drawings for the Thunderbolt.

CHRYSLER *Thunderbolt* THE CAR OF THE FUTURE

WILLS'S CIGARETTES

"THUNDERBOLT" (CAPTAIN G. E. T. EYSTON)

△ Though it was not offered for sale, a publicity brochure (top) was prepared for the Chrysler Thunderbolt. Six cars were made and all were eventually sold to private individuals. At least two survive.

△ The car (above) for which Chrysler's Thunderbolt was named — the Land Speed record car in which Captain George Eyston set a new record of 357.53mph at Bonneville Salt Flats, Utah, in September 1938. It was powered by two 12-cylinder Rolls-Royce aeroengines, was more than 30 feet long, and weighed 7 tons. Chrysler obtained Eyston's permission to use the name.

painted bone-white and with pleated leather interior which was used around both cockpits and in the door panels. Roberts had originally planned a swept forward windshield, but this was vetoed (wisely) by Keller. An interesting touch was the provision of rear-view mirrors for the rear cockpit passengers. Six Newports were built, some of which were colored dark green with tan leather interiors. A white example was used as the Pace Car for the 1941 Indianapolis 500 race.

If the Newport was modern looking, the Thunderbolt was definitely futuristic and would not have looked out of place in the 1960s. It was styled by Alex Tremulis, who was also working for Briggs. It was shorter than the Thunderbolt and seated three on a wide bench seat. Unlike the Newport's dipped fender line, the Thunderbolt had a straight-through line with no dip or belt molding of any kind, like the post-war Kaiser-Frazer. Both front and rear wheels were covered, there were concealed headlights and no recognizable grille – air intakes were below the bumper. Like the Newport,

the body was aluminum, with a stainless-steel molding running right around the lower part. When he saw the design, Keller asked how they were going to bend it around the front end. Tremulis said they would make that section of brass and plate it. That pleased Keller, who said, "Sometimes you stylists think like engineers and make sense."

The Newport and Thunderbolt both used a stock Chrysler L-head straight-eight engine, and rode on stock chassis, 127½ inches for the Thunderbolt, and 143½ inches, Chrysler's longest, for the Newport. Six were made of each, of which four Newports and two Thunderbolts survive. One of the surviving Newports, now in the National Automobile Museum at Reno, Nevada, was owned by playboy millionaire Henry J. Topping, who customized the car with his name on the hubcaps and valve covers; he also replaced the Chrysler engine with a Cadillac V8. The cars certainly achieved their purpose of putting Chrysler at the forefront of styling ideas, and they traveled the country at shows in 1940 and 1941.

△ 1941 CHRYSLER WINDSOR CONVERTIBLE
Chrysler styling in the early 1940s was up-to-date, with pontoon fenders, fully-integrated headlights and a bold horizontal grille. Only after the war did they lag behind as a result of Chrysler president Kaufman T. Keller's conservatism. The Windsor was the cheapest Chrysler line, using a 241½-cubic-inch six cylinder engine. It was priced at $1,315, while the eight-cylinder New Yorker convertible cost $1,548.

OWNER: ROBERT LUTZ, CHRYSLER CORPORATION

A HAT WEARER'S MARKET

Like most American manufacturers, Chrysler entered the post-war era with slightly warmed-over 1942 styling. The only exceptions were the Town & Country models – four-door sedan, two-door hardtop and convertible, with station-wagon appearance – thanks to their white ash frames with shaped plywood panels. The 1946 catalog showed five styles: a roadster, a brougham, a two-door club coupe, a four-door sedan and a convertible. Of these, the roadster was never built, and only one brougham and seven coupes were made, but the sedan and convertible were made in small numbers, selling at high prices. A regular six-cylinder Windsor sedan cost $1,561, while a similar style Town & Country cost $2,366, reflecting the amount of hand work involved in the wooden bodies. (Ford and Mercury had similar-looking cars, but they had steel bodies with wooden strips.)

ART OF THE AMERICAN AUTOMOBILE

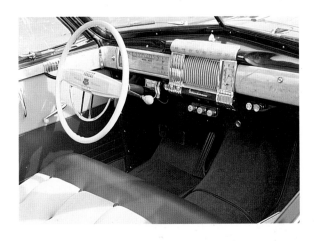

▽ 1941 CHRYSLER WINDSOR CONVERTIBLE
Steering column gearshift was adopted by Chrysler in 1939, and in 1941 Vacamatic semiautomatic transmission was offered.

▽ 1941 Chrysler convertibles introduced rear quarter windows behind the B-pillar. Trim options included Highlander, Scottish plaid and leatherette, and Navajo, based on a Native American pattern.

Town & Country Chryslers, particularly the convertibles, were popular in Hollywood. Marie McDonald had one, as did Leo Carillo, best known as the Cisco Kid's sidekick, Pancho. His carried a steer's head mounted above the grille, while the animal's hide was used for the seats and door panels. The cars featured in movies as well; historian Beverly Rae Kimes observed that "they were usually in the hands of the gambler or 'the other man,' this possibly because they were considered too rakish for forthright upstanding heroes."

The Town & Country cars may not have made any profit for Chrysler, but their publicity value was excellent. The regular Chryslers sold well in the post-war seller's market, and Kaufman Keller was not one to indulge in change for its own sake. Early in 1948, he was asked if Chrysler planned any changes that year, and he replied that he saw no reason why it should. Then Ford brought out its radically changed '49 models in the summer, and Keller sanctioned a new line of Chryslers and accompanying models from Dodge, De Soto and

Plymouth. Oliver Clark had been succeeded by Henry King, who was allowed little latitude when styling the '49 Chryslers. Keller was particularly conservative about headroom. In an address to the Stanford University School of Business in the summer of '48, he said "Many of you Californians may have outgrown the habit, but there are parts of the country containing millions of people, where both the men and the ladies are in the habit of getting behind the wheel, or in the back seat, wearing hats." When he saw some of the new offerings from rivals, he observed "we build cars to sit in, not to piss over."

The result was a fairly undistinguished line of cars for 1949, the main difference from their predecessors being larger trunks and four windows for the sedans rather than six. Though Chrysler had its best year in 1949, with 1,122,095 cars made by the group, and another record year in 1950, it was overtaken by Ford that year. Clearly the hat wearers were dwindling in numbers and something had to be done about Chrysler design.

VIRGIL EXNER'S FORWARD LOOK

As there was at least a three-year lead for new models, nothing could be done immediately. When changes did appear, they were the work of Virgil Max Exner, who had been invited by Keller to join Chrysler's design department in 1949. Born in Ann Arbor, Michigan, in 1909, Exner trained as an artist at Notre Dame, then worked in an advertising agency before joining Harley Earl in the Art & Colour Section in 1934. His best-known legacy from his GM days was the 1938 Pontiac, which he styled after Frank Hershey had moved on. Exner, in turn, left GM in 1938 to join the Raymond Loewy Studios, where he was responsible for the radical post-war Studebakers (see Chapter 11). He never got along with Loewy, and was happy to move to Chrysler.

It may seem surprising that the conservative Keller would welcome an innovative stylist like Exner, who had been responsible for America's most radical post-war production car. However, he knew that Chrysler needed some charisma for publicity purposes, something to continue the legacy of the Newport and Thunderbolt. In 1949 Chrysler was in the position of Pontiac in 1933. It had a brand-new engine, a hemi-head overhead

◁ △ 1960 PLYMOUTH XNR ASSIMETRICA. Named for Virgil Exner, this two-passenger roadster showcar was built by Ghia and after display by Chrysler was sold to the Shah of Iran. It was built on a modified Valiant chassis; the bumper/grille arrangement would be seen in production on the 1971 Plymouth Barracuda and Satellite.
▽ Virgil Exner (1909-73) with one of his fins, circa 1957.
PHOTOS: CHRYSLER CORPORATION

ART OF THE AMERICAN AUTOMOBILE

valve V8 that would be an industry leader, but no new car to put it in. Exner came up with the K-310, a sleek two-door five-passenger coupe with wrap-around rear window and chromed wire wheels. Other features included a spare wheel molding on the rear deck, later to be used in many of Exner's designs, though the wheel itself rested on the trunk floor, flush-mounted door handles and free-standing taillights, which were later seen on the production C-300.

The K-310 (named for Keller and the 310hp V8 engine) was built by Ghia of Italy, starting a long connection between the two companies, and made the rounds of autos shows in 1951. Exner and his modelers produced a scale model which was cast in plaster and sent to Ghia in Turin. There was never a full-size clay; Ghia's skilled panel beaters built in the metal from the plaster model.

Because K. T. Keller was particularly fond of the K-310, limited production was planned, but projections showed that it would be unrealistically expensive. In Virgil Exner's words, "... we got it all costed out to be put into production. But as we

△ A later Exner clay sent to Ghia in Turin, Italy, in April 1952 (top). The dropping door line is more pronounced than on any of the cars actually built; this is possibly a predecessor of the 1953 De Soto Adventurer.
PHOTO: CHRYSLER CORPORATION

△ Exner's first Chrysler showcar was the K-310 of 1951 (above left and right). It was built on a Saratoga chassis, construction being by Ghia. Among many innovations was the spare wheel molding on the rear deck, later used on the production Valiant.
PHOTO: GHIA SPA

◁ 1952 CHRYSLER C-200 CONVERTIBLE
Generally similar to the K-310, apart from its soft top, the C-200 was the main showcar for 1952. Like the K-310 it used a 125½-inch Saratoga chassis, and was 220½ inches in overall length. The gunsight taillights later saw production on the Chrysler C-300.

◁ 1953 DE SOTO ADVENTURER COUPE
Chrysler spread its showcars among different divisions. The Adventurer, designed by Virgil Exner and built by Ghia, was the first to come from De Soto. A four-passenger coupe on a 111-inch wheelbase, it was Exner's favorite showcar, and he drove it for three years as his personal car.

▽ ▷ 1954 DE SOTO ADVENTURER COUPE
Adventurer II, De Soto's second showcar, was longer than the first but seated only two passengers.

PHOTOS:CHRYSLER CORPORATION; GHIA SPA

found – as all the car companies found out when they began considering anything like this – you have to have a completely separate set-up for it. It wasn't practical to put in separate facilities here in the U.S., and that left Italy or maybe England, but their production facilities weren't big enough to make anything profitable out of a car like this." Not that the prototype was particularly costly; Exner estimated that its total cost was around $20,000; as he said in 1972, "You can't even buy a custom windshield for that nowadays."

In 1952 the C-310 was joined by a convertible on similar lines, called the C-200. Both were on the 125½-inch Saratoga chassis; there was also a coupe with somewhat different styling on the 119-inch New Yorker chassis called the Special. In modified form it became a production model in Europe, with

Ghia making 400 of them for the European market only, in 1954. However, C. B. Thomas, president of Chrysler's Export Division, had a slightly altered version of the 1952 Special, which was called the Thomas Special. Another coupe made by Ghia, the 1953 d'Elegance, was reworked by Ghia's Luigi Segre into the design that Karmann offered on the

Volkswagen Beetle chassis from 1955 to 1973.

Between 1950 and 1961, 26 different idea cars were made for Chrysler, mostly bodied by Ghia. All the early ones were Exner designs. They carried names of all four Chrysler Corporation divisions; Exner's favorite was the De Soto Adventurer I, a four-passenger coupe on a 111-inch wheelbase with 170hp Firedome V8 engine and outside exhaust pipes and mufflers, which he drove for three years as his personal car. It was painted off-white, with a black leather interior. Though some of the later ones, such as the gas-turbine powered Chrysler Turboflite, were way out in design, the idea cars provided many styling points which were put into production a few years later. These included the spare wheel molding in the rear deck, irreverently known as the toilet seat deck (1959 Plymouth Fury, 1960 Valiant), wire wheels and free-standing taillights (1955 Chrysler C-300 and Imperial), and flush door handles.

Apart from the Chrysler Ghia coupe, the only idea car to bring forth a production model was the

ART OF THE AMERICAN AUTOMOBILE

△ ▷ DODGE FIREARROW II ROADSTER
◁ 1954 DODGE FIREARROW III COUPE
Dodge's showcars followed the pattern of American
design by Exner and Italian construction by Ghia.
Firearrow I was a mockup only, but II and III were fully
functioning cars, a roadster (this page) and a coupe
respectively. There was also a convertible, Firearrow IV.
All used the 241-cubic-inch V8 engine and had a
119-inch wheelbase. The convertible was put into
production by Gene Casaroll as the Dual Ghia; it was
little changed in appearance, though slightly larger
engines were used.

PHOTOS: GHIA SPA

1953 Dodge Firearrow. The design was bought by Detroit-based enthusiast Gene Casaroll who put it into production in 1955 as the Dual-Ghia. A total of 117 were made up to 1958, followed in 1960 by a further series of 26 Dual Ghia 6.4s, with bulkier bodywork and 6.4-liter Chrysler 300 engines.

Unlike Harley Earl or Bill Mitchell, on whom colleagues generally agree even if they weren't always complimentary, Virgil Exner earned mixed opinions. To design executive Bill Brownlie, he was "a warm, personable, father-like figure, intensely interested in car design, who loved cars and hated administration." George Motorojescu, a clay supervisor, found him "very personable, very intense. He was an easy guy to work with because he always knew what he wanted." However, to Dave Cummins, he was "a reclusive, unapproachable,

pre-occupied individual." Certainly he spent a lot of time in his studio, over which he demanded complete control.

Years later, Cummins had reason to revise his opinion. "During his [Exner's] terminal illness, as it turned out, in the summer of 1973, I believe, I found myself assigned to a hospital room for some minor surgery, and to my great surprise, my roommate was Ex. He was in periodic pain and had great difficulty sleeping, so he would politely ask if I was awake at, say 2 a.m., and then proceeded to tell me a great deal of his life story. I was enthralled, of course, and think he was glad to have a 'fella designer' to talk to at all hours. He could not remember me from the Chrysler days – no surprise at all to me – but he surely made up for all the earlier inaccesibility during that week. I don't think

I ever met a more kindly, gentle and yet articulate person, ever. He was simply wonderful!" Another junior designer at the time, Fred Schimmel, says of Exner, "He was more refined than Elwood [Engel, his successor], but really didn't let his own personality come out."

Cliff Voss, Exner's second in command, recalled, "Originally K.T. would pick the renderings and the body engineers, headed by U. L. Thomas, would lay out the body draft based on the rendering. The draftsmen would follow the clays, not the stylists. The stylists were not allowed in the clay rooms! Ex demanded control over clay modeling and approval of die models, if he was to stay, and K.T. agreed. It was a first at Chrysler."

According to Dave Cummins, an interesting aspect of the Chrysler studios in the 1950s was that

△ The Chrysler 300-C was a 1957 model, so this clay probably dates from at least three years earlier. A major difference in the front end is that the production car had four headlights. The grille surround was similar, but the grille itself was simpler, with an egg-crate pattern and no vertical chrome bar. At the rear, the fins lacked the kick-up of the clay.

◁ An experimental 300-C with fins similar to the clay above. It has a very heavy appearance, and it is hardly surprising that it was kept in the engineering department and not put on display.

PHOTOS: CHRYSLER CORPORATION

△ 1955 CHRYSLER C-300
A new model for 1955 and the progenitor of a line of
high-performance Chryslers. In it Exner combined the
grille of the new Imperial with a lowered New Yorker
hardtop body. Under the hood was a 300hp Hemi.
OWNER: OTTO ROSENBUSCH

the clay rooms where the full-size models were built
and developed were across the hall from the styling
studios where the artwork was done. "This was
perhaps brought about by the fact that the Chrysler
modelers were union, and the designers were non-
union; a unique set-up. Clay rooms and studios

were freely accessed by mutual personnel within
any one studio, but we didn't have the right to visit
other clay rooms or studios."

Bill Porter has a very high regard for Exner. "His
work was very sophisticated in form and pattern.
His understanding of form, in my view, exceeded

that of Earl – it was much more sophisticated. The shape of the cars that he did, especially the 1947 Studebaker and the late cars at Chrysler, show this. And after he left Chrysler, when he did those retro cars for the American Copper Institute – even though we laughed at them because they were so neoclassical. We laughed at them because they seemed corny; nevertheless when you examined them they were very, very beautiful. Exner really was good." (Interview with Nicky Wright, 1994)

In 1955 Virgil Exner's cars burst on the scene. All four divisions were restyled, the total program costing in the region of $250 million. Longer, lower

and wider than previous models, they featured "The Forward Look," an eager, straining-at-the-leash appearance which was particularly noticeable in the Plymouths. These were a truly radical departure from the rather stodgy, dumpy-looking 1954 models; the front of the fenders formed a hood over the lights and were slanted forward at an angle of about 30°. The windshield was wrapped around at the top and bottom of the A-pillar. This was slanted rather than vertical as on the GM wraparounds, which gave easier access. The '55 Plymouths not only looked longer, they were longer, by ten inches. This necessitated rebuilding

▽ ▷ 1955 CHRYSLER C-300
The C-300 was the first of the Letter Cars, so called because annual changes were indicated by letters attached to the 300. These ran from the 300B of 1956 to the 300L of 1965. Confusingly, this first model was the only one to have the letter in front of the number, and there was also a 300C of 1957. Only 1,692 of these lovely cars were made in the 1955 season which for the 300, did not start until February 10.
▷ The engine was a 331-cubic-inch V8, at 300hp the most powerful American engine of the year. It had two four-barrel carbs and a full-race camshaft.
OWNER: OTTO ROSENBUSCH

the production line, to give an extra 27 feet. It was voted "The Most Beautiful Car of the Year" by the Society of Illustrators, a remarkable achievement for a mass-produced popular car which had never had any previous claim to style. To accompany their appearance, the '55 Plymouths had the marque's first V8 engines.

De Sotos and Dodges were less striking, but a great improvement on their 1954 predecessors. This was thanks to a greater use of color, in two-tone combinations and, on the De Soto Fireflite Coronado and Dodge Custom Royal Lancer, three tones. In all, the Chrysler Corporation offered 56

△ FLIGHT SWEEP I AND II
These were built on 1955 De Soto chassis and did the show circuits in 1955 and 1956. Flight Sweep I (front) was finished in bronze and white, with matching leather upholstery. It was 43½ inches high, 7 inches lower than a regular De Soto.
◁ The counterbalanced deck lid of Flight Sweep I. The spare wheel was in the lower part of the lid and the molded cover in the upper.
▷ Rear view of Flight Sweep I.
PHOTOS: CHRYSLER CORPORATION

solid colors and 173 two-tone combinations on the 1955 models. Two years earlier, Exner had been predicting the importance of color: "… Plymouth will establish a new era in styling with the introduction of a new series of cars whose interiors, right down to floor mats, will be keyed harmoniously to their two-tone exteriors."

The other two stars of the 1955 line were the Chrysler C-300 and the Imperial. For the first time, the latter was designated a separate marque rather than a model of Chrysler. It would carry this status until 1975. The C-300 was a high-performance two-door coupe whose styling was a clever combination of a lowered New Yorker hardtop body with the

divided grille from the Imperial. Engineered by Bob Roger, the tuned 331-cubic-inch hemi V8 gave 300hp and propelled the 4,000-pound car up to a maximum of 130mph. The colorful auto writer Tom McCahill described it as "as solid as Grant's tomb and 130 times as fast." A bit of journalist's license there, as tombs do not move at all, but we know what Tom meant. In addition to the grille, the C-300 borrowed from the Imperial the free-standing taillights which Exner had first used on the K-310. Known as "microphone" or "gunsight" taillights, they had little amber-colored lights at the front which enabled the driver to use them as a parking aid in the dark as well as in daylight.

The 1956 Chryslers used the same body panels as in 1955, but Exner contrived to give them a new look by raising the rear fenders with fins. Cadillac was no stranger to fins, but at Chrysler the whole line, from the budget-priced Plymouth up, was given the fin treatment. They were not all the same; on the Plymouth the fender sloped forward from fin top to bumper, mirroring the slope of the front fenders, while Dodge's sloped forward with a little

△ The Norseman was intended to be Chrysler's leading 1957 showcar, but it was lost when the liner *Andrea Doria* sank en route to New York. Its most unusual feature was the cantilevered roof which had no windshield pillars.

notch three-quarters of the way down. Chrysler and De Soto fins sloped the opposite way. They were still quite modest compared with what was to come for 1957. Then, once more, Plymouth led the way.

Using the apt advertising slogan "Suddenly it's 1960," the '57 Plymouths were the most advanced looking of the five-marque Chrysler range. From their hooded quad headlights (in fact, single headlights flanked by large parking and signal lights) to their large flamboyant fins, they were all new. Even more than the 1955 Forward Look cars, they looked taut, eager and poised for take-off, as their ads claimed. Like other Chrysler cars, they were lower than the competition from GM and Ford, with much airier passenger compartments. The chief designer working under Exner was former GM stylist Homer LaGassey, who said that one of their main aims was to change the proportion of glass to sheet metal. In the typical early 1950s cars, this was about one to three, but in the '57 Chryslers it came closer to one to two. Pillars were very thin so that, in the words of Jeff Godshall, a historian who worked in Chrysler's styling department, "the roof, or what little there was of it, seemed to float above the body, anchored by the slimmest of pillars."

The Plymouths were the most striking of the Corporation's '57 models because of their fins which were sharply kicked up halfway along the deckline. The other cars had fins which sloped gradually, though their height at the rear was as great as that of the Plymouth. Even the 149½-inch wheelbase Crown Imperial limousines had the fins, though they were less noticeable behind the enormous body of the luxury limousine. For the first time, the 1957 Imperials shared no body panels with Chrysler. Dodge's fins were actually set on top of the rear quarter panels and were accentuated by separate colors.

Exner was a firm believer in the practical advantages of fins. Using a plastic scale model of a De Soto sedan in a wind tunnel at the University of Detroit, he found that road holding was improved and steering corrections reduced by as much as 20 percent in strong crosswinds. As he wrote in a paper presented to the Society of Automotive Engineers: "Most of the force of a side wind acts on the front portion of a finless car, tending to make it veer from its course. When fins are added, a large surface is presented at the rear of the car, directing the side wind so that its force is better balanced around the car's center of gravity, which acts as a pivot point. Thus the additions of rear fins equalized the force about the pivot point, resulting in less tendency of the wind to turn the car off its course."

With all respect to Exner, one wonders if this was the prime reason for the fins, which GM and Ford as well were into by 1957, or if it was rationalizing a styling decision. Paul Wilson, author of *Chrome Dreams*, had his doubts. "A halfhearted attempt was made to persuade people that they were functional in helping directional stability, but few believed and few cared. Immediately everyone knew why they were there, as a prop for the owner's fantasies." Fins disappeared by the early 1960s, yet no one reported worse handling and steering than before.

▽ ▷ 1957 DODGE CORONET CONVERTIBLE
Like other cars from Chrysler Corporation, the 1957 Dodges embodied Virgil Exner's Forward Look, with a reverse slope to the front fenders and dramatic, swept-up fins. These made the roof look lower than it actually was. The two-tone color schemes were chosen to enhance the fin line. The cars were longer, lower and wider than any previous Dodge. There were three series: Coronet, Royal and Custom Royal. Coronets were the lowest priced, and the sedans could be had with six-cylinder or V8 engines, convertibles only with the V8. This car cost $2,842.
OWNER: DOOR PRAIRIE MUSEUM

T HE VALIANT

Though the disappearance of fins coincided with Exner's departure from Chrysler in 1961, there was one model which was pure Exner and also finless. This was the Valiant, Chrysler's entry in the compact car field in which Ford and Chevrolet were also competing with the Falcon and Corvair. It was built in the Dodge plants, and sold by Plymouth dealers, yet, for its first season, 1960, it was regarded as a separate brand. Thereafter, it became a Plymouth.

Unusual because of its unitary construction and the slanting of the engine at 30°, it needed fresh styling to complement its place in a new market.

Exner went for what he called "a strong automobile look" with "directed motion." Above all, he did not want the look of a scaled-down large car. "Chopping off front and rear overhang, squeezing in the sides and dropping the roofline was not the answer." The first sketches show a two-door sedan with distinct fins, to be expected in 1957 when the project began, but Exner rejected this as lacking in the European look he wanted. No fewer than five full-size clays were made before he and his staff were satisfied.

The Valiant was developed and tested in the greatest secrecy. Under the designation Project A-901, it was worked on in its own premises, a trim brick building at 403 Midland Avenue, Detroit, and became known as the "Mystery of Midland Avenue." When the time came for it to be tested at the proving grounds, the test cars were not permitted to pass certain marker points, beyond which the road would be visible from public highways.

In its production form, the Valiant was a six-window sedan with a short rear deck and a bold rectangular grille. Exner admitted that he raided the files of show cars; in particular, the horizontal line running from the front wheel arch and rising sharply to arc over the rear wheel was derived from the 1953 Chrysler d'Elegance. The rear deck carried the dummy spare wheel cover which had been tried on the K-310, and which was featured on some 1959 Plymouths.

The Valiant, which had begun as Project A-901 in May 1957 and had since mid-1958 been under serious development, including the building of 32 prototypes, was launched on October 29, 1959. It sold 194,292 units in its first season, well behind the Ford Falcon's 435,676 and Chevrolet's unconventional Corvair at 250,007. Though the Valiant was not the runaway success Chrysler had hoped, it continued with the same basic styling through the 1962 season, after which it was restyled on more conventional lines by Exner's successor, Elwood Engel. Though undistinguished in itself, the new Valiant was the source of a sporty coupe that Chrysler built in response to the Ford Mustang. Named the Barracuda, it had a very large rear window in the fastback style; at 14.4 square feet, it was the largest area of glass ever used on a production car.

A mid-season model, launched on April 1, 1964, the Barracuda was initially a model of Valiant, carrying the Valiant signature and V-shaped blue and red Valiant emblem. It was called the Plymouth Valiant Barracuda, though only for one year. For 1965 it was simply the Plymouth Barracuda, though still with the Valiant emblem at the lower center of the rear window. For 1966 it gained its own barracuda fish emblem in the center of the grille.

△ 1958 DE SOTO FIREDOME SPORTSMAN
The Forward Look was continued on 1958 Chrysler cars, though styling changes were minimal. Quad headlights were not standard because some states had not approved them. De Soto front fenders were designed to accept one or two lamps each, as local laws permitted.
OWNER: LEO GEPHART

△ Fred Schimmel's drawings for projects in the 1960s and early '70s. Clockwise from top right: a Barracuda study from the Elwood Engel period; the Hummingbird two-door coupe by Schimmel from the Exner era; an Engel design, 1970; two personal luxury cars by Exner.

▷ Schimmel's designs for Valiant wheel covers.

DRAWINGS: COURTESY OF FRED SCHIMMEL

A new body was featured for 1967, with a smaller rear window and a more complete fastback line, without any break caused by the rear fender. In 1970 a third-generation Barracuda, with notchback styling was launched. Several stylists contributed to the various Barracudas. The grille of the initial 1964 model was by Dave Cummins, and taillights by Fred Schimmel, Fred Froberg and Miller Johnson. The 1967 body was by John Herlitz and the fastback roof by Milt Antonick, with the rear end by Fred Schimmel.

Another high-performance Plymouth of the era was the Road Runner coupe, based on the Satellite B-body designed by John Herlitz (now Chrysler Corporation's Vice President of Design), with high performance and a relatively low price. Named after

ART OF THE AMERICAN AUTOMOBILE

◁ ▽ 1968 DODGE CHARGER COUPE

Totally restyled for 1968, the Charger lost its bulbous fastback, and acquired a more lithe semi-fastback rear end with a characteristic recessed rear window. Concealed headlights gave the front end a very clean look. Five engine options were available: 318, 383 (one-barrel carb), 383 (two-barrel carb), 426 and 440 cubic inches. The latter two were only used in the R/T (Road/Track) series. The most powerful of all was the 426 Hemi, which gave 425hp. One Charger R/T became a TV star, "The General Lee" of the *Dukes of Hazzard* series.

OWNER: RON SMITH

the cartoon character with permission from Warner Bros. to use the name and cartoon image, the Road Runner debuted in 1968. Even the bird's "beep-beep" call was imitated in the car's horn. Styling was begun by Fred Schimmel, but his lower dropping form wasn't liked, and Pete Loda was given the model to complete. The rear end was Schimmel's.

Dave Cummins was the chief designer in the K-car studios, the compact series made from 1981 to 1990 badged as Dodge Aries and Plymouth Reliant. The Chrysler LeBaron joined them for 1982. The K platform was used for more sporty cars badged as Chrysler Lasers or Dodge Daytonas. During Cummins' regime, convertibles were reinstated. Dropped by Chrysler in 1970 and by all American makers from 1976, the convertible had died because of anticipation on roll-over legislation. "One day when all was going well," says Cummins, "I called up our legal department and asked how the legislation had turned out. 'Oh, it never happened – all we really have to do is to take the impact loads of a frontal crash through the doors…' So that was it! When I told our vice-president Dick Macadam this information, his jaw dropped to the ground he was

so dumbfounded. I think he relayed this to our planners, and in about six months I started hearing more and more about convertibles until we finally had them… at least through *Cars & Concepts* in a cut-coupe form. Of course, they really came into their own with the J-body LeBaron, expertly built as a convertible on the assembly line rather than farmed out." This was syled by Steve Bolanger, aided by John Bucci.

However, so much had changed since the demise of the convertible that no one in the corporation knew how to engineer a folding top. They had all retired or died. "So we found a retiree who did know how and he made the first layout in his basement for us – incredible!"

Dave Cummins believes that the orginal design of the J-body coupe and convertible was a one-man effort, which is extremely unusual and perhaps a reason for its cohesive, handsome appearance. "When the clay was shown, I am told, Iacocca liked the car a lot. He turned to the audience and declared something to the effect that, 'Okay, now, we've everyone here, VPs of planning, styling, engineering, manufacture, sales. This is a good car, understand? Don't any of you guys screw it up!' "

△ TRANSATLANTIC PARTNERS
Nash put Italian-styled cars into production in the early '50s; their Italian partner was Pinin Farina. Here a Pinin Farina sedan body appears on a Nash Ambassador chassis. It was exhibited at the 1955 Turin Show.

CHAPTER TEN

THE ITALIAN CONNECTION

After World War II, Italy was the place to go for
inspirational design.

BEFORE WORLD WAR II, styling as expressed by custom coach-building was seen in France, Britain, Italy and the United States, but after the conflict Italy took an indisputable lead as traditional coach-builders in other countries faded away. Therefore any American company wanting to tap European inspiration would logically turn their attentions to Milan and Turin.

Two American companies, Chrysler and Nash, looked to Italy in the early 1950s, though only Nash put Italian-styled cars into production. Though Chrysler's partnership was with Ghia, its first Italian-bodied car, a fastback four-door six-window sedan built as a private venture in 1950, in fact came from the Turin firm Pinin Farina. Believed to use a New Yorker chassis, it appeared at a number of European shows, but was not commissioned by Chrysler, and had no successors. The following year, the first of the Ghia designs appeared for Chrysler, ordered by the American company. Christened the Plymouth XX-500 and built on a stock 118½-inch Plymouth chassis, it was also a fastback four-door sedan. It provided no discernable influence on future Plymouth styling, with its severe lines and minimal ornamentation, though its wire wheels were seen on Virgil Exner's Ghia-built

designs and they went into production on the 1955 C300. Subsequent Ghia-built Chryslers had little styling input from Turin, as they were mainly executing Exner's ideas.

Nash's partner was Pinin Farina, which built a custom sedan on the 1950 Ambassador chassis in 1951. The production Nash at that time was an all-enveloping fastback sedan nicknamed the "bathtub." A controversial design springing from a 1943 exercise by Holden Koto and Ted Pietsch, it had sold very well in its first two seasons, 1949 and 1950, but by 1951 was meeting resistance, partly because its all-enveloping shape made wheel-changing difficult, and any mechanical work was more expensive than on cars from the Big Three. Nash was ripe for a new design, and president George Mason instructed his assistant, George Romney, to do whatever it took to secure a contract with Pinin Farina. The exact cost to Nash is not known, but a tangible expense was the gift of a Nash Ambassador to Battista Farina, whose nickname Pinin was used in the company name. In 1961 it became one word, Pininfarina. The Farina-bodied prototype was studied for several months before management decided to use it in preference to a Nash design. In fact, substantial changes were made before the design went into production. The sloping hood and rear deck were leveled out to give

a more horizontal look, and the quarter windows behind the rear door were eliminated. The Farina cars had 25 percent more glass area than their predecessors and, Nash claimed, the widest seats on the road. Surprisingly, the half-covered front and rear wheels were retained, despite complaints about wheel changing.

For the 1952 season, the Statesman with a six-cylinder engine and the Ambassador with an eight

▽ 1951 PLYMOUTH XX-500
The first of Ghia's designs for Chrysler. The interior was upholstered in Bedford cord and leather. The curved windshield and fastback six-window styling did not have any impact on future Plymouth models.

△ 1952 NASH-HEALEY

This was America's first production sports car of the post-war era. The original slab-sided British body was replaced by this graceful design, both styled and built by Pinin Farina. As a result, the "production line" ran from the Nash factory at Kenosha, Wisconsin, to the Healey factory in England, where the engines were mounted on the chassis, and then on to Turin, Italy, where bodies and chassis were brought together, and finally back to Kenosha. No wonder the price was high – $5,128, and even then Nash lost money on every car.

OWNER: WALLY HERMAN

1952 NASH-HEALEY
This car was the child of a shipboard meeting between Nash boss George Mason and British sports car maker Donald Healey.
OWNER: WALLY HERMAN

were launched. Nash's president George Mason wanted to capitalize on the Farina connection, and realizing that the name meant next to nothing to the American public, he arranged for Farina-designed cars, a Cisitalia, a Fiat and a Lancia to share in dealer displays.

Apart from the sedans, the Nash-Healey sports car also received the Farina treatment. It started life as an Anglo-American hybrid and finished up as an Anglo-Italian-American hybrid. The first Nash-Healey of 1950 was a marriage between the lightweight sports-car chassis that Donald Healey had been making for four years, and a 232-cubic-inch Nash six-cylinder engine, which gave more power than the 149-cubic-inch Riley four that he had used hitherto. Healey had planned to use a Cadillac V8, but sailing to New York on the *Queen Elizabeth*, he fell into conversation about cameras with George Mason. A friendship sprang up, and

▽ 1953 NASH-HEALEY
There were no styling changes on the 1953 models,
though there was an additional style, a hardtop coupe
on a longer wheelbase. Total production of Farina Nash-
Healeys was 402, of which 90 were coupes.
PHOTO: NATIONAL MOTOR MUSEUM, BEAULIEU

Healey was invited to stay with the Mason family in Detroit, where he was told, "If you don't get engines from Ed Cole, come back and see me." Cole, head of Cadillac, couldn't help as he was fully committed to making engines for his own cars, so Healey accepted Mason's offer, and the Nash-Healey was born.

In its original form, the Nash-Healey used a British body designed and built by Panelcraft, simple in style (though not particularly graceful) and fronted by a vertical Nash grille which Healey called the "Joe E. Brown" grille. Though the cars performed well, Mason was not very happy with their appearance, so he called on Pinin Farina for a complete redesign. Out went the Joe E. Brown, to be replaced by a sloping grille with only two horizontal central bars, and headlights mounted inboard, next to the grille. The body had a slightly

△ A Pinin Farina sedan body on a Nash Ambassador chassis, shown at the 1955 Turin Show, the *Salone Torino*. The grille and headlight design is close to that of the Nash-Healey.
▽ The Palm Beach coupe on a Rambler chassis was Farina's last styling exercise for Nash. By 1956, when this showcar was made, Nash was part of American Motors.

dropped belt line, with a sculpted rear fender which had a tiny kick-up behind the wheel, a sort of embryo fin. The whole car was transformed from a rather ungainly hybrid – American grille grafted onto British body – to a handsome integral design.

Unlike the Nash sedans, the Healey bodies were not only designed but built in Italy, which necessitated a complex production program. Engines and transmissions were shipped from the Nash plant at Kenosha, Wisconsin, to Healey's little factory at The Cape in Warwick, England, where they were fitted to the chassis and transported on to Pinin Farina in Turin. There they received their bodies, and the completed cars were shipped back to the U.S. This extended production line was a major factor in the high price, $5,128 in 1953. When a Corvette cost only $3,515 and a Jaguar XK-120 only $3,945 at port of entry, it is understandable that there were no long lines at Nash dealers for the Healey. Even at $5,128, Nash was losing money on every car sold, because it is estimated each cost around $9,000. A total of 402 Farin-bodied Nash-Healeys were made. Nash's contract with Pinin Farina ended in 1955, and was not renewed. By then Nash was part of American Motors, and cost-cutting economy cars were the order of the day. Farina built one car on the new Rambler chassis as a styling exercise. Named the Palm Beach, it was a two-passenger sports coupe with an unusual front

end, quite unlike the Nash-Healey. A large central oval air intake was flanked by two smaller ovals containing the headlights. The oval intake had appeared on some custom designs by Farina on Lancia and other European chassis, as well as on a very ungainly Cadillac, but it never saw production and neither did the Palm Beach.

In another Italo-American operation, Hudson, Nash's partner in American Motors, contracted with

▽ Between 1950 and 1961 Ghia built 27 showcars for Chrysler, including these two Darts of 1957. The Super Gilda (below) was a convertible, while the Dart (bottom) was a hardtop. It was tested in a windtunnel, and to aid aerodynamics a full bellypan was used. It was a running car, powered by a Chrysler 300-C engine.

Touring to build bodies for its Italia, but these were designed by Frank Spring, whose work is discussed in Chapter 16.

Cadillac's prestigious Allante, made from 1987 to 1993, was styled by Pininfarina, and the bodies were built in Turin, necessitating what was called the longest production line in the world. The modified Eldorado frames were flown out to Turin in specially adapted Boeing 747s, where the bodies were made in a plant separate from ordinary PF production. They were then flown back to Detroit to be fitted with engines and transmissions. Though they claimed Pininfarina styling, the Allantes were not very different to look at from other Cadillacs. Their grilles were individual to the model, and they differed from other Cadillacs in being two-passenger cars, but they had no great distinction. This, and initial problems of build quality, resulted in disappointing sales. The 1993 Allantes, with 290bhp Northstar 32-valve engines, four-speed automatic transmissions and improved steering and suspension, were much better cars than the '87s, but production was halted after several thousand had been made.

◁ 1989 CADILLAC ALLANTE
▽ 1990 CADILLAC ALLANTE
This was another Italian-American car with a
transatlantic production line, though it was not as long

as the Nash-Healey's, since there was no detour to
England. The Allante was built on an Eldorado frame
shortened from 108 to 99.4 inches.

PHOTOS: NATIONAL MOTOR MUSEUM, BEAULIEU

△ RAYMOND LOEWY (1893-1987)
As well as being responsible for the design of Studebakers, Loewy and his company had a hand in designing everything from refrigerators to Coca-Cola's classic bottle. He is seen here with the SI locomotive he designed for Pennsylvania Railroad.
PHOTO: RAYMOND LOEWY DESIGN

CHAPTER ELEVEN

RAYMOND LOEWY

"Ex was a designer and Loewy was a promoter,
a promoter/designer, you might say."

Bob Bourke, manager and chief designer at Loewy's studio

RAYMOND LOEWY WAS one of the more controversial designers, not popular with many of his colleagues and, by some, not regarded as a true stylist. "He was not a car designer. He wanted to be," said Bill Mitchell. However, Chrysler stylist Dave Cummins considers this view unfair. Bob Bourke, who worked with Loewy and Virgil Exner, observed "Ex was a designer and Loewy was a promoter, a promoter/designer, you might say." Nevertheless, several important cars have been associated with Loewy, as well as a wide variety of industrial and domestic appliances, shop interiors, and railroad locomotives. This diversity is one of the charges held against him. Those with gasoline in their veins do not think that cars and iceboxes can have anything at all in common. "Car designers don't give a damn about iceboxes," said Mitchell.

Raymond Loewy was born in Paris in 1893, the son of an Austrian father and a French mother. Though he spent a lot of time sketching, especially trains and cars, he says that he did not consider drawing as a career until he was on board the liner *France*, bound for New York, in 1919. His sketch of a girl was auctioned for charity, and the buyer happened to be the British consul in New York City. He offered to put the young man in touch with magazines, and within a few years Loewy was well known as an illustrator, and also did window dressing for such stores as Macy's and Bonwit Teller. His first industrial commission was to redesign the Gestetner duplicating machine, which he "streamlined" by covering up the belt drive and separate drawers in a smooth cabinet.

Raymond Loewy had always enjoyed drawing cars, and in 1928 he filed a patent for a "combined automobile body and hood"; this was an interesting design with sharply V-ed windshield, short stubby

fenders, and a separate running board. It never progressed beyond the drawings, but in 1931 he was introduced by a friend from advertising to the Hupp Motor Car Corporation. He restyled the 1932 Hupmobiles, the most striking features of which were the cycle-type fenders which hugged the wheel contours. Though it was not a trend-setting design like the Graham Blue Streak, it was another breakaway from the traditional long clam-shell fender, and an echo of his 1928 design. The wheels themselves could be covered with chrome-plated disks for five dollars extra. This was certainly an improvement over the wooden-spoked artillery wheels, though the alternative wire wheels were handsome enough anyway. Loewy's disks anticipated those on the 1953 Studebaker Starliner, one of his most successful creations. The radiator was given a slight V-shape, and in place of Northup's H with dagger and castle came an ornament above the radiator: an open ring with the letter H inside it. Unusually, it was meant to be viewed from the side rather than the driving seat, so it was in line with the hood.

Loewy had planned a more radical design, with step plates instead of running boards, and to demonstrate his ideas to Hupp management, he built a four-door phaeton with step plates, at a personal cost of around $18,000. Though it was not adopted by Hupp, Loewy toured Europe in this car, gathering prizes at several Concours, at Dieppe, Le Touquet and Cannes.

Hupp was sufficiently pleased with Loewy's work on its 1932 models to give him a clean sheet for the '34s. These were more streamlined than anything on the road except the Chrysler Airflow, and they had better proportions, with a longer hood. The headlights were faired into the side of the hood, which was very simple with no louvers, while the skirted fenders were of tear-drop shape. The windshield, while not a full wraparound like the GM cars of the 1950s, was a three-piece structure with small side pieces which gave a slight wraparound effect. The rear of the body was aerodynamic in shape and included a spare wheel cover molded in the trunk lid. The design was continued without major change through the 1936

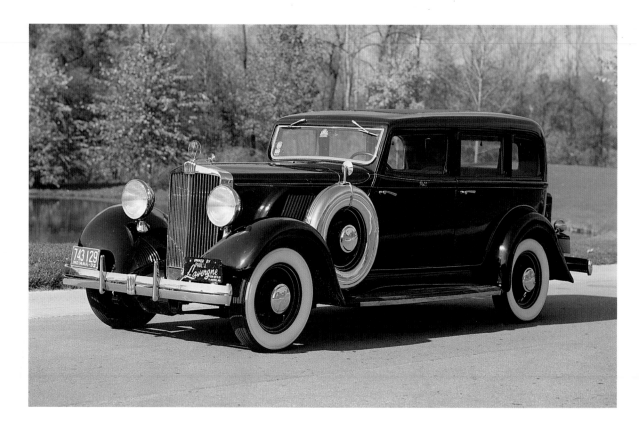

▷ 1932 HUPMOBILE MODEL 226 SEDAN
The first production car from the drawing board of Raymond Loewy, this car was distinguished by its wheel-hugging cycle-type fenders. The 226 had eight cylinders; cheaper sixes had conventional fenders.
PHOTO: NATIONAL MOTOR MUSEUM, BEAULIEU

ART OF THE AMERICAN AUTOMOBILE

season, but financial malpractice within the company denied the aerodynamic Hupps the success they deserved. The last were assembled from parts in stock in July 1937, and the 1938 models were much less adventurous. They owed nothing to Loewy, who was by then a consultant to Studebaker.

L OEWY'S STUDEBAKER YEARS

Apart from his contract with Hupmobile, Raymond Loewy was busy in the mid-1930s with work on refrigerators for Sears Roebuck and Frigidaire and locomotives for the Pennsylvania Railroad. In 1936, however, he was invited back into the automobile world by Studebaker executives. It took two years for him to agree, and then on his own terms. Resenting the conservative influence of certain people at Hupmobile, he stipulated that although his office would be in the Studebaker plant, it would be a Loewy office, and Studebaker personnel would only be admitted by invitation. The executives at South Bend presumably accepted this autocratic demand as the price of getting the country's best-known designer. Because of his work with locomotives and refrigerators, together with a considerable flair for self-publicity, the name of Loewy was very much more familar to the public than that of Harley Earl. Loewy's picture and comments featured in Studebaker advertising, which never happened to Earl.

His influence was first seen on the 1938 Presidents and Commanders, which were a considerable advance over the 1937s. In particular, the State Commander and the President had semi-faired headlights of oblong shape, tapered to a rounded back which was faired into the fenders. Never backward in coming forward, Loewy pro-moted the new Studebakers energetically, and as a result of keen lobbying, *The Magazine of Art* voted the Studies "Car of the Year" for 1938, 11 years before the award was officially made by *Motor Trend* magazine.

For 1939, front ends were restyled again, with headlights fully faired into the fenders and twin low grilles flanking a pointed prow. This applied to the larger Studebakers, Commanders and Presidents, but 1939 also saw a brand-new smaller car, what

would today be called a compact. Named the Champion, this had different styling from other Studebakers, with a central, bold-chrome grille with horizontal bars flanked by vertical bars. The Champion's body was less inspired, but an important step was the absence of running boards.

Lightness was all important in the Champion, which was promoted as an economy car aimed at the budget-minded buyer. Research showed that 90 percent of car-owning families had weekly incomes of $60 or less, of which 10 percent went into their automobiles. Fuel consumption was a major anxiety, so the Champion's average of 20½ miles per gallon was an important selling point, when compared with 17 from Plymouth, 18 from Chevrolet, and 16 from the Ford V8-85. Apart from the small block Ford V8-60, which never sold well, the Champion had the smallest displacement engine (164 cubic inches), and the lowest weight (2,375 pounds). This fitted very well with Loewy's philosophy. A strong advocate of lower weight rather than higher power, he had about 40 big

△ 1939 STUDEBAKER CHAMPION SIX SEDAN
The Champion was Studebaker's third attempt at a compact car, and was the most successful. Loewy's studio gave it different styling from the larger Studebakers. The fully recessed headlights, used on all models, were new for Studebaker that year.

posters reading "Weight is the Enemy" displayed around the studio, and even mounted on the floors, covered with plastic. In this he was in accord with Studebaker management: "... parameters primarily involved reduced weight," he said. "There were no problems as I was dealing with intelligent people who understood that weight was the enemy." To save weight, he used a lot of aluminum trim.

The Champion was a great success, very encouraging for Studebaker, whose two previous attempts at smaller cars, the Erskine and the Rockne, had been far from bestsellers. The Champion sold 72,791 units in the 1939 calendar

The 1946 Studebakers were rare cars, being carry-overs from the 1942 models, and only made from December 1945 to March 1946, when the radical new "coming-or-going" cars appeared.

year, and overall Studebaker sales were up an astonishing 86.7 percent over 1938.

When describing the Champion, or later Studebakers, as a "Loewy design," you must bear in mind that Loewy was not a hands-on designer, and that most of the actual work was done by his associates and submitted to him for approval. In this he was like Harley Earl, yet Earl has always had the higher creative reputation. Part of the reason was that Earl was a pure automobile man, a gasoline-in-the-veins character, while Loewy's talents and interests were very widespread. By 1939 he had offices in London and New York, and after the war in Paris and São Paulo as well. Clare Hodgman, who was mainly responsible for the 1939 Champion, said, "Mr. Loewy was always involved with a number of projects at the same time. His policy was

to hire competent people he could trust to do the firm's commissions. The design work for the Champion – all preliminary sketches, drawings and quarter-scale models – were done in the Loewy studios in New York. After approval, full-size clays and the first metal prototypes were built in South Bend." After completing his design, Hodgman had to take it for approval to the London office, where Loewy just happened to be at the time.

Virgil Exner, who has been credited for the '39 Champion, in fact, did not join the Loewy studio until most of the work had been done. He was involved with the 1940 Champion, and, of course, was a key figure on the radical post-war Studebaker.

The 1941 Studebakers represented the high point of pre-war Loewy design, especially the top-of-the-line President. The pointed prow was flanked by lower grilles than before (Hodgman had pleaded for a lower grille on the 1939 Champion but it was rejected, not by Loewy but by Studebaker management). Like the Champion, the President lacked running boards, and the rear fenders were sculpted over the wheel arches. Two lines of four-door sedan were offered, the six-window Cruising Sedan (W-body) and the four-window Land Cruiser

(B-body), which in profile, resembled GM's C bodies as fitted to Oldsmobiles, Pontiacs and Buicks. The De Luxe model featured two-tone exteriors and color-keyed interiors. In mid-season came a new body, the two-door five-passenger Sedan Coupe (F-body).

E XNER'S POST-WAR STUDEBAKERS

Soon after the war halted passenger car production in February 1942, a government order went out that no human or technological resources should be used to develop post-war models. This was supposed to release all available talent for the war effort, and also to ensure that all manufacturers started out on a equal footing after the war. Inevitably, the directive was not followed, and we have seen that Ford worked on quite a number of post-war designs from 1943 on.

The Loewy studios had one advantage though, they were not part of a manufacturing company, so the rule did not apply to them. In fact, they had very few staff as most had joined the military, but Virgil Exner stayed on and was joined by Holden

Koto in the fall of 1943. Other stylists in the studio included Bob Bourke and Dick Caleal.

Certain parameters had been agreed between Loewy and Exner; the car was to have a full-width body, originally slab-sided, but Exner decided early on to include some sculpting to break up the slab. It was also to have a curved windshield and a wraparound rear window, with a large rear deck. Several stylists, including Exner and Koto, were assigned to produce quarter-scale clays of how they thought the post-war Studebaker should look. Unfortunately, Exner and Loewy were not getting on; Exner felt that his boss was claiming credit for designs, while he had actually only promoted the designs of others. The result was that, in Loewy's words, "he was not cooperative and became a disruptive element... he often bypassed me and made a big play for Roy Cole."

Cole was Studebaker's vice-president for engineering, who was also disenchanted with Loewy and resented the independence of his studio. "We'll never get anything out of this guy Loewy," he said. "We'll just waste time talking to him." Exner had found a natural ally in Cole, and pretty soon he was working on a clay of his own, in

the basement of his house, with clay, lighting and equipment provided for him by Cole. During the day he still worked on his design for Loewy, and at night on his own. We can imagine which model claimed the bulk of his attention and enthusiasm. Cole followed the Exner design closely and secretly asked Budd to make a full-size wooden mock-up. He may also have seen to it that the Loewy studio was furnished with incorrect dimensions, a 110-inch wheelbase and 67-inch width, while the Exner model had a 112-inch wheelbase and 70-inch width. An alternative theory is that Cole didn't give Loewy false figures, but simply allowed him to go ahead with the smaller dimensions, which were those of the pre-war Champion.

Late in 1944, Cole called a full board meeting and showed them Exner's full-size mock-up and the clays from the Loewy studio. The board accepted the Exner version without hesitation. Loewy's reaction was predictable: "In my experience of over 50 years, I have never seen such a case of despicable behavior," he said in an interview with Richard Langworth years later. He sacked Exner on the spot, but the design still went ahead, with Exner fully on the Studebaker payroll. He worked directly

under Cole, in his own design department at the Studebaker proving grounds.

The post-war Studebakers were announced in April 1946 as '47 models, though none reached the showrooms until June. They proved sensational. The coupes were the most way-out, with enormous wraparound rear windows, and fear decks that seemed as long as the hoods. In fact, the rear deck from window to rear of trunk lid was 45 inches, and the hood 48 inches, but the proportions were more equal than any other contemporary car. They immediately provoked cries of "Are you coming or going?," so the cars came to be nicknamed the "coming-or-going Studebakers." At the time of their appearance, their full-width bodies were unique to the industry apart from the Kaiser-Frazers, and those had straight slab sides with no molding. Exner's design had a bold molding at the rear fender point and, therefore, much more character.

It is difficult to know the balance between the contributions of the Loewy studio and of Exner in these Studebakers. The basic layout had been decided before Exner left to work on his own, but he definitely designed the front end, with a more complex grille than before. In fact, the grilles differed between the low-priced Champion and higher-priced Commander. Two- and four-door sedans were offered in both lines, also coupes and convertibles, the latter the first open cars from Studebaker since 1939. They sold very well, lifting Studebaker from tenth place in the industry in 1947 to ninth in 1948 and eighth in 1949. Thereafter, with the arrival of genuine post-war cars from the Big Three, they dropped a little, though ninth place was held through 1953.

As one would imagine from a brand-new design, little change was made for several years, the first important one being the spinner grille for 1950. By then Loewy had regained the styling contract for Studebaker, and the idea of the spinner was his,

◁ In 1946 the Champion was the only line, and had four models, two- or four-door sedans, and three- or five-passenger coupes. Stylewise, they differed little from the 1942s. Total production was 19,275, of which 3,750 were coupes. The three-passenger cost $1,002 and the five-passenger $1,044.

being actually worked out in detail by Bob Bourke, who had become manager and chief designer for Loewy. Loewy celebrated the adoption of the spinner by mounting a propeller which revolved in the wind on the nose of his personal car. Coincidentally, Bourke was also responsible for the slightly different spinner on the 1949 Ford (see Chapter Six). There were a lot of changes at that time; Exner stayed with Studebaker but apparently didn't do very much; at one point he was asked back to the Loewy studio, which seems surprising. He refused and soon left to join Chrysler, where he did his most famous work (see Chapter 9). Gordon Buehrig was briefly Loewy's chief designer, before going to Ford in 1949. Bourke remained until the mid-Fifties.

THE STARLINER

Apart from the spinner grille, no great changes were made to the Studebaker for several years. In 1952 a new grille replaced the spinner, a low horizontal shape of no great distinction, which some dubbed the "clam digger," though Loewy favored it over the spinner. Public reaction to the latter had not been as good as hoped, and a face-lift enabled Loewy to lower the hood. "I always objected to the high hood," he said.

The 1953 Studebakers were all new. The most striking model was the Starliner coupe, largely the work of Bob Bourke. Work began in 1951 on what was planned as a one-off showcar to tour the auto exhibitions in the same manner as GM's Le Sabre

▽ 1950 STUDEBAKER CHAMPION REGAL DE LUXE
This was the second generation of genuine post-war Studebakers, and was distinguished by the spinner grille. This was Loewy's idea, but the detail work was done by Bob Bourke, who was also responsible for the similar front end design on the 1949 Ford.

▷ 1953 STUDEBAKER CHAMPION STARLINER
Familiarly known today as the "Loewy coupes," the Starliner hardtop and Starlight coupe were among the best-looking American cars of the 1950s. From the Loewy studio, Bob Bourke and Holden Koto both submitted designs, and it was Bourke's that was chosen. They used a longer wheelbase than the sedans and both came in Champion and Commander series.
PHOTOS: NATIONAL MOTOR MUSEUM, BEAULIEU

ART OF THE AMERICAN AUTOMOBILE

did. Bourke and four of his designers were given a free hand to create their idea of a new body form, making drawings followed by quarter-scale clays. When it came to the full-size clay, the two sides were worked on by separate teams, Holden Koto with three assistants doing the right side, and Bourke with two assistants doing the left. The main difference lay in the B-pillar, which had a sharp reverse angle in the Bourke design, parallel to the A-pillar, while Koto's was more curvaceous and at an angle of about 45° to the A-pillar. Both had side molding; Bourke's finished in the door, while Koto's extended some way behind the door. Bourke's taillight mounting was also at a reverse angle, like

the B-pillar, while Koto's panel roughly paralleled his B-pillar, with the lights projecting behind it.

These designs were done while Raymond Loewy was away in Europe, and when he returned he voted for Bourke's design, though Koto says that the rank and file in the studio preferred his. The design also pleased Studebaker boss Harold Vance, who authorized it as a production car. The only major change, whch Bourke did not approve of, was the insertion of a quarter window, whereas his design had a single piece of glass between A- and B-pillars, as on the later Camaro and Firebird. The front end was low and simple, with a hood sloping down to twin openings, which could hardly be

called grilles as they had only a single bar across the middle.

Inevitably dubbed the "Loewy coupe," the new design went into production as part of the 1953 Studebaker line, in both Champion and Commander series. The sedans and Starlight coupes had similar front ends, though they were higher overall. The Starliner did not have a trouble-free debut. With the launch only weeks away, it was discovered that the front sheet metal did not fit properly to the body, and quality problems plagued the design during its first year. Its very success went against it, for demand for the coupes turned out to be four times higher than for the sedans, whereas

Studebaker had expected the proportion to be the other way around. Production of the coupes could not be increased that quickly (actual production figures were nearly equal, with coupes outnumbering sedans by about 2,000 units) and the company ended the model year with a disappointing 169,599 cars built.

The 1954 Studebakers were little changed, apart from some vertical bars in the grille which did not improve their appearance, and for 1955 the front ends became much heavier and more chrome-laden. This was a management decision, resulting from the success of the highly chromed Harley Earl designs for Buick and Cadillac. Loewy was not in agreement with this. "It has been the designer's sad experience that a great majority of the people love chrome, and love it dearly…" he lamented.

By 1955 the Loewy studios had less influence at South Bend. Management tended to blame declining sales on the "un-American" look of his cars, so they began to dictate to the studio what they wanted, instead of Loewy deciding on an ideal design and selling the idea to management. In the

fall of 1954, C. K. Whittaker, vice-president of sales, sent down a directive to Bourke for an attention-grabbing design based on the Starliner shell without too many expensive alterations. The result was named the President Speedster; it had a heavier front end with more chrome on the bumpers and big, underslung fog lights called bumperettes. The body carried Speedster scripts and checkered flag emblems, while striking three-tone color schemes were offered, quite different from those on other Studebakers. It was a classic example of Sorensen's "Let's just deluxe-y the hell out of these cars" philosophy, and it worked, at least in the short term, though Bourke never liked it. "We hammered up the 1955 line with that big chromium snout-like grille. It was completely out of context." Only 2,215 President Speedsters were sold in the 1955 season, but it always was intended as a limited production specialty car.

For 1956 the car was redesigned as the Hawk, the main external difference being a big square grille with thin mesh bars, taken from a projected large luxury sedan which never got beyond the clay

▽ 1953 STUDEBAKER COMMANDER STARLIGHT COUPE
The Commanders were the higher-priced line of Studebaker, with a 232.6-cubic-inch V8 engine giving 120hp, while the Champion used a 198.6-cubic-inch six of 85hp. This Starlight coupe cost $1,955 as a Champion and $2,213 as a Commander (shown here). They were much better looking than the sedans which rode on a shorter wheelbase, and demand was four times greater.
OWNERS: DICK AND JANET RIGBY

ART OF THE AMERICAN AUTOMOBILE

stage. It was certainly an improvement on the '55, but lacked the purity of the original Starliner. The top model, the Golden Hawk, which used a Packard V8, had small fins which, says Bourke, he kept as restrained as possible, while still pleasing sales. The '56 Hawk was the last design from the Loewy studios for Studebaker for seven years, for with the Packard merger, Loewy's contract was dropped.

A VANTI

The Hawk was continued up to 1964 in various manifestations, from 1961 styled by Brooks Stevens. Studebaker's bread and butter came from the compact Lark sedans, which were successful when introduced in 1959, but sales were badly hit by compacts from the Big Three. In February 1961 Studebaker gained a new president in Sherwood Harry Egbert, who decided that the company needed a brand-new car to boost its image. Although Studebaker still had its own styling department, he contacted Raymond Loewy. After

consultations at South Bend, Loewy rented a building near his home in Palm Springs, California, and with three assistants, went to work on the new car. Egbert had set an almost impossible deadline of the New York Show in April 1962, just 13 months after from his first meeting with Loewy. Any Detroit production man would have said that such a deadline was absurd, but Egbert was not an automobile man, having come from McCulloch superchargers in California.

The Avanti was, in fact, not all new. There was neither time nor money for that, so it rode on the shortest of the Lark chassis with a stock Studebaker 289-cubic-inch V8 engine, but Loewy's body was quite new and bore no resemblance to anything previously done by Studebaker or by anyone else.

Its proportions were more European than American, with a long hood and very short rear deck, razor-edge front fenders, air intakes being below the bumpers and no grille at all. Unlike contemporary American cars, it had almost the same overhang at the front and rear, which added to the long hood/short body effect. The body had a

distinctive "Coke-bottle shape" and perhaps it was no coincidence that Loewy's company had been, in fact, responsible for the final look of the classic Coca-Cola bottle. The Avanti's nipped-in waistline when seen from above, with a slight kick-up behind the door, which was widely imitated later. In a sketch dated March 1961, Loewy scribbled alongside the Coke-bottle drawing, "Like Jaguar, Ferrari, Aston Martin, Mercedes, Lotus, Osca, Stanguellini, Cooper etc." The body featured a built-in roll bar, and there was a large wraparound rear window, later seen in the Plymouth Barracuda and Rambler Marlin.

Loewy's team – John Ebstein, Robert Andrews and Thomas Kellogg – produced a clay in just over

▽ 1954 COMMANDER REGAL STARLIGHT COUPE
With the '53s being such freshly styled cars, it is hardly surprising that very little change was made for the 1954 season. Externally the '54s were distinguished by an egg-crate pattern in the horizontal grille.
PHOTO: NATIONAL MOTOR MUSEUM, BEAULIEU

◁ △ 1963 STUDEBAKER AVANTI COUPE
Seven years after Studebaker ended its contract with the Raymond Loewy Studios, the stylist was called back to design a new car to boost the company's falling sales. The long hood and short body were quite new to Studebaker, as was the plain front with no grille.

▷ The Avanti's dashboard was a model of simplicity with no frills. This car has optional Flightomatic automatic transmission.

▷ The standard engine in the Avanti was a 289-cubic-inch V8 which gave 240hp, or 289hp with a supercharger.

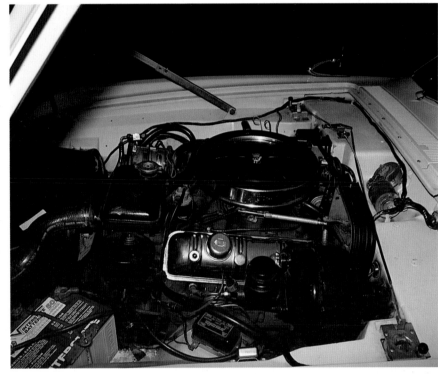

two weeks and took it to Egbert for approval. Studebaker's Bob Doehler had the job of making a full-size clay from Loewy's model, and began with sectional drawings made from the model and then blown up to full size. From these, modelers Harold Davidson and H. Levoy Schryer produced a full-size clay, with numerous small changes being made along the line at the suggestion of Egbert, Loewy and Doehler, as well as Studebaker's chief of engineering Gene Hardig. The windshield was made more vertical because Egbert bumped his head when trying to sit down in the seating buck, and the Coke-bottle effect was smoothed out a little. The model had quad headlights, but they proved too expensive and twins were substituted. Mounted just inside the razor-edge fender fronts, they were very good-looking, and the change from quads was probably a good idea.

The full-size clay was finished in 40 days from the start of work in Palm Springs, and once Egbert had received approval from the Studebaker board, production could go ahead. There had been some debate about the material for the body, and fiberglass was chosen as being cheaper and quicker to manufacture. The anticipated production of 1,000 cars per month did not justify tooling up for a steel body. The leading maker of fiberglass bodies for automobiles was the Molded Fiberglass Products Company of Ashtabula, Ohio, which was already making bodies for Corvettes. Studebaker naively thought this would ensure trouble-free production but, in fact, there were many problems with the alignment of body to chassis, resulting in delayed production. Although the prototypes were ready just in time for the New York Show in April 1962, the first production model was not completed until June. All production Avantis were considered as 1963 models. Even then, output was slow, and many who had ordered Avantis canceled and bought a Corvette instead. It was the story of the Chrysler Airflow and Cord 810 all over again. Far from achieving 1,000 a month, Studebaker made just 3,834 Avantis in the 1963 model year, and 809 in the 1964. In fact, production ended in December 1963.

However, the Avanti line lived on until quite recently, for after Studebaker dropped it, the dies, parts and rights to the name were bought by Nate Altman and Leo Newman who set up Avanti Motors Corporation, using Corvette engines. They made the coupe virtually identical, and in the 1980s new owners added a convertible and a four-door sedan.

The Avanti was Loewy's last automotive design. Later, in the '60s, he produced Skylab designs for NASA, but the only suggestions that were taken up were the color schemes, the coveralls for the crew, and the Garment Storage Modules. After the death of his partner Bill Snaith in 1974, Loewy let many of his clients go, and in 1976 the New York office was closed. He retained the London office, which survived his death in 1987 and still functions today.

△ GORDON BUEHRIG (1905-1990)
After a brief spell at GM's Art & Colour section he returned to the Auburn-Cord-Duesenberg empire where he designed his most famous cars, the Cord 810s and 812s. Buehrig went on to work for Raymond Loewy, the American Sports Car Company and Ford, from which he retired in 1965. He is pictured here in his Duesenberg studio in Indianapolis, circa 1930.

CHAPTER TWELVE

GORDON BUEHRIG

"Somehow it looked like a beautiful thing that had been born
and just grew up on the highway."

Anonymous admirer of the Cord 810

GORDON MILLER BUEHRIG (1905-90) will always be remembered, rightly, for the Cord 810 of 1936, yet his career spanned more than 30 years, and he was also responsible for some other beautiful cars, including the Duesenberg Beverly and the Auburn 851; he also influenced the post-war Studebakers, and Fords from the mid-'50s.

Born in Mason City, Illinois, Buehrig studied liberal arts at Bradley Polytechnic in Peoria. He was expelled from class on one occasion because the instructor saw that his notebook was full of drawings of automobiles. In 1924 he joined the Gotfredson Body Co. of Wayne, Michigan, which made bodies for Jewett, Peerless and Wills Sainte Claire. A move to Dietrich two years later took him into the realms of custom coachbuilding, which was followed by

stints at Packard, General Motors (in the Art & Colour Section, where he was to return in 1934), and Stutz, for whom he designed the fabric bodies used on the company's Le Mans sports cars of 1929. In that year, worried by Stutz's lack of prospects, he joined Duesenberg as chief body designer. He was still only 25 years old.

Duesenberg did not build its own bodies, but Buehrig designed them to the point where they could be put into three-dimensional form by any of the coachbuilders which Duesenberg used. Probably his best-known design was the Beverly four-window berline, which was made by Murphy. It had a compact four-door sedan body with a sizable luggage trunk at the rear. The rear seating was strictly for two, with an armrest which could be removed "when a more intimate seating arrangement is desired." It was not a fold-up rest as in

▽ 1929 DUESENBERG MODEL J LEBARON
This convertible sedan was one of Gordon Buehrig's designs put into practice by LeBaron. The absence of radiator shutters make this an early Model J. These had V-shaped radiator cores, but a change to the cheaper flat core necessitated the shutters to keep the V shape.
OWNER: DOOR PRARIE MUSEUM

◁ △ 1933 AUBURN V12 BOAT-TAIL SPEEDSTER
A predecessor of Gordon Buehrig's Type 851 speedster, this V12 and earlier Auburn speedsters were the work of Al Leamy.
OWNER: DUKE DAVENPORT

modern cars, but a panel which had to be detached and stowed elsewhere. Murphy built about 12 Beverlys and sold them for $16,500 in 1932, equivalent to around $330,000 in the mid-'90s. Other notable Buehrig designs included the Derham tourster and Brunn torpedo phaeton.

In 1933 Buehrig was lured away from Duesenberg by Harley Earl, becoming yet another of the luminaries who worked for GM's Art & Colour Section at one time or another (he had worked for GM briefly before joining Duesenberg). Shortly after joining Art & Colour, he had an altercation with his boss, having the great temerity to disagree publicly with Our-Father-Who-Art-in-Styling on the subject of the front end, which Harley said represented 90 percent of a car's

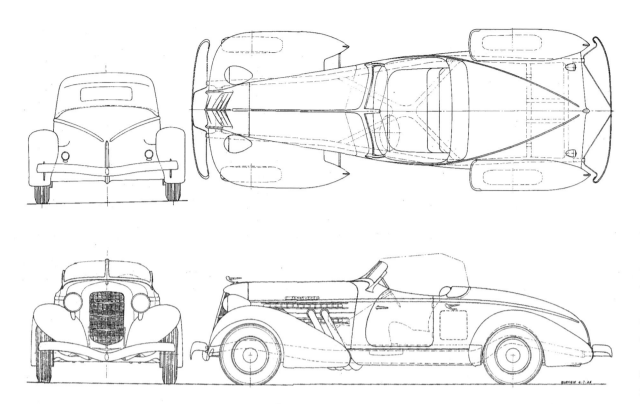

appearance. Buehrig observed that he had been designing Duesenbergs for five years, and they all had the same front end. "Some of them were very beautiful automobiles, and some of them were very ordinary looking, but they all had the same front end."

He did not record Earl's response to this but, of course, the difference between the two men lay in the markets they were aiming for. Duesenberg had, in a remarkably short time, established itself as a glamour car par excellence. It was recognizable by its radiator and therefore, as with Rolls-Royce, it would be crazy to alter it. (Though some custom body builders did disguise it a few years later.) Earl, on the other hand, was styling cars which had to compete for a mass market with rivals which might be only slightly different mechanically. So a striking appearance, led by the front end, was vital to success.

In November 1933 Earl held a competition for an aerodynamic car, and Buehrig headed one of the four teams. Another team was Frank Hershey's,

△ Line drawings of the Auburn 851 speedster. These were made by Gordon Buehrig in 1968 from original data in his files dated July 1934.

PICTURES: AUBURN-CORD-DUESENBERG MUSEUM

△ A 1935 Auburn 851 speedster receives admiring attention at the Bonneville Salt Flats in Utah. Here Ab Jenkins drove this car in 24-hour endurance runs sponsored by the Firestone Tire Company.

△ The exceptionally sleek lines of the 1935 851 speedster are well shown in this rear view. All speedsters carried a plaque verifying that they had been driven by Ab Jenkins at a speed of at least 100mph.

ART OF THE AMERICAN AUTOMOBILE

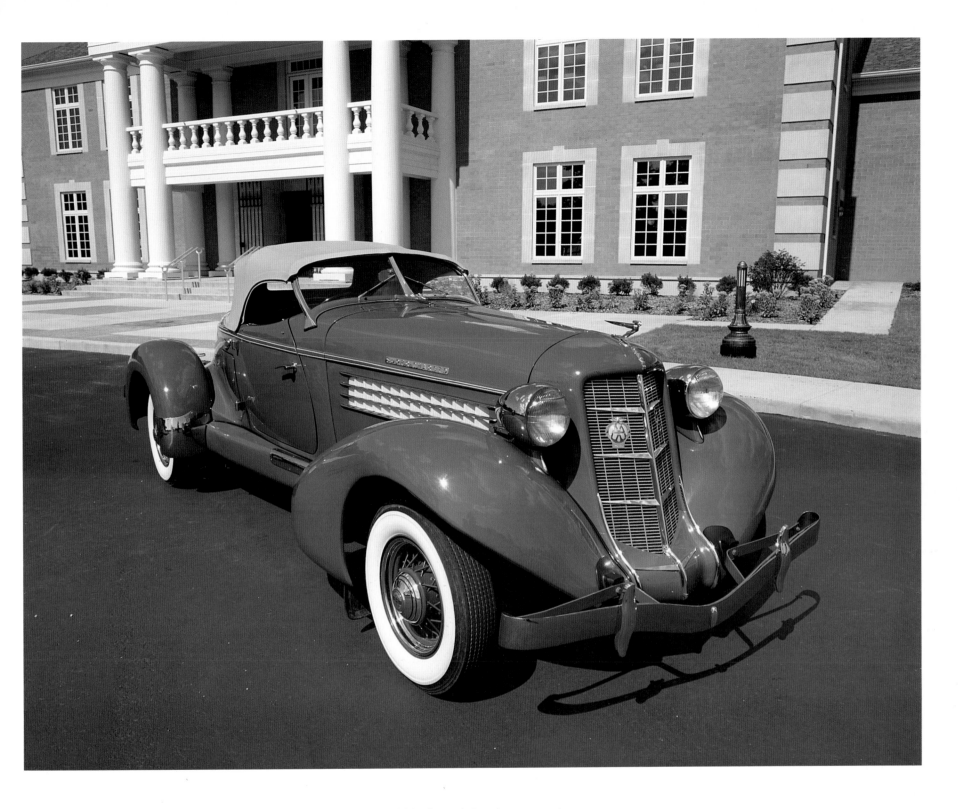

△ 1936 AUBURN TYPE 852 BOAT-TAIL SPEEDSTER
There were virtually no changes between the 1935 and
1936 models of Auburn, though designation progressed
from 851 to 852. Cord probably lost money on every

speedster sold (at $2,245), but they attracted customers
into the showrooms. Though 1937 Auburns were said
to be on the way, they never arrived.
OWNER: AUBURN-CORD-DUESENBERG MUSEUM

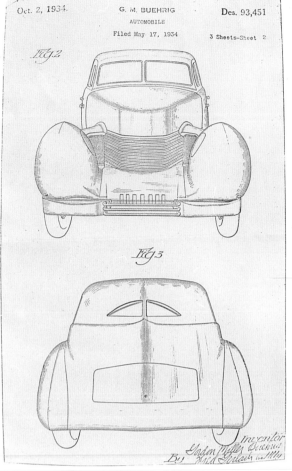

△ 1936 AUBURN BOAT-TAIL SPEEDSTER
This model was designed by Buehrig in a brief interval in his work on the new Cord 810.
▷ Drawings in support of Gordon Buehrig's patent application of May 1934 for what became the Cord 810, showing the headlights in the side of the fenders. This car was built on a rear-drive Auburn chassis.
PICTURES: AUBURN-CORD-DUESENBERG MUSEUM

which came up with the Pontiac Silver Streak. Buehrig's design was very striking, with a pointed prow to the hood and a radiator grille which wrapped around it and extended back a foot or more to large, egg-crate type air intakes on each side. Though the design was greatly modified later, it was the basic shape of the Cord 810. A panel of judges chaired by Earl voted it last in the contest, but another judging, by the studio men alone, voted it first. One can see why Earl was unimpressed; he was interested in a mass market, and for that even the Cord was too way out; the original design was even more so.

A BEAUTIFUL THING THAT JUST GREW UP ON THE HIGHWAY – THE CORD 810

Before the design emerged in its final shape, it went through several changes. After six months in Art & Colour, Buehrig returned to Duesenberg, where he was asked to design a small car which would make the famous name available to middle-income purchasers. He came up with a four-door six-window fastback sedan whose front end was derived from his GM proposal, though the egg-crate intakes were much reduced in size, and in front of

them, opening from the inside of the fenders, were the headlights, which the original proposal seems to have lacked altogether. One reason for Earl's disapproval, perhaps – "Where are the goddam lamps?" A full-size prototype was built on a straight-eight Auburn chassis, and Buehrig filed a patent for the design on May 17, 1934, which was approved on October 2. In the application it was described as "an ornamental design for an automobile."

Before he had even filed the patent, Buehrig was transferred from the baby Duesenberg to a more urgent project, that of redesigning the 1934 Auburn, which had been badly received. His outstanding legacy was the 851 speedster, which put the pointed tail used on the big V12 Auburns of 1932-34 onto the more modestly priced straight-eight 851. It and the restyled sedans and phaetons

lasted for two seasons; then disappeared along with the rest of the Auburn-Cord-Duesenberg empire.

When he returned to the Duesenberg project in the summer of 1934, Buehrig found that two not-unimportant changes had been made – it was to have front drive and it was no longer a Duesenberg but a Cord. As the first Cord, the L-29, had front drive, Errett Lobban Cord thought it appropriate that the new car should follow suit. Perhaps also he was itching to have his name on a car again. Buehrig went to work on the new car, changing the six-window sedan to a four-window layout, and extending the grille right around the hood to the scuttle. Although the Cord design was pretty close to the baby Duesenberg, Buehrig said that they did not refer to the latter when working on the Cord. In an interview with C. Edson Armi, he disclaimed

any close influence between the two. "We didn't pay any attention to that [Duesenberg] when we did this one [Cord]." The Duesenberg was down in the warehouse when they were styling the Cord, so any reference would have been just in the designer's head.

The front drive involved changes, which Buehrig thought for the better "... the front end of the small Duesenberg is rather dull. There is nothing going on. On the Cord we had the transmission up front, and the radiator sat right over the front axle, right above the differential." To get a linkage from the Bendix Selectric hand-vacuum gearshift forward to the transmission was a problem,

◁ The 1935 prototype Cord 810 was very close to the production version, though the headlights are still mounted in the sides of the fenders rather than the front.
▽ The first Cord 810s come off the production line at Auburn's second factory in Connersville, Indiana, in February 1936.
▽ Introduction of the Cord 810. Left to right: Ray Faulkner, President of the Auburn Automobile Company; Curt Hilkey, Production Manager; and Arthur Landis, Vice-President.

PHOTOS: AUBURN-CORD-DUESENBERG MUSEUM

▷ The Cord 810 at the National Automobile Show at the Grand Central Palace, New York City, in November 1935. For show purposes, only one headlight is open. The lights were opened manually, though at least one owner modified his to use electric power.

PHOTO: AUBURN-CORD-DUESENBERG MUSEUM

but it was solved by putting the wires under a raised portion of the apron. This raised section, essential from the engineers' point of view, was also an aesthetic improvement. "It added some interest in this area, which was pretty blah," Buehrig said.

The Duesenberg's inside mounted headlights were also seen on the original Cord proposal, but when engineering decided to make the fenders in a different way, there was room for the lights in front, though they were still retractable.

The Cord nearly didn't happen because of financial problems in the Cord empire. When Buehrig returned from his honeymoon at the beginning of 1935, he was told the project had been canceled. Then, sometime between January and July, more finance became available, thanks to a big contract for kitchen cabinets, most of which went to Montgomery Ward. The Cord project was reactivated, but with very little time available, as a running car had to be ready for the New York Auto Show opening on November 2. They had three months and 26 days to build and test a prototype, complete tooling and have production cars ready for the show. The Automobile Manufacturers' Association did not look kindly on prototypes and insisted that at least 100 examples should be made of any car exhibited. Since no production line could be set up in time, the 100 had to be made by hand. Even so, the cars which made it to the show lacked transmissions, as the four-speed boxes with vacuum control just could not be made in time.

Shortage of time and money led to improvisations which, in some cases, contributed to the car's appearance. The doors were paired, the left front and right rear using the same stampings, as did the right front and left rear. Rear doors required only an additional trim die. The result was a well-balanced appearance from the side view. Other cost-cutting measures included using obsolete Sheller

steering wheels, to which Buehrig added a horn ring with a special hub cover to give it an individual look.

The situation with bumpers was similar; a salesman from Buckeye Bumpers of Springfield, Ohio, came in to the factory one day, and his model was better than the one Buehrig's men had come up with, so it was adopted, with no tooling costs involved. They used existing door handles by Doelher-Jarvis, with big, round Tenite knobs added. On the first prototype the wheel covers were plain round disks. When overheating of the brake drums was diagnosed, George Ritts, head of the experimental garage, simply punched ten holes in the disk, solving the heating problem and giving the Cord one of its distinctive points.

The paradox of this Cord is well set out by Dan R. Post, author of the first history of the car: "It was built primarily as a functional transportation vehicle of superior performance. Whenever art conflicted with utility, utility won." Yet it turned out to be one

of the most beautiful cars ever to grace American roads. Gordon Buehrig's favorite tribute runs as follows... A new owner was followed by a friend who was seeing the car for the first time. Later, he told the owner, "It didn't look like an automobile. Somehow it looked like a beautiful thing that had been born and just grew up on the highway."

Sadly, the Cord 810 did not become such a success in the showrooms, despite glowing tributes from visitors to the 1935 Show, and from foreign dealers ("Congratulations – Cord hottest thing since Rome burned sold 11 cars please cable price," London). As with the Chrysler Airflow, the four-month delay between show launch and the delivery of the first cars was fatal. Many orders were canceled by impatient customers, and those who bought were unhappy with glitches such as transmissions shifting back to neutral without warning.

Also, the Cords were expensive; from $1,995 for a Westchester sedan to $2,195 for a two-door

One of four models, two of which were sedans, the Westchester was $100 cheaper than the Beverly, at $1,995. The difference was limited to upholstery patterns; plain, simple broadcloth for the Westchester, pleated or ribbed pattern on the Beverly. This was also available with folding or fixed center armrests front and rear.

PHOTO: NATIONAL CAR MUSEUM, BEAULIEU

phaeton, prices well above any Buick and most Chryslers, and $300 more than the lowest-priced Cadillac. Granted, to the connoisseur they were better-looking than any of these, but there weren't too many connoisseurs around. The supercharged 812 models were added to the line for 1937, but they were even pricier, $2,960 to $3,060. Production ended in August 1937 after just under 3,000 had been made. U.S. sales totalled 2,320, with the balance being exports for which there aren't any statistics. The state-by-state breakdown is interesting, from a high of 353 in California down to three in Nevada, two in North Dakota and one in Arkansas. Even these beat Vermont, whose cautious citizens bought not a single Cord 810.

The Cord's fame has never died; in 1951 the New York Museum of Modern Art chose it as one of the ten finest examples of industrial styling of all

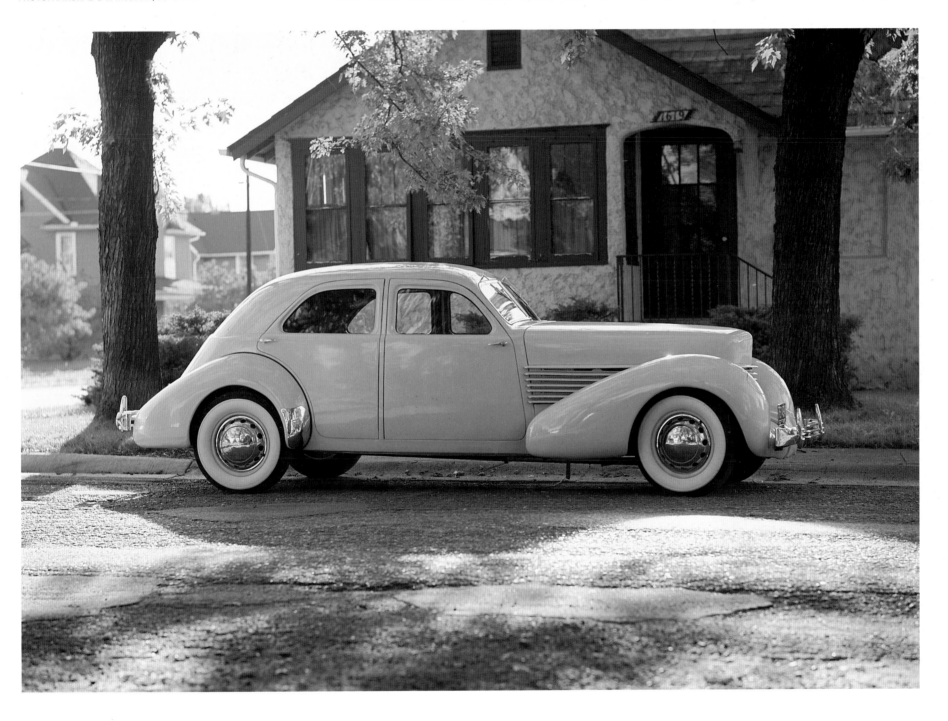

△ ▷ 1937 CORD 812 BEVERLY SEDAN
812 was the designation for all 1937 model Cords which had integral trunks instead of the fastback of the 810s. The 812 range included Custom models on a longer wheelbase, identified by eight hood louvers rather than seven. The Custom line included a Beverly sedan and a Berline with a chauffeur's division.
OWNER: NILA MUZZILA

time, and several replicas were offered between 1964 and 1970. Cord bodies were used by Graham and Hupmobile for their Hollywood and Skylark models of 1939-41, though these had different grilles and external headlights, which made for a less harmonious appearance. They also had six-cylinder engines and rear-wheel drive, and sold in a lower price range than the Cord.

LIFE AFTER CORD

After leaving Cord in 1936, Gordon Buehrig worked for the Budd Corporation for about three years. At the time Budd was making doors for Packard and truck bodies for Ford and Dodge, but no passenger car bodies. Buehrig produced several designs for them, including the Wowser, a small economy sedan

ART OF THE AMERICAN AUTOMOBILE

with the body stamped in two halves and a seam running down the middle of the roof. Budd took up neither this nor any of his other suggestions, so he resigned. During the war he worked for Consolidated Aircraft at San Diego and for Goodyear Tires, afterward joining Raymond Loewy's studio, which was responsible for the early work on the '47 Studebaker. In 1948, with ten friends, he formed The American Sports Car Company to build a radical two-passenger coupe which they called the Tasco. Each invested $5,000, but the total of $50,000 was a slender sum to launch a new car on. They used a modified Mercury frame and a Mercury V8 engine boosted with dual carburetors and cast aluminum Edelbrock cylinder heads. Body design was, of course, down to Buehrig, and he came up with a striking coupe with an airplane-like cockpit and all four wheels enclosed in separate fenders, the front ones turning with the wheels. Made for Buehrig by Derham, the body was aluminum and the fenders fiberglass, a material almost unknown in auto construction in 1948. The car handled well, though Buehrig wished he had waited a year to get the 1949 Ford chassis with independent suspension; as he said, "Hindsight is easy." Like so many similar projects, the Tasco failed through lack of money, and Buehrig's attempts to interest aircraft firms like Beech, Consolidated, Ercoupe and Lockheed came to nothing. The prototype went back to Derham, which sold it, though it was returned to the company for restoration work in 1970.

In 1949 Buehrig joined Ford, taking charge of one styling studio and soon concentrating on station wagons. His best-known work was the 1952 Ranch Wagon, a two-door design which broke away from the wooden bodies Ford was making and the imitation wood models favored by Chevrolet. In fact, Plymouth made the first all-steel wagon with no paneling on it in 1949, but the Ranch Wagon was much more stylish, with a single window running from the B-pillar to the rear. While Buehrig was at Ford, he also tried to sell his idea of transparent roof panels, which he had used on the Tasco. The Thunderbird seemed an ideal subject for this, and Ford Division president Robert McNamara showed initial interest, but then dropped the idea. It eventually saw production as a detachable panel on the 1968 Corvette, though Buehrig had nothing to do with this.

After retirement from Ford in 1965, Buehrig taught at Los Angeles' Art Center College of Design. In his later years he was much in demand as a speaker on the subject of car design.

△ AMOS NORTHUP (1889-1937)
With the Reo Royale to his credit, Northup went on to
style the mold-breaking 1932 Graham Blue Streak
which, with its fender skirts and other innovations,
could have passed for a 1935 car in an age when
design was changing very rapidly. Graham's advertising
proclaimed it "the most imitated car on the road."
Northup is pictured here pointing to the mural of the
Cars of the Future at the Murray Corporation in 1934.

Amos Northup, Unsung Hero of Design

"A genial, stocky, lively man who's never gotten anything near full credit for all he really did."

Special Interest Autos

ONE OF THE definitive steps toward modern design came in 1932 when the Graham Blue Streak adopted fender skirts. This simple step, so obvious to later generations, was one of the first moves toward the integrated, streamlined shape and was widely copied the following year. Another step, also seen on the Graham, was to give the radiator grille a backward slope. Both were the work of Amos Northup, yet his name is virtually unknown compared with those of Earl, Mitchell, Gregorie and Hershey.

Amos E. Northup was born in Bellevue, Ohio, in 1889. His first important design commission, for Wills Sainte Claire, was a relatively small high-quality car built by Henry Ford's former production manager and chief engineer, Childe Harold Wills. It lasted only from 1921 to 1927, and Northup left in 1924 to join the Murray Corporation of America.

Formed in Detroit in 1912, Murray was a major supplier of bodies to medium-sized car makers who did not have large body facilities themselves. These included Jewett, Hupmobile, Marmon, Reo and Willys-Knight, while, from 1930 Murray became increasingly involved with Ford, a connection which lasted until 1950. The company had a design studio as early as 1925, in which Northup looked after the production bodies and Ray Dietrich, lured away from LeBaron, designed the custom styles.

The first body in which Northup had a definite influence was the 1928 Hupmobile Century Eight. Hupp had introduced its first eight in 1925, but like Pontiac in 1933 and Chrysler in the early '50s, it lacked a suitable body to adorn their new machinery. Such a body arrived with the 1928 models. The fresh styling began with a new radiator, higher than before and with a colorful new emblem consisting of an H with a dagger behind it, pointing down at a crenellated castle. This emblem

was replicated in the center of the bumper, but only for 1928. The headlights were larger and bullet shaped, while the fenders were longer and slenderer. The closed cars had stylish visors above the windshield. A double-dropped frame allowed for lower bodies, which could be purchased with two-tone color schemes. Overnight Hupmobile's image changed from a fairly plain-Jane make to a style leader. This was continued in several subsequent models, though not under Northup's direction.

▽ ▷ 1936 HUPMOBILE 618G SEDAN
Hupp brought out a brand new line for 1934, styled by Raymond Loewy, aided by Amos Northup. For 1936 a waterfall grille was introduced. Six- and eight-cylinder engines were offered in '36; this 618G has a 101hp six, while the 621 had a 120hp straight eight.
PHOTO: NATIONAL MOTOR MUSEUM, BEAULIEU

ART OF THE AMERICAN AUTOMOBILE

ART OF THE AMERICAN AUTOMOBILE

THE REO ROYALE

The next important design from Northup's pen, while he was still at Murray, was the 1931 Reo Royale Eight. Reo, always a middle-class car, moved up into the luxury market with the 125hp straight-eight Royale, though at $2,845 it was quite a bargain. While the lesser Reos retained conventional styling, the Royale saw several new concepts combined to make a truly innovative car, though perhaps not many people recognized it at the time. Northup worked mainly at night on the Royale, for he claimed that inspiration glowed best by candlelight.

The Royale had a vertical radiator but the grille was V-shaped with a thin chrome surrounding band. The fenders were droopily curved and extended farther over the front wheels than on previous cars. This had the practical effect of trapping less air beneath the fenders. Northup's assistant Julio Andrade, whom he had brought with him from Wills Sainte Claire, and who would go on to become an important stylist under Harley Earl, said that aircraft experts had pointed out that conventional fenders would produce lift at high speeds. Certainly the British owner of another Royale, the fabulous Bugatti, reported that at speeds in excess of 80mph, the front wheels actually left the ground, and on one occasion the fender was torn right off by wind pressure.

Northup was granted two patents for the Royale's front end, one for the ensemble, fenders, grille shell and hood, and one for the grille shell alone, but there was a lot more to the Royale than that. The windshield was slightly slanted, and above it there was a curve up to the roof, in place of the peak which had seemed modern on the Hupmobile only three years before. At the rear a double curvature panel swept down to conceal the fuel tank. The widest point of the body was at the front seat, which was half-an-inch wider than the rear, in contrast to most contemporaries, and which could seat three comfortably.

The Royale was well received. *Automobile Industries* described its styling as "the most radical departure in lines that has been made for some time," while the *SAE Journal* of January 1, 1931, called it the outstanding design of the year. It won first prizes in Concours d'Elegance in Rome and Zagreb, Yugoslavia, of all places. Unfortunately, its appearance coincided with the second worst year of the Depression (1932 was the absolute bottom in terms of car sales). Sales from September 1930 to August 1931 were 2,736 cars, out of a total for Reo of 6,762. Breakdowns for individual models are not available after that, but as Reo's total dropped to 3,870 in 1932 and 3,623 in 1933, the last year for the big Royale Eight, total Royale sales are unlikely to have been more than 5,000.

THE GRAHAM BLUE STREAK

Northup's greatest contribution to the progress of styling was the Graham Blue Streak. This was also a Murray product, though there have been suggestions that Graham made its own bodies, certainly from 1933 onward. Probably the bodies were finished, assembled, painted and trimmed in the Graham shops at Wayne, Michigan, and Evansville, Indiana, but the stampings came from Murray. It is likely that Murray pressed ahead with a new design for Graham with the intention of selling it, just as they had done with the Reo Royale.

Graham was something of a phenomenon in the American auto industry. The three Graham brothers made trucks for Dodge in the '20s, bought the Paige car company in 1927, and the following year launched a four-car line which sold 73,195 cars in the first season, a record for a new make. The cars were not particularly exciting to look at; and by 1931 the Depression had brought sales down to 20,428.

◁ 1931 REO ROYALE COUPE
Advanced features of Amos Northup's second important design included the V-shaped grille and the curved front to the roof. The Royale had a 125hp, 354-cubic-inch straight-eight engine and a 135-inch wheelbase.
PHOTO: BUD JUNEAU/IMAGE PORT

▽ 1931 GRAHAM 822 CONVERTIBLE SEDAN
An example of Graham styling on the eve of the mold-breaking 1932 Blue Streak.

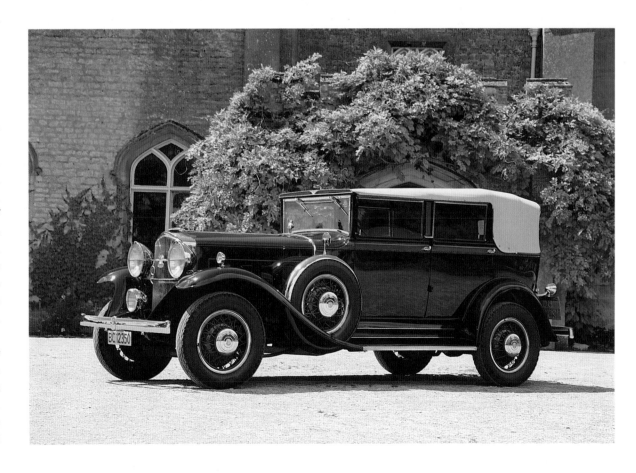

▷ 1931 GRAHAM 822 CONVERTIBLE SEDAN
Before Northup got his hands on the Graham, it was a
classic 1920s-looking car, with vertical radiator and
windshield, and clam-shell fenders. All this changed
with the advent of the Blue Streak (opposite) in 1932.

▷ 1934 GRAHAM BLUE STREAK
This design was a mold-breaker with its skirted front
and rear fenders, sloping grille and windshield. This
1934 model is hardly changed from the first in 1932.
PHOTO: CHAN BUSH/IMAGE PORT

The Blue Streak Eight, launched for the 1932 season, was a complete break, and set several trends for the industry.

Some of the Blue Streak's features, including the curved front fenders, which now reached almost down to the bumper, and the curved top, had already been tried by Northup on the Reo. The windshield also sloped a little, reflecting the backward slope of the radiator grille. Below the grille, between it and the bumper, was a splashpan which concealed the frame cross-members and shock-absorber mounts visible in other cars. The feature for which the 1932 Graham is best remembered, though, is the fender skirt, creating a round space for the front wheel. The upper line of the fender was the same as before, but the lower was curved around the front wheel, the panel behind it being the skirt. This concealed the chassis with its inevitable accumulations of dirt, but also made the fender a more important statement in the car's appearance, leading to growing height and eventual integration into the hood and doors. The Graham had small skirts over the rear wheels as well.

For anyone accustomed to cars of the later 1930s, it is hard to understand the importance of the 1932 Graham. Suffice it to say that it could easily have passed for a 1935 car, in an age when design was changing very rapidly. In 1933 almost all American car makers adopted fender skirts and sloping grilles, with the exception of Chrysler, which waited until 1934. While it cannot be proved that the Graham influenced them all or that no other designer was thinking about fender skirts in 1931-32, it was Graham who put them into production.

As we might expect, the Blue Streak was received with delight by the automotive press. "Should the new Graham model be preeminently successful this year, we believe that the speed with which rear-engined and fully streamlined cars come onto the market will be accelerated by many months." (*Automotive Industries*, February 13, 1932)

Despite its innovations, the Blue Streak did not sell very well; the Depression forced Graham sales down from over 20,000 in 1931 to 12,858 in 1932. The design was barely changed for 1933, when advertising rightly proclaimed it "the most-imitated car on the road."

OTHER NORTHUP DESIGNS

At least three other cars have been credited to Amos Northup, though for two of them the claims are uncertain. In 1929 Willys commissioned a few roadsters finished in plaid colors for show purposes.

These were definitely Northup's work, but some sources say that he did another car for Willys, the budget-priced, four-cylinder Model 77 of 1933. It was by no means a thing of beauty, though one innovation was its headlights, which were partially faired into the fenders, anticipating 1937 Fords and 1938 Studebakers.

In 1938 the Graham company tried to boost its flagging fortunes with a striking new body style christened Spirit of Motion. Ruder critics dubbed it the Sharknose, by which name it has been known ever since. Instead of a rearward sloping grille, the 1938 Grahams leaned forward, like photos of early racing cars. It also had squared headlights fully faired into the fenders, and full skirts over the rear wheels. Amos Northup did most of the work on this Graham, aided by the company's own William Nealey. He never saw it in production, for in February 1937 he slipped on an icy sidewalk, cracked his skull and died of his injuries shortly afterwards.

△ HOWARD DARRIN (1897-1982)
On his return from Paris, where he had worked with Tom
Hibbard, Darrin built custom bodies on Packards for glamorous
clients which culminated in the Darrin Victoria in 1939.
After the war, still freelance, he made custom bodies for
Cadillacs and Lincoln Continentals, and produced several
designs for Kaiser, including the Kaiser-Darrin.

CHAPTER FOURTEEN

HOWARD DARRIN

"If I had continued with General Motors, I am afraid I would
have at best become an assistant to the assistant to the
vice-president of design, truly a fate worse than death."

Howard Darrin

U NLIKE MOST OF the designers discussed so far, Howard "Dutch" Darrin had a good career as a stylist and bodybuilder in Europe, working in Paris in partnership with Tom Hibbard (see Chapter One). Born in 1897, he was an electrical engineer with Westinghouse in 1916 when he was invited by John Willys to design an electric gearshift for his cars. America's entry into World War I the following year put an end to the project and, perhaps more crucially, took the young Darrin to France with the U.S. Army. There he decided he might prefer working with cars to being an electrical engineer, and he developed a love for France that led him to settle there after the war.

In his partnership with Tom Hibbard, he styled a number of bodies which were built initially by Van den Plas, and later in their own Paris workshop. He also had some involvement with the major U.S. manufacturers on his many visits back home. In 1926 he suggested to Edsel Ford an updated Model T, which was rejected, and a year later he was invited by Dodge to modernize its cars, including developing a sloping windshield that was rejected as being too expensive (by 30 cents per shield). In 1929 he was given a one-year contract with General Motors to build special bodies on Cadillac (and one Chevrolet) chassis, which went to the top brass, including the Fisher brothers. However, a misunderstanding on the styling of the Buick, which led Harley Earl to think that Darrin had coined the phrase "pregnant Buick" led to his hasty departure. In retrospect, Darrin thought all these unsuccessful brushes with big manufacturers to have been a blessing. "If I had continued with General Motors, I am afraid I would have at best become an assistant to the assistant to the vice-president of design, truly a fate worse than death." As it was, he became an independent stylist, doing the three things he liked best in the world, building cars, flying airplanes and playing polo.

After his partnership with Hibbard ended in 1931 when Hibbard returned to the U.S. to join Ford, Darrin formed a new partnership with a French banker named Fernandez. Though Fernandez was not active in design, he provided the finance for a successful business – as Darrin put it,

"We had the most modern factory in France and the most important showroom on the Champs Elysées." Some of the most beautiful bodies of a beautiful era were built by Fernandez et Darrin, including several on Hispano-Suiza and Packard chassis, and a coupe de ville on a Duesenberg J for Greta Garbo.

In 1937 Darrin returned to America, and on the strength of a friendship with Darryl Zanuck went to Hollywood and set up a small shop in an old bottling plant on Sunset Strip, where he executed one-off designs for celebrities. Lacking the money for a plate-glass window, he displayed the cars in the open and built them behind a plywood partition ten feet back from the "showroom." The open location led more people to stop and stare than if the cars had been inside a showroom. His first effort was a two-passenger Ford for Percy Morgan, followed by a Packard 120 two-passenger convertible with lowered radiator and cutaway doors for Dick Powell.

This was not his first link with Packard, for Hibbard & Darrin had built several bodies on

△ ▷ 1934 PACKARD ROADSTER
This is a good example of the rather staid styling typical of Packard in the 1930s; it is hardly surprising that a company accustomed to cars like this would react warily to such a radical design as Darrin's 1939 Convertible Victoria. The vertical radiator gave way to one with a slight slope from 1935 onward, but the general tone was conservative, appealing to Old Money rather than the ostentatious buyer.
OWNER: DOOR PRARIE MUSEUM

Packards in the '20s, but it led to an important connection with the Detroit firm. With his partners Rudy Stoessel and Paul Erdos, Darrin built a striking town car on a 1930 Rolls-Royce Phantom II for the socialite Countess Dorothy di Frasso. Born Dorothy Taylor in Watertown, NY, the countess was an inveterate party-giver and great rival of movie star Constance Bennett. Her wish to outdo Bennett's Rolls led her to commission Darrin to build what he called his best-constructed car and his proudest achievement. Paneled in aluminum, it had very low lines for a Rolls, with a sharply slanted windshield and running boards with a gap between front and rear doors.

After the Dick Powell two-passenger Packard, Darrin built a four-passenger version, also with cutaway doors, for Packard's annual dealer show in Detroit. The car was damaged in an accident on the way to the show, but Darrin's colleague Arthur Fitzparick parked it in the proving grounds and attracted an enormous amount of attention from the dealers. One even threatened to cancel his Packard franchise unless the company built the car.

Packard was reluctant to offer a limited-production sporty car for several reasons. It would be obviously expensive, and in 1938 the company was concentrating more on medium-priced cars like the 120 than on the labor-intensive Big Eights and Twelves. Half the workforce was engaged on the Senior Packards, which represented only 8 percent of the output. Another reason was that sporty Hollywood-type cars had never been part of Packard's image, and third, they had reservations about a coach-built body. The wood-framed, metal-covered bodies that Hibbard & Darrin had built for Packard tended to warp and rattle after a few years, and they were the only experience the company had of Darrin's work. Packard board chairman Alvan Macauley hesitated, "Well, Darrin, I don't know if we want to take a chance on this – we have to put our name on it and stand behind it, you know." Darrin's response was to climb on the hood and jump up and down. Macauley was horrified, but Darrin demonstrated that the aluminum cowl could stand up to such abuse, having no wooden frame underneath.

This apparently convinced Macauley, who was aware of the tremendous dealer enthusiasm, so he agreed that the car could go in the 1939 catalog under the name Packard-Darrin Victoria. Cautiously, his first order was for only five cars.

Output was very limited anyway, so dealers were told they could keep any Darrin on the showroom floor for at least 30 days, even if it had been sold on the first day. This pleased the dealers, who saw its virtue as a crowd puller. Even if few bought a Darrin, visitor numbers increased by up to 300 percent when one was on display.

The Darrin Victoria was a beautiful car, using the standard Packard grille, lights and bumpers, with a lowered and lengthened hood. The fenders were Darrin's design, the windshield was raked at a greater angle than the regular Packard and there were no running boards. The doors were not cut away to allow elbow room as on some British sports cars, but sloped gently from front to rear, with the line then sweeping slightly up below the top. All

Darrin Victorias were built on the 127-inch wheelbase, but could be had in the 120 line, with a 282-cubic-inch engine or in the Custom Super Eight 180 line with 356-cubic-inch engine, both in-line L-head eights. Prices in 1940 were $3,819 for the 120 and $4,593 for the 180. Darrin also made a few four-door versions, which were called convertible sedans, on a 138-inch wheelbase and priced at a whopping $6,332. Some problems with flexing of the chassis were encountered; on early cars the doors wouldn't open and close when passengers were sitting in them. It was discovered that Darrin had been supplied with closed-car chassis, which relied on the rigidity of a steel body to keep them taut. Chassis for convertibles were more rigid and were supplied from then on.

As the small plant on Sunset Strip could not cope with demand, Darrin had to look for new facilities. He found them at the former Auburn-Cord plant at Connersville, Indiana. This arrangement lasted through 1940, then Auburn closed its automotive division, and Darrin found a new builder at the Cincinnati, Ohio, plant of Sayers & Scovill. They were known as ambulance and hearse builders, and the first Darrin Victoria off the line was followed by a hearse. "Such strange partners; it was quite a sight," said Darrin.

The Darrin Victoria was continued in the 1941 catalog, along with other custom offerings such as the all-weather cabriolet by Rollston and various town cars and limousines by LeBaron. Total production was five in 1939, about 50 of

ART OF THE AMERICAN AUTOMOBILE

◁ △ 1940 PACKARD DARRIN CONVERTIBLE VICTORIA
These cars were completed in the former Auburn-Cord factory at Connersville, Indiana. Packard supplied chassis intended for convertible bodies, as these gave the rigidity lacking in a "sedan chassis."

△ This radiator ornament was $10 extra. Packard's traditional ornament was a cormorant.

OWNER: DUKE DAVENPORT

Macauley would be on the West Coast in ten days' time, and wanted to see a design for a new Packard body. The fee would be $1,000 a day if he could meet the deadline. Darrin managed to come up with a quarter-scale clay. It is difficult to say at this late date how much of the original clay was translated into the production Clipper. Certainly some points, like the line straight through from front to rear fender and the absence of running boards, were modified during the design's passage through the Packard styling studio. The straight-through fender was considered too radical, so it tapered out halfway through the front door while there were running boards, but was concealed under a bulge line at the bottom of the doors. Darrin considered this particularly unsuccessful. Nevertheless the Clipper was a smooth, modern-looking design, with headlights in the fenders and two wide horizontal grilles flanking the traditional Packard vertical shape, though narrower than on any previous car. A memo from chief engineer Clyde Paton to president George Christopher in 1944 stressed, "The present Packard radiator grille profile has been demonstrated to be an acceptable mark of identity. Great caution must be exercised in changing this detail."

There are those who challenge Darrin's major role in the Clipper. According to Richard Langworth, writing in *Special Interest Autos* in 1980, a member of the in-house team said, "We all submitted designs, including Darrin, (George) Walker, (Bill) Flajole, and Packard. Management eventually selected about 90 percent of the Gubitz car. I've heard all the other claims, but it was Gubitz's car almost entirely." (Werner Gubitz was Packard's head of styling at the time.)

The Clippers were announced in April 1941 as mid-season models, though some regard them as 1942 models. Initially offered in one model, with the 282-cubic-inch engine on 127-inch wheelbase, by 1942 the style had spread down to the six-cylinder 110 and up to the big eights, the 160 and 180. The only Packards with traditional styling were the long-wheelbase sedans and limousines, and the convertibles. There was never a cataloged convertible Clipper, though Darrin made a few specials, including one for his friend Errol Flynn. With some modifications, the style was continued on all Packards from 1946 to 1948.

the 1940 models, 35 of the 1941s, and 15 of the 1942s.

By 1941 Darrin had become involved in a much bigger job for Packard, styling the new low-to-medium-price Clipper line. In 1940 Packard styling was more traditional than that of any other American make. The hood was still fronted by a vertical grille, the headlights were mounted externally beside the hood, fenders were relatively separate from the hood, and all models had generous running boards. This might have been acceptable had they been competing only in the rarified market of the luxury car, but since the launch of the eight-cylinder 120, followed by the even lower-priced six-cylinder 110, they were aiming for the same markets as the Mercury and low-to-mid-price Buicks. Here styling was a vital selling point. "Packard was so afraid of GM they couldn't see straight," said Darrin.

Early in 1940 Darrin was contacted by Packard president Max Gilman, who told him that Alvan

THE POST-WAR KAISERS

Immediately after the war, Darrin built some customized Cadillacs and Lincoln Continentals with cutaway doors and fenders following through from front to rear, which he sold for about $8,600 each. (A regular Cadillac convertible cost $2,556 when they became available in 1946.) He was then invited to New York by Charlie Schwartz, a partner in Dillon, Read, to meet the Lehmann brothers, bankers who also owned a large chain of stores. The idea was that Darrin would design and build a low-

priced car which could be sold through the stores, rather as Sears Roebuck did with the Allstate a few years later. The original plan was for a three-wheeler, but Darrin talked them out of that idea, and the prototype that Darrin built was a four-wheeled convertible with straight-through fender lines and a remarkable list of hydraulic power assists. Not only was the top power-operated, so were the window lifts, jacking and doors. According to Richard Langworth, no other car had power-operated doors until the Mercedes-Benz 600 limousine of 1964. The body was made entirely of

△ ▷ 1953 KAISER DRAGON SEDAN
Launched in March 1950 as a 1951 model, the new Kaiser sedan was one of Howard Darrin's more imaginative designs for the company at Willow Run, Michigan, and made up for the dullness of the 1947-50 models, with which he was not happy. Two-door models were available as well as four-doors. The Dragon was a special-trim version made only in 1953. Not so special was the engine, a flathead six by Continental, when the Kaiser's rivals were getting V8s.
OWNER: STAN BLOCK

fiberglass, with only four outer panels, hood with front fenders, doors and deck with rear fenders.

During his preliminary discussions with the Lehmanns, Darrin was introduced by Schwartz to Joseph Frazer, who had acquired Graham-Paige with a view to producing a post-war car. He would shortly go into partnership with Henry Kaiser, though the car design was Frazer's and it was he who asked Darrin to design it. The relationship between the Darrin convertible and the Kaiser-Frazer sedans is close and somewhat complex to sort out. Darrin built a quarter-scale model of his convertible in 1945, then became involved in the KF project, and finished off the convertible after he had completed his work for Frazer. The grilles are very similar, as are the straight-through fenders, though the convertible does not have such a slab-sided look, being shorter and having only two doors. Its hood was six inches lower than the Frazer, while the fiberglass body gave a curb weight of 2,400 pounds (the Frazer sedan weighed 3,340 pounds). As they used the same engine, the 100bhp Continental six, the convertible had obviously peppier performance. Alas, production problems associated with the fiberglass body prevented its manufacture, and only the single prototype was made. It was destroyed in a flash flood at Darrin's home a few years later.

Although he stipulated that any design he did for Frazer could not be changed by engineers, Darrin's design was considerably altered between drawing board and production. In particular, the rear deck was raised, Darrin said, because they wanted a rear engine; the curved sides were flattened, doubtless in the interest of cost; and the extended rear fender line was removed. Darrin was so displeased with the result that he declined to have his name anywhere on the car. With hindsight the Kaiser-Frazer design is not unpleasing, but could be described as a copybook exercise in full-length fender design, with no imaginative flair about it. However, it was the first all-enveloping American car, debuting several months before the more imaginative Studebaker.

Darrin was not so disillusioned with the Kaiser-Frazer organization that he refused a commission to design their next cars, and these showed much more flair. Darrin began work in the fall of 1948, for a 1951 launch. The work was not easy, as Darrin recalled in an interview with *Automobile Quarterly* in 1968. Joe Frazer had told him that Kaiser was working on some new designs which would not be to Darrin's liking.

"So I flew to Willow Run; they wouldn't let me into the styling department, didn't want to pay my royalties. I pointed out that I had a contract, that I would give $5,000 to the workmen's fund if they'd let me in, and that I would take no longer than ten days to do whatever I was going to do. Finally, someone sneaked me in, and I saw the cars they were considering and decided I'd better get to work. The staff wasn't overly cooperative. They wouldn't give me any workmen at all, just one helper from their staff whom they sent home every night promptly at five o'clock. So I procured some of the clean-up help from the factory, gave them $10 or $15 a night, and we proceeded to put together two tons of clay for my version of the 1951 Kaiser."

His original design called for curved doors extending into the roof, but these did not see production. However, the car was lower than any other American car, and had 700 square inches more glass area than its nearest competitor. The windshield was distinctive, with a dip in the center, nicknamed the "Darrin dip." The styling was complemented by an exciting range of colors both outside and inside, the work of "color engineer" Carlton B. Spencer.

Darrin's last work for Kaiser was a two-passenger sports car which was known as the Kaiser-Darrin 161; the figure was for the displacement of the six-cylinder F-head engine. This was designed in his Hollywood workshop and, like the 1946 convertible, used fiberglass for the body. It was a beautiful design, with the fender line sloping down through the door, to meet a kick-up over the rear wheel arch. This feature was also seen in the prototype roadster Darrin did for Crosley, and, like the windshield on the '51 Kaiser, was also known as the "Darrin dip." The most controversial aspect of the design was the small, curved top and pointed bottom grille. "It looked like it wanted to give you a kiss," said Kaiser stylist Bob Robillard (but there was always a rivalry between the in-house stylists in Michigan and the flamboyant freelancer from California).

A point that upset Darrin deeply was the raising of the headlights. Those on the early prototypes (there were 62 protos in all) were found to be too low for state lighting laws, so the Kaiser stylists raised them by lifting the line of the front fenders which, Darrin said, bent the middle section and gave the car an "uphill" look. His solution would have been to use larger wheels and tires. These

came from the Henry J compact sedan, as did the engine and chassis, and Darrin contended that a sports car needed more rubber on the road anyway.

The Kaiser-Darrin's doors opened by sliding into the front fenders, but they did not slide all the way, making entry and exit less than easy. An advanced feature was the fitting of seat belts; this was only the third example of belts in an American car. By 1954, when the Kaiser-Darrin finally went into production, they were alone. Of the previous belt providers, Muntz was out of production, while Nash had dropped them, as they gave a negative image, promoting the idea that Nashes weren't safe.

By the time the Kaiser-Darrin appeared in the showrooms, Kaiser had merged with Willys, so the production cars used the Willys six engine, slightly more powerful than the Henry J unit, but also of

▽ ▷ 1953 KAISER DRAGON SEDAN
Among the Dragon's distinguishing features were the "Darrin dip" in the windshield, and a larger area of glass than any other American car. It had gold-plated exterior trim, wire wheels, a padded top usually made of "bambu" vinyl, this material also being used for the dash and parts of the door panels and seats. Among many options were tinted glass, whitewall tires and dual-speaker radio. The owner's name was engraved on a gold medallion on the dash.

ART OF THE AMERICAN AUTOMOBILE

161-cubic-inch displacement. Kaiser sedans were now made at Willys' plant in Toledo, Ohio, but the Kaiser-Darrins were built at Kaiser's special-products factory in Jackson, Michigan, where the last 1951 Frazer Manhattans had been made. The Darrins were well equipped, but they were not great performers with only 90hp, strained to reach 100mph, and were pricey at $3,668. A Corvette cost somewhat less at $3,523, but gave 150hp. Only 435 Kaiser-Darrins were made before Kaiser-Willys withdrew from car production altogether. Darrin bought 100 left-over bodies and chassis, fitted them with 270hp Cadillac V8 engines which made them really potent performers, with a top speed of 140mph. At a price of $4,350, they sold easily.

The Kaiser-Darrin 161 was Dutch's last production design, though he worked on a number of projects and prototypes during the rest of his long life. These included a fiberglass two-seater sports car on the German DKW chassis, of which 30 were made and sold under the name Flintridge DKW Darrin; a sedan for Studebaker dealers in Israel, a proposal for a luxury Packard with doors which slid forward to give access to the rear seats and backward for the front seats, all electrically operated, and a Rolls-Royce Silver Shadow with extended front and rear ends, of which at least one was built. He died in 1982 at the age of 85.

△ ALAN H. LEAMY (1902-1935)
Working for the Auburn Automobile Company, Leamy designed
the 1929 Cord L-29, America's first front-drive production car.
He joined GM's Art & Colour section in 1935 where his designs
were admired by Harley Earl. However, he was sadly cut short
in his prime.

CHAPTER FIFTEEN

AL LEAMY

"The first really new automobile design to appear on the
market for many years."

MoTor on the Cord L-29

△ Watercolor by Al Leamy of a phaeton, dated March 12, 1928. Leamy has painted himself in at the wheel.
ILLUSTRATION: AUBURN-CORD-DUESENBERG MUSEUM

▷ 1929 AUBURN CABIN SPEEDSTER
Borrowed aircraft features included wicker seats, an all-aluminum body, altimeter and compass. Leamy's contribution to the design has not been confirmed; some credit race driver Wade Morton, but Leamy had greater design experience, was at Auburn during the period and he did produce drawings for a four-door car of similar shape (see Page 235). The original was destroyed by fire in 1929; this is a faithful replica.
OWNER: DOOR PRAIRIE MUSEUM

FEW WOULD DENY that one of the most significant American cars of the interwar period was the Cord L-29, with its front-wheel drive and exceptionally low lines. The Auburn speedsters of the early 1930s, though less innovative, were also very striking cars. Yet the man behind the looks of these two marvels has been largely overlooked, doubtless because of his tragically short career.

Alan H. Leamy was born in Arlington, Maryland, in 1902, and grew up in Columbus, Ohio, where his father was district manager of the Welsbach Company, makers of gas mantles. Like many boys, he drew cars incessantly during his school years and was also interested in architecture. His first job, however, was selling real estate in New Jersey, from which he was rescued by his father, who recommended him to a former Welsbach colleague who had become chief engineer of Marmon. Al worked as a stylist at Marmon from March 1927 to April 1928, but was unhappy with the conservatism of the Indianapolis company. Like Harley Earl, he was a great admirer of the European luxury car,

especially the Hispano-Suiza, and he also favored pastel colors. Had he stayed at Marmon a little longer, he would have found a sympathizer in Walter Dorwin Teague, who styled the V16, which had both low lines and attractive color schemes.

Hearing that E. L. Cord was planning a new front-drive car, Leamy wrote asking for a position in the Auburn Automobile Company. He was interviewed by the engineer responsible for the front-drive technology, Cornelius van Ranst, who was sufficiently impressed with Leamy's drawings to recommend him to Errett Cord, who hired him as chief stylist. How many people he had in his "department" is not known, but as Auburn was a very small outfit compared with the Big Three or even a medium-sized company like Hupmobile or Graham, there cannot have been a large styling department. Throughout his time at Auburn, Leamy had only a relatively small office on the second floor of the Auburn administration block.

The most striking Auburn was the two-passenger speedster built for the Pacific Southwest Automobile Show in February 1929. Resembling an airplane on wheels, the Cabin Speedster had wicker seats, and an all-aluminum body coming to a sharp point at the rear. This was familiar on open cars, but almost unknown on closed ones, apart from a few streamliners built in Europe for racing. Leamy has never been directly credited for the Cabin Speedster, though he produced drawings for a four-door closed speedster with a similar tail. However, the Cabin Speedster had cycle-type fenders, which were never seen on anything of Leamy's, either drawings or actual cars. E. L. Cord credited the Cabin Speedster to Wade Morton, a racing driver who set many records for Auburn. But could a driver who had no previous record in styling come up with such an original design?

As Cord was responsible for three makes of car — Auburn and Duesenberg, as well as his new front drive — there was plenty of work for young Leamy. He has never been directly credited with the front

△ Al Leamy at work in his small studio on the second floor of the Auburn administration building, circa 1930.

△ Children of Leamy's friends could not pronounce his name; the closest one got was "Owl Meany." Leamy produced this drawing in 1933 as a gift to the children.
ILLUSTRATION: AUBURN-CORD-DUESENBERG MUSEUM

◁ The designer in his 1931 Auburn 8-98 speedster.
PHOTOS: AUBURN-CORD-DUESENBERG MUSEUM

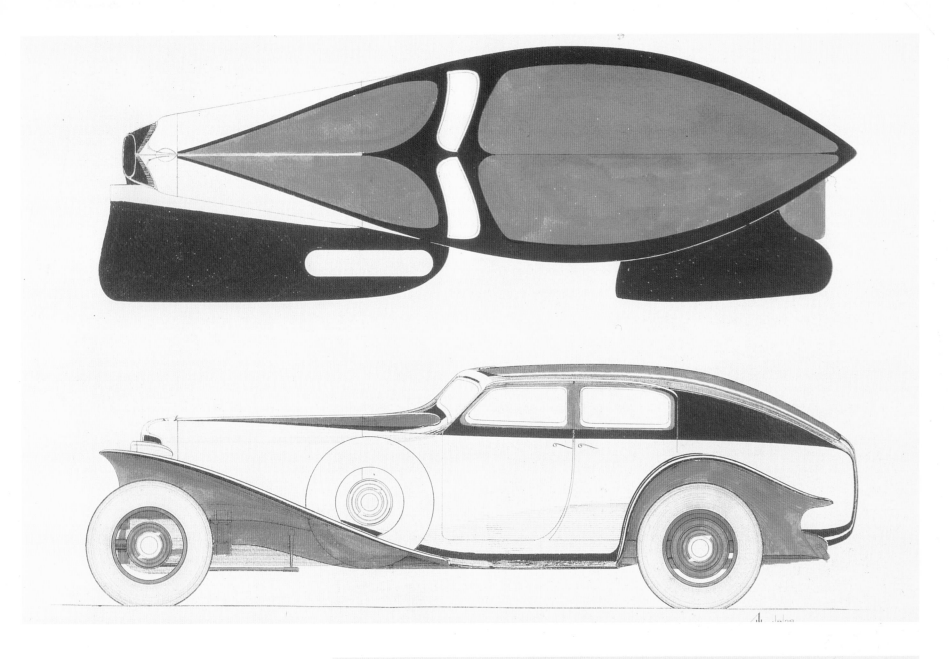

△ Watercolor rendering of a Leamy design for a four-door cabin speedster on the Cord L-29 chassis, dated 1929.

▷ Another design for the Cord L-29, a two-passenger car which Leamy called the Le Mans Speedster. Sadly, Cords never raced at Le Mans, nor did Auburns.

ILLUSTRATIONS: AUBURN-CORD-DUESENBERG MUSEUM

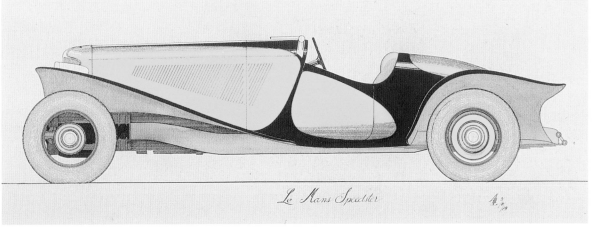

Le Mans Speedster

▷ Two Leamy designs for hood ornaments.

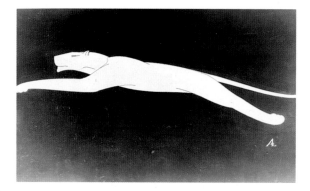
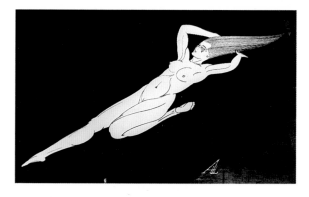

▽ A 1929 Cord L-29 cabriolet at the Chicago dealer's showroom for Auburn, Cord and Duesenberg cars. The banners refer to the Grand Prix and Cup of Honor at Monte Carlo, both awarded to the Cord. The design also won honors at Concours in Berlin and Prague.
PHOTO: AUBURN-CORD-DUESENBERG MUSEUM

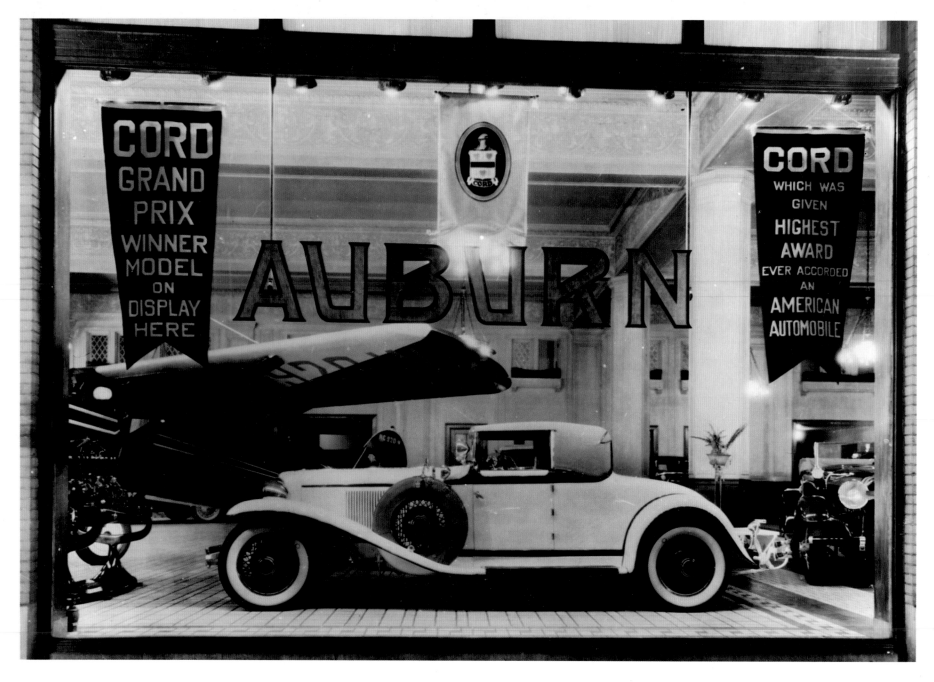

end of the Duesenberg Model J, yet it was clearly under development from the time that he joined Auburn in August 1928, and there was no one else there of comparable talent. The wide shoulder of the radiator, which tapered slightly toward the bottom, was echoed in the Cord, and in some designs Leamy did for Auburn at about the same time. The Duesenberg gave him no chance to exercise his interest in integrated design, marrying hood and bodywork, as bodies were styled by Gordon Buehrig and built by outside companies. Buehrig did, however, admit that the Model J's radiator and fender line were too perfect for him to change in any way.

The Cord, named the L-29 for the year of its introduction, was another matter, and Leamy had full control over the whole car. The set-back radiator, necessitated by the front drive, was a gift to any stylist, as was the low chassis. (The Cord's slight V to the radiator was copied by Chrysler's Oliver Clark on the 1931 Chrysler models.) Using these parameters, Leamy created some superb styles. The fenders, still unskirted, of course, flowed into the running boards with a particular flair, and the bodies, though of classic type for their periods, benefitted greatly from the low chassis. Four styles were offered, a six-window sedan, four-window

△ 1930 CORD L-29 COUPE
This is a unique car built by the Hayes Body Corporation to the design of Alex De Sakhnoffsky, as an inducement to Cord to order bodies from Hayes. In this aim it failed, but it remains one of the most beautiful cars of its era. The curved belt line and absence of running boards give it a more rakish look than the regular Cords. It won the 1930 Concours d'Elegance in Paris, where it arrived at the last minute, after being driven by its designer from Grand Rapids, Michigan, to New York City, shipped on the *Leviathan* to Le Havre and then driven to Paris.
PHOTO: NATIONAL MOTOR MUSEUM, BEAULIEU

△ 1930 CORD L-29 COUPE
The De Sakhnoffsky Cord was acquired by Brooks
Stevens in 1938 and customized with fender skirts and
aerodynamic headlights. He later realized that these
were a mistake and the car was restored.

brougham, phaeton-sedan (four-door convertible) and cabriolet. In addition, some custom styles, including a town car and a speedster, were built by Murphy on the L-29 chassis.

Hailed by *MoTor* magazine as "the first really new automobile design to appear on the market for many years," the L-29 sold about 5,200 units up to 1932, when the Depression forced Cord to end production. Meanwhile, the Auburns had received the Leamy treatment, in particular the 8-98 line introduced for 1931. Just as he had capitalized on the low chassis of the Cord, so he used the Auburn's higher frame to make an equally distinctive car. In particular, in the boat-tail speedster which joined the 8-98 line in the fall of 1931, Leamy made no attempt to disguise the height of the hood, but capitalized on its length and on imaginative color schemes. Auburn's introduction of a V12 engine for 1932 gave an additional eight inches to the hood length. The combination of the lines of the 8-98 speedster with the extra length produced a massively impressive car. It cost only $1,600, a remarkably low price for such a stylish car. Comparable V12s were much more expensive: Cadillac ($3,495), Lincoln ($4,700), and Pierce-Arrow ($3,450). The lowest-priced Auburn V12, the coupe, cost $975, the only 12-cylinder car ever to sell for under $1,000. Unfortunately, there were few buyers for a flashy two-passenger speedster at any price in 1932, and after two years the Auburn V12 was dropped. Leamy styled the 1934 Auburn sixes and eights, which were less than successful, and Cord brought Gordon Buehrig back to restyle the line for 1935.

The situation was difficult. Buehrig admired Leamy's work, especially on the L-29, yet he was hired to replace the 1934 and given four helpers. Leamy left in the summer of 1934 to join Fisher Body Company, moving a year later to GM's Art & Colour Section under Harley Earl. Here he produced some ideas for the La Salle which were greatly admired by Earl. Sadly, Leamy never had a chance to prove himself at GM; a routine diphtheria injection led to septicemia, from which he died in the summer of 1935.

△ Two views of a proposal by Leamy for a 1935 Graham sedan. The narrow grille is reminiscent of the 1934 La Salle, while the pontoon fenders, headlights and enclosed rear wheels are quite advanced. It is a better-looking car than the one Graham actually built in 1935.

◁ Leamy made several designs for Auburn, including this two-door sedan which never progressed beyond a quarter-size clay.

ILLUSTRATIONS: AUBURN-CORD-DUESENBERG MUSEUM

△ FRANK SPRING
Spring influenced Hudson styling for many years, however
he was best known for the 1948 "step-down" Hudson in
which the floor was dropped below the frame sides, so
you stepped down as you got into the car.

CHAPTER SIXTEEN

FRANK SPRING

"Well, boys, I have good news for you. Management and
I have decided that, as of today, we've passed the Buick."

Frank Spring, 1948

FRANK SPRING IS best known for one of the most distinctive American cars of the '40s, the "step-down" Hudson, yet his career spanned more than 35 years, and he didn't begin life as a designer. Born into a wealthy West Coast family, he earned his mechanical engineering degree from the Paris Polytechnic in 1914, and after service with the U.S. Signal Corps, he became an engineer with the Courier Car Company of Sandusky, Ohio. In the early 1920s he joined the Walter Murphy coach-building company in Pasadena as an efficiency manager, and in 1924, when Murphy's general manager George R. Fredericks drowned in an accident, Spring took over as general manager. William Murphy, uncle of coachbuilder Walter, was a friend of the Lelands, which led to the younger Murphy taking the Lincoln agency for California. In December 1926 they changed the agency to Hudson-Essex. Possibly Spring had links with Hudson already, though this has not been proven. Certainly Murphy built bodies on Hudson chassis, and in 1931 Spring moved to Hudson.

Like Harley Earl, Spring was not a hands-on designer. Strother McMinn, who worked for him at Hudson, says that he made assignments and supervised the design activity, but never put pencil to paper. Frank Hershey says that he might specify or indicate a preference, but never invented a design. He was more interested in gadgets and ingenious constructions than in the overall lines of the body. In his time at Murphy, he adapted a design by the Swiss coachbuilder Gangloff in which the front and rear doors were hinged at the B-pillar, allowing the glass drop frames to be very close together. This made for a light and airy interior with maximum visibility. Spring improved on the Gangloff design by substituting an aluminum forging for Gangloff's light fabrication. This forging extended to the floor level and helped to eliminate side distortion of the body, even when the top was removed, as on a convertible sedan. Murphy called such cars "Clear Vision" models and used the design in sedans, convertible sedans and town cars.

▽ ▷ 1948 HUDSON COMMODORE SEDAN
The "step-down" Hudson was a big step forward in design, with the floor dropped below the frame sides and the rear wheels located inside the frame. Body and frame were combined in what was called Monobilt construction. Frank Spring led the styling team.
OWNER: GLEN STALEY

▽ ▷ 1948 HUDSON COMMODORE SEDAN
The Hudson's low lines were an immediate hit with the public, and total sales in the first three seasons were 429,165. Unfortunately, it was a difficult design to update and the same shape was continued up to 1954, by which time the style was behind that of competitors.

In the late 1920s, ties between Murphy and Hudson grew stronger, and although the coachbuilder continued to do work on prestigious makes like Duesenberg and Cord, it offered a line of "semi-custom" bodies on Hudson chassis in 1928. These included a seven-passenger sedan, a convertible landau sedan, a victoria, a fixed-head coupe and a rumble-seat convertible coupe. They were all

ART OF THE AMERICAN AUTOMOBILE

on the long-wheelbase Hudson and were very expensive at $5,000, compared with $1,250 to $1,925 for regular models.

As Murphy had no facilities for any degree of quantity production, the bodies were made by Biddle & Smart to Murphy designs. The idea was that the cars would be sold to "community leaders" in selected areas, so that the general public would be impressed to see a prominent citizen in a Hudson, when he might more usually be expected to drive a Cadillac or Lincoln. The semi-customs were only listed for the 1928 season, but for 1929 similar styles were made for Hudson by Biddle & Smart and by Briggs.

In September 1931 it was announced in the automotive press that Frank Spring had been appointed style engineer at Hudson, though he had, in fact, been working there for several months. Like all other car makers except General Motors, Hudson did not have a styling department up to that date. As Don Butler said in his *History of Hudson*, "Before styling began to emerge as a necessary factor, stylists were rare, and body engineers applied whatever untrained styling touches they could muster."

Frank Spring's influence at Hudson was first seen in the 1932 models which had slightly V-ed grilles with chromed bars, and a greater slope to the windshield. This was the year that the low-priced Essex Terraplane, which had rather similar styling to the bigger Hudsons, was launched. Spring designed one Terraplane sports car with cutaway doors, lightweight fenders and no running boards. Its hood length indicates a straight-eight engine, though officially there was no Terraplane Eight until 1933. However, the sporty body was never put into production in the U.S., although various British-bodied Terraplanes had cutaway doors.

Hudsons were never style leaders in the 1930s, but the company kept up with current trends such as fender skirts (from 1933), while the fencer's mask grilles on the 1936 models were certainly eye-catching. The sports-car-loving Frank Spring would doubtless have liked a lower body line, but Hudson was run by a hat-wearing conservative, Edward Barit who, like Kaufman Keller at Chrysler, insisted on a high roof line. It is all the more remarkable that Barit eventually succumbed to the charms of Frank Spring's most revolutionary car, the so-called "step-down" Hudson, which was launched in October 1947.

◁ Hudson offered two engines in the 1948 cars, a new 262-cubic-inch L-head six (shown here) giving 121hp, and a straight eight of 254 cubic inches, also a L-head and giving 121hp. For 1951 the six was enlarged to 308 cubic inches and 145hp, helping Hudson to many successes in stock car racing.

△ The Commodore's interior features included a cigarette lighter and walnut-grained instrument panel.

THE "STEP-DOWN" HUDSON

A good story about the "step-down" Hudson is that Frank Spring built a prototype in 1941, showed it to Edward Barit, who complained that it was too low, and that the car was relegated to the roof of the Hudson factory until after the war, when Spring retrieved it, smartened it up and re-submitted it to Barit who, having driven it, was enthusiastic and ordered it into production. Unfortunately, the timing is all wrong for the story to be true. The first scale model was not made until 1943, and no prototype can have been running until 1945. Spring certainly oversaw the design, as he had done on all Hudsons since 1931, but the actual work should be credited to designers Robert Andrews,

Arnold Yonkers and Bill Kirby, and chief modeler Arthur Michel, all working under Spring's chief assistant Arthur Kibinger. Spring also brought in Englishman Reid Railton, who had built Hudson-powered sports cars under his own name before the war and was the designer of the Land Speed Record car, Railton-Mobil Special. It is not certain what Railton contributed to the design, but Andrews recalled that he was only seen twice in the Hudson studio.

The core of the Hudson design was an engineering feature. The floor was dropped below the frame sides, so that one stepped down over the frame side members on entering, hence the name. The rear wheels were mounted inside the frame members. Around this frame Spring and his team designed a low, six-window, all-enveloping sedan with a short rear deck. It had the lowest center of gravity of any American car. The grille caused some heartache among the stylists, who had come up with a high horizontal shape, gracefully curved at each side and mounted between the headlights. Below was a substantial double-bar bumper with a single central overrider. Management thought it too radical, so the final design ended up with a lower grille derived from the 1946-47 model, with a single bumper and four overriders.

According to Andrews, Frank Spring was aiming at the 1942 Buick as the style to mark, and once he considered that their design was better than the Buick, they could go ahead. One day he came into the office and said, "Well, boys, I have good news for you. Management and I have decided that, as of today, we've passed the Buick." It may seem a trifle unambitious to model a new car on a four-year-old design but, in fact, the 1948 Buicks were little different from the '42s, and there would be no radical change in Buick lines for several years. The Hudson certainly seemed all new, and it attracted rave notices at its launch. "Sparkling style of an advance character," said *Automotive Industries*, while the normally cautious British *The Motor*, called it "… something of a sensation… a daringly original innovation which enables an outstandingly low car to be roomy, strong and of normal weight."

Four styles were offered on the 1948 Hudsons – four-door sedan, two-door brougham, two-door club coupe and convertible. Two engines were available, a six and an eight, and two levels of trim, Super and

Commodore. The new Hudsons sold very well at first: 143,697 in calendar year 1948; 142,462 in 1949; and 143,006 in 1950. Unfortunately, the semi-unit construction bodies were very hard to restyle in any significant way. The grille was changed for 1951 and again for 1954, and various trim modifications were made, but the same basic shape continued until the end of the '54 season. By then, what had seemed daring and advanced six years earlier was old hat. Rivals had completely new body shells, and even racing successes, and a new 145hp engine could not keep sales up. They dwindled to a miserable 32,287 in 1954, and for 1955 the individual Hudson was no more. The merger with Nash resulted in a "Hash," Nash bodies with Hudson engines.

Alongside the bigger Hudson was a compact car, the Jet, launched in 1953. Spring had ambitious plans for a really striking small car, but the Hudson management decided they wanted something like a scaled-down 1952 Ford, and that is what they got. Some idea of what the original Jet design might have looked like can be seen from the Italia, a limited-production car styled by Spring but built in Italy by Carozzeria Touring. It was intended to be a

△ The 1948 Hudson was offered in two series – the Super and the higher-specification Commodore (shown here). Prices ran at around $150-$220 more for the Commodore. Both engines were available in each model. As well as the sedan, there were coupes for three or six passengers and a convertible.

specialty car in the manner of the Corvette or Thunderbird, but was a fixed-head coupe with seating for four passengers. It is rumored that a free hand with the Italia was Spring's compensation for having his Jet design ignored. Although they always watered down his designs, Hudson management did not want to lose Spring to another company.

The Italia was quite unlike any previous Hudson, with a sloping hood lower than the fender line, headlights surmounted by hoods which ducted air to the brakes, and a simple mesh grille not unlike a Ferrari. The bumper was sharply raised to a point in the center, making an inverted V, inside of which was a badge. The door tops were extended into the roof line, and the windshield was a wraparound structure with pillars leaning forward.

The Borrani wire wheels were partially covered front and rear.

The Italia's engine and chassis came from the Jet; in fact, complete Jets were shipped to Milan, where the bodies were cut off, leaving only the floorpan, cowl and some bracing at the rear. Hudson ordered 25 Italias from Touring, but it is believed that only 19 or 20 were delivered; at $4,800 they did not sell easily. Spring also designed a four-door version on the Hudson Hornet chassis, called the X-161. It was planned to be the regular Hudson sedan for 1957, but the merger with Nash forestalled that idea, and only one X-161 was made. Shortly afterward, Frank Spring died in an automobile accident; at least it was not in one of his own designs, but a little Nash Metropolitan.

▽ 1953 HUDSON SUPER JET FOUR-DOOR SEDAN
Hudson's compact car, made in 1953 and '54, was not pleasing to Frank Spring. His plans for a really striking small car were watered down to something like a 1952 Ford. It was made in two-door Coupe-Sedan and four-door Sedan versions, and used a 202-cubic-inch six engine. Jet production was 35,367 for the two seasons.
PHOTO: NATIONAL MOTOR MUSEUM, BEAULIEU

△ RICHARD TEAGUE (1923-1991)
When Teague arrived at American Motors, where he was to stay
for 23 years, he had already worked at General Motors and at
Packard, where he styled the Panther and Request showcars.
At American Motors, he styled the Gremlin and the Pacer, two
of the most controversial designs of the '70s.

CHAPTER SEVENTEEN

RICHARD TEAGUE

"You gotta love automobiles and have gas in your blood."

Richard Teague

DESCRIBED AS AN automotive renaissance man, Dick Teague had a career in design which spanned almost 50 years, including 23 years as vice-president of styling at American Motors. In addition to designing cars, he was an avid collector, owning more than 300 cars. In a phrase reminiscent of Bill Mitchell, he said, "You gotta love automobiles and have gas in your blood." He certainly did both.

Richard A. Teague was born in Los Angeles on December 26, 1923, and was in the movies at the age of five, playing girl characters under the stage name Dixie Duval in *Our Gang*. His teenage years saw him styling hot rods, working with such gurus of tuning as Ed Iskendarian and Stu Hilborn, and in 1942 he got his first professional job with Northrop Aircraft Corporation. Teague also said that luck was an essential ingredient in a successful styling career, and he got his break when a friend told him about an ad for "a prospective automobile designer" to come to Detroit. He was interviewed by Frank Hershey, and was hired to work in GM's "Planet 8" (Fisher's Body Plant 8). From there he moved to the Oldsmobile and Cadillac studios; his first creative work was the Rocket 88 hood ornament for Oldsmobile.

In 1954 he was invited to join Hershey at Packard, but after three months his friend left for Ford, and Teague found himself as Packard's chief stylist. James Nance had recently taken command of the old-established but now-floundering Detroit company, and was determined to restore its prestige with some long-wheelbase sedans and limousines, and the glamorous Caribbean convertible. Nance was not an automobile man, having come from GM's Hotpoint division, and Teague encountered problems with his boss's impatience and impossible deadlines. However, nothing is impossible with sufficient motivation, and Teague found himself redesigning taillights over a single weekend. These were the "cathedral" lights, so-called because of the

gothic arching of the rear fender over the light, that went on 1955 Packards and were continued for '56. Teague also designed Cadillac-like fins, never seen on a production Packard, though he did put them on the Predictor, a 1956 showcar based on a Clipper chassis, with power-operated top and rear windows, retractable headlights and swivel seats.

In addition to styling regular Packards, Teague was responsible for two other showcars, the Panther and the Request. The former was a fiberglass two-passenger roadster to compete in the Thunderbird/Corvette market, though it would probably have been considerably more expensive. Four were built in 1954, two with McCulloch superchargers which gave a top speed of 131.1mph when timed at Daytona Beach. Among their styling

features was Packard's first wraparound windshield, which reached the production cars in 1955. They had hooded headlights and a low tail, accentuated by a drop-line molding which ran from above the front wheel arch to the lower part of the rear arch. The effect was the exact opposite of the upswept, finned rear end of the Predictor. The Panthers were built by the Mitchell-Bentley Company of Ionia, Michigan, and after the Studebaker-Packard merger they were sold to private individuals. All exist today, a fortunate fate as showcars and prototypes are often destroyed after their publicity potential is exhausted. In fact, the Predictor also survives, in the Studebaker National Museum in South Bend, Indiana.

The Request was, to the writer's eyes, the best looking of Teague's showcars, yet it was the least

◁ △ 1966 RAMBLER MARLIN
Richard Teague's original design for something to chase Ford's Mustang was for a smaller car. However, AMC boss Roy Abernethy, who liked big cars because he was a big guy, insisted that it go on the Rambler Classic wheelbase. The price was $2,601, and only 4,547 were sold in the 1966 model year.
PHOTOS: NATIONAL MOTOR MUSEUM, BEAULIEU

original, consisting of a vertical, pre-war type Packard grille on an unmodified 1955 Patrician with Caribbean trim and paintwork. Its wire wheels were options on all Packards at the time. As Teague pointed out, it wasn't a simple graft of old grille onto a new body. "We never did have that concave

undercut to the tiara (grille) in the '30s. But you couldn't just take a 160 or a 180 grille and put it on another car – it had to look right." The name Request came from Teague, logically as dealers had been asking repeatedly for a return to the classic Packard vertical grille. Had finance and Packard organization been better, the Request might have seen production, but the company was already committed to the 1957 models and after that Packards simply became Studebakers with a different grille.

T WENTY-THREE YEARS AT AMERICAN MOTORS

After an unhappy 18 months at Chrysler where none of his proposals were accepted, Teague took up the post of Assistant Director of Styling at American Motors in September 1959. Within three years, he became Styling Director, and two years after that, Vice-President of AMC.

In the early 1960s, AMC Ramblers were budget-priced, low-image cars, and it took Teague several years to alter that situation. January 1964 saw the Tarpon, a showcar based on the Rambler American platform. A fastback two-door coupe, it was presumably launched to anticipate the arrival of the Mustang three months later. It was attractively styled, but the chassis was too small for a V8 engine, which any car with a claim to sporty performance would have to use. Also AMC president Roy Abernethy did not like small cars. "He liked big cars because he was a big guy," said Teague. Abernethy's response to the Tarpon was, "Well, heck, Teague, why don't you just put it on the Rambler Classic wheelbase? That way you've got

△ ▷ 1968 AMERICAN MOTORS AMX
The most successful pony car from AMC, the AMX was a shortened, two-passenger version of the Javelin. Like the Mustang, it came with several engines giving a variety of characters, from a relatively tame 232-cubic-inch six to a wild 390-cubic-inch V8. This gave 315hp and 0-to-60mph in 7.2 seconds.
OWNER: ED GRIMES

V8 availablity and you've got more room inside it."

So, reluctantly, Teague scaled up his little coupe into a full-size six-passenger car, and the result was the Marlin. To add insult to injury, while Teague was in Europe, Abernethy told styling to add another inch to the roof height. Teague was never happy with the Marlin's proportions. "If you've got a long roof, it doesn't come off unless there's a long hood." The original Marlin of 1966 rode on a 112-inch wheelbase, but for 1967 the 118-inch Ambassador chassis was used. Although it was an even larger car, Teague put the extra two inches into the hood length. It was somewhat better looking than the '66, but Marlins still did not sell. It was great pity that the Tarpon was not put into production, for it had neat, compact lines that would have competed well with the Mustang, and by mid-1966 AMC had a more compact V8 which would have fitted under Tarpon's hood.

The Marlin's successor was a much more promising car. The runaway success of the Mustang convinced chairman of the board Robert Evans that AMC must have a pony car in their range. He ordered a series of ideas cars which were collectively called Project IV. Among them was a

short wheelbase fastback coupe with a rumble seat which Teague called AMX. Although none of the Project IV cars saw the production line, the AMX design was held in reserve and appeared in modified form as a short, two-passenger Javelin. The Javelin was a direct response to the Mustang, Camaro and Barracuda, and had quite a resemblance to the Camaro, with its belt line kick-up behind the door and a similar grille.

The original AMX was styled by Teague and first seen as a non-running fiberglass showcar early in 1966. It was well received, and Evans authorized the building of a running steel-bodied car by Vignale in Italy. Evans liked it so much that he asked Teague to design it for production, using as many Javelin components as possible. (Originally a fiberglass body had been considered, but it

proved unacceptably flimsy.) The wheelbase was shortened by 12 inches, from 109 to 97 inches, the roof and quarter panels were changed, and a new hood and grille were used. However, many Javelin components did appear on the AMX, including the bumpers, front fenders, back lights and trunk lid. At first the two-passenger car was to have been called the Javelin II but it needed an image distinct from the four-passenger, so Teague suggested AMX, from the 1966 showcar. This was his coinage anyway, while Javelin was thought up by AMC's marketing men. Considering how much of the Javelin went into the AMX, it is remarkable how the lines of the original showcar were replicated in the production AMX.

Despite commendable performance on the racetracks, including five wins in the SCCA Central Division races of 1969 to take the championship, the AMX did not sell well enough to satisfy new AMC president William Luneburg, and it was dropped after the 1970 season, with 19,134 having been made. Javelin production over the same three years was 125,347.

In the late 1940s, George Mason, president of Nash, had argued that if an independent car maker were to succeed, it had to offer something different from the Big Three. This led to the compact Rambler, which became the staple model of American Motors when Nash merged with Hudson. The same views were held by Robert Evans in the '70s: "We can't be just another pretty face on the road, Teague – we've got to be different."

In complying with this philosophy, Teague came up with two of the most controversial designs of the decade, the Gremlin and the Pacer. The first was AMC's entry in the sub-compact market. Launched in April 1970, it anticipated the competition from Ford's Pinto and Chevrolet's Vega. AMC's limited finances meant that, unlike these, it could not be an all-new car; Teague used the front end, hood and doors from the compact Hornet, and fitted a 96-inch wheelbase by designing a sharply cut-off tail with very little overhang. It could never be called handsome, but it was certainly different. As Teague said, "Nobody would have paid it any attention if it had looked like one of the Big Three." *Car & Driver* said of the Gremlin, "Probably the most conspicuous of its virtues is styling. It's brisk and efficient and it borrows from no one." Total tooling costs

were only $5 million, and AMC sold 700,000 of the little beasts.

The next small car from Teague was even more idiosyncratic. Whereas the Gremlin had been a genuine sub-compact car, the Pacer was conceived as a roomier small car, mainly for urban use, with a very wide body; "the first wide, small car," it was billed. The hood was very short, as it was designed to hold a Wankel rotary engine; the glass area was enormous, and the body was almost wider than it

was long. Teague sketched it hastily during a conference on new sub-compacts, and comments on its appearance varied greatly, though few were complimentary. "A football on wheels," was one, while Denise Frostick, French-born wife of the prominent British journalist Michael Frostick, observed of theirs "*Mais oui, elle est comme une grosse grenouille, mais elle est charmante*" ("Yes, it's like a big frog, but it is charming").

Teague had planned to use urethane bumpers,

▽ 1971 AMERICAN MOTORS PACER HATCHBACK SEDAN
Whatever you thought of the styling, and most people did not think very highly of it at all, there was no mistaking the Pacer. Its window area was greater than any other American car, and its body almost as wide as it was long. The short hood was intended to house a GM-built Wankel rotary engine, but when that failed to materialize, AMC had to use a stock 258-cubic-inch six.
PHOTO: NATIONAL MOTOR MUSEUM, BEAULIEU

ART OF THE AMERICAN AUTOMOBILE

By 1979 the Pacer line had been extended to comprise a station wagon as well as the hatchback, and engine options included a 304-cubic-inch V8. The grille had been extended higher into the hood, which did not improve its appearance. The Pacer wagon came in three lines, De Luxe and Limited sixes at $5,189 and $6,189 respectively, and Limited V8 at $6,589.

OWNER: EBER SCHMUCKER

but they were too expensive, and the Pacer ended up with steel bumpers which gave the front end a heavy appearance. When GM didn't come up with the Wankel engine, AMC used their standard sixes, joined by a 305-cubic-inch V8. Just over 280,000 Pacers were sold in six seasons, so, as Teague said, "It was no Edsel." Tony Lapine, designer of the Porsche 928, admitted that the rear end was inspired by that of the Pacer.

Although Dick Teague stayed with AMC until 1984, he did not have a great deal to do with a line that was in decline, and ended by making foreign designs. He was responsible for the restyled Jeep Cherokee launched in 1984 and still made in 1995. When AMC started offering small Renault front-drive sedans under the names Alliance and Encore, all Teague was able to do was to change the grille and rear bumpers, and improve the interior. After retirement, he returned to California where he enjoyed his car collection until his death in 1991.

△ BILL PORTER

The designer with his 1995 Buick Riviera. Technology has advanced
enormously since Porter started out, but it's creativity that still counts.
"When I'm shaping a car, getting its contours right, at some point it
seems to take on its own life. In fact, at some stage you have to stop
working and listen to it…"

CHAPTER EIGHTEEN

PRESENT AND FUTURE STYLING

"It may be that one day we won't build three-dimensional models. We'll scale and section that image in the computer."

Irv Rybicki, GM Vice-President, Design

ART OF THE AMERICAN AUTOMOBILE

ON A VISIT to the United States in the fall of 1994, the author was struck by the un-Americanness of the current car scene. It is only a slight exaggeration to say that, as far as the passenger cars are concerned, downtown Boston could be downtown Paris, Munich or Tokyo. Of course, many of the cars are foreign, but the average American car of today has little of the distinction of past eras. The fins, the wide rear decks, and the chrome-laden grills of the 1950s have been submerged in a blandness imposed by safety regulations, fuel economy and the enormous cost of new models, which inhibits imaginative design. With investment costs of up to $3 billion for a new model, auto manufacturers have to play it safe, which means looking to international markets and, increasingly, international input into new designs.

When Ford replaced their American-designed Pinto sub-compact in 1981, it turned to the Escort, an international design conceived by Ford's Powertrain research group in Dearborn but engineered in Britain and Germany. This Escort's replacement of 1990 was engineered by Mazda in Japan and is a close relative of Mazda's 323. Moving up a size, the Ford Tempo and Mercury Topaz, hardly inspired designs but at least from American drawing boards, have been replaced by the international Mondeo, made in Britain and Germany. As with the Escort, many of the new models have considerable input from the U.S. but the result is a design indistinguishable from a European car. Even Cadillac has gone European with the LSE (Luxury Sedan Eurostyle). Shown at the Detroit Show in January 1994, and planned for production in 1996, it is no more than an Opel Omega with lengthened front and rear and a Cadillac grille.

Federal regulations have also imposed a certain uniformity on car design, though there have been useful spin-offs. In the 1950s and '60s bumpers were cosmetic components which the stylist could vary according to his whim, integrating them with the grille or reflecting grille design in some way. Then came the regulations on 2½mph and 5mph-impact, which resulted in bumpers projecting farther at front and back, and giving the cars a heavy appearance. This was particularly unfortunate in a small car like the Chevrolet Vega, as the bumpers were disproportionately large compared with those, say, on a Cadillac. However, by the mid-'80s softer deformable material came into use and bumpers were integrated into the body shape, as on the Corvette from 1984 onward. This meant that the car became a total form, with no add-on shapes at front or rear.

Although less distinctively American than in earlier decades, American cars today are by no means boring or all alike. The low point was probably the late 1970s when stylists were struggling with the shorter wheelbases imposed by the fuel crisis, yet were still using concepts from the big-car era. It took ten years for design to accommodate the new parameters and now, nearly 20 years on from the cars that so upset Dave Holls — Chevrolet Malibu, Chrysler K-car and Ford Fairmont — we have many exciting designs. In particular, Bill Porter's 1995 Buick Riviera, Chrysler's imaginative Neon compacts, and Concorde and LHS larger sedans, Lincoln's Mark VIII coupe, and the current Corvette and Camaro/Firebird, all show real flair.

Bill Porter, who styled such important cars as the second generation 1970½ Firebird, 1984 Corvette and 1985 Buick Electra, has some interesting insights into the creative process, which he feels has

◁ 1995 BUICK RIVIERA COUPE
For 1995 the famous name of Riviera went onto an all-new car, with a new 232-cubic-inch V6 engine and a sleek two-door five-passenger coupe body. The platform is shared with the Oldsmobile Aurora four-door sedan.
◁ The 1995 Buick Riviera coupe with its stylist, Bill Porter.

not been stifled by current trends. "When I'm shaping a car, getting its contours right, at some point it seems to take on its own life. In fact, at some stage you have to stop working and listen to it ... 'What are you trying to tell me that you want to be?' Sometimes it tells me — it sounds ridiculous but in practice there is some kind of exchange there — you are giving it life, and at the same time it is telling you what it wants to be. Other designers have recognised this too." (Interview with Nicky Wright, 1994)

Less successful artistically, yet distinctively American, are the big rear-drive V8s which reappeared for the 1991 season. After being marginalized in the ranges of the Big Three since the mid-1980s, the traditional American gas-guzzler was resurrected for those buyers who were tired of shoe-box sized compacts, the hat-wearing customer who, Kaufman Keller believed, was so important in the 1950s. In January 1991 Chevrolet completely restyled their Caprice six-passenger sedan, giving it rounded, lozenge-shaped lines and plenty of overhang front and rear. European commentators might dub it "the Moby Dick school of styling," but it was a good aerodynamic shape, giving a drag coefficient of 0.33 compared with 0.41 for the 1990 Caprice. Buick and Oldsmobile versions were made as well,

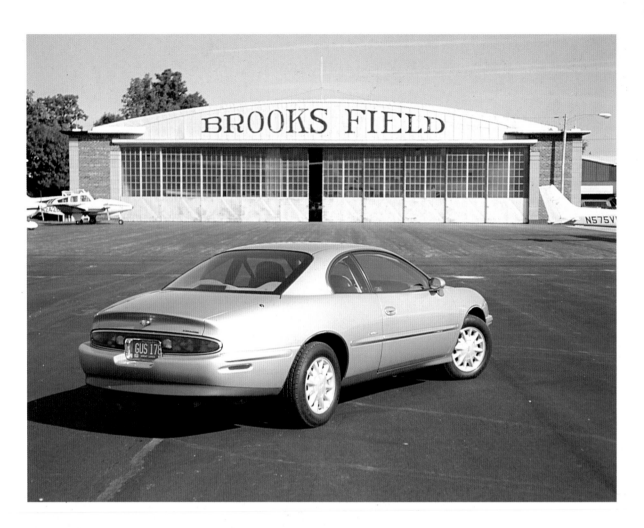

COMPUTER-AIDED DESIGN

There has been much talk about the role of the computer in car design, and whether it will help or hinder the stylist's creativity. Dave Cummins is clear that it is not a substitute for the human imagination, but that it can speed up that work. "Few uninitiated people really understand the role that a computer can, or more aptly cannot, play in designing a form. I can't emphasise too strongly that there is no substitute for a creative mind inside a human skull which has the ability to make the rest of the body set down a design — no computer does this on its own. The first step is always done by a human being. What computers can do is to speed up the process from that point in the development of the theme with variations, alternative views, surface development, illustration, presentation, communication of data, etc. Because of this, the designer is infinitely more capable of creating more and better design work in every sense of the word." (Letter to Nick Georgano, 1994)

Irv Rybicki, General Motors' current vice-president of design, similarly stresses the time factor. "A problem I always had when I was a designer up on the boards was that I had more ideas swimming through my head than my hand could possibly put on the page. It takes several hours to lay out an automobile, render it and get it up on the wall. If we could speed up that process, we would have a better selection. I see the day when a designer will sit at a computer terminal and create in just a matter of minutes an image that flashes through his mind, put it in the computer bank and create another one.

"Perhaps he would decide that the face on the first one was great, but that the body shape and upper and tail end on the second one are very good. So he can bring the face out of the memory bank and bring it all together in a new car. Now he has an image he really has confidence in. Then he'll project that image right out into space in holographic form and in full scale, and he'll be ten feet away from a full-scale model. He can walk around the image and look at the face, look at the tail and get a feel. It may be that one day we won't build three-dimensional models. We'll scale and section that image in the computer." (Interview with C. Edson Armi, 1985)

◁ △ The 1995 RIVIERA
This car represents a comeback for Buick's styling studios. Owing quite a lot to the Lucerne concept car shown in 1991, its oval grille is reminiscent of a Pininfarina-bodied Jaguar sports car first seen in 1978.
◁ The V6 engine gives 205hp in normally aspirated form, 225hp with a supercharger.
◁ Bill Porter designed the Riviera's exterior and Paul Tatseos designed the interior, which has a rather retro,1960s look.

the Roadmaster and Custom Cruiser. These were all big cars, nearly 18 feet long, weighing nearly 4,000 pounds and with trunk volumes of 20.4 cubic feet. The Roadmaster station wagon, with rear seats flat, had a volume of 87 cubic feet. The wagon was described by *Road and Track* as "decidedly un-trendy, with its floating ride and vinyl wood-grain appliqué," but it has sold well.

Ford's versions of the rear-drive V8 are the Ford Crown Victoria and Mercury Grand Marquis. Styling followed that of the smaller Taurus and Sable sedans. Unlike the GM cars, which used existing engines, the Fords have new modular overhead cam V8s which are more powerful than the larger units used in previous big Fords.

FUTURE STYLING

Attempts at predicting the future of car styling are about as imprecise as any other form of forecasting. One has only to look at ideas of "cars of the future," produced over the past seven decades to see how out of line they were. Some 1920s prophecies featured way-out ideas like a short hood or no hood at all, fins on the top and wings, yet they still had heavy-spoked wheels and separate headlights and fenders, which were to disappear in the next decade. Similarly 1950s ideas cars, like John Tjaarda's son Tom's Selena, with van-like, cab-over controls and engine bay cut at the back, have not yet come to production, and probably never will.

The general shape of the present automobile is unlikely to change for some time with one exception already present. This is the MPV or "people carrier," a cross between a station wagon and a van already made by Ford (Aerostar, replaced by Windstar in 1994), GM (Chevrolet Lumina,

Oldsmobile Silhouette, Pontiac Trans Sport) and Chrysler (Plymouth Voyager, Dodge Caravan). This practical layout, with a capacity of eight or nine passengers on a relatively short wheelbase, is slated for production by most major car makers (Ford of Europe and Volkswagen have a joint design), and America is likely to follow with new versions from the Big Three. The MPV is sometimes called the one-box design, as in profile there is only the passenger compartment, with no hood or trunk. France already makes a small one-box sedan, the Renault Twingo, and this might be adopted by the American industry, though doubtless in a larger model than the 135-inch-long Twingo.

▽ ▷ 1995 BUICK RIVIERA COUPE
The Riviera name has always been reserved for a particularly special kind of Buick, from the first hardtop of 1949, through Bill Mitchell's coupes of the 1960s, to Bill Porter's design for the 1990s.

styling and a V6 engine. Insiders believe that it will be on sale by mid-1995.

Among less sporting machinery, Bill Porter's 1991 Buick Lucerne concept coupe has inspired many aspects of the 1994 Riviera, including the flat-oval horizontal grille, itself derived from a Pininfarina-bodied Jaguar. The Lincoln Contempra luxury sedan which was exhibited at the 1994 Detroit Show is likely to become the 1996 Continental, the first Lincoln to use Ford's new modular V8 engine. Among the Contempra's new-age features are tap-sensitive windows to trigger door opening, as there are no door handles.

Whatever the future brings, the stylist's role will continue, and despite all the commercial and technical constraints, it will be essentially the role of an artist. Bill Porter recalls a philosophy teacher who said that manufactured objects such as cars, just as much as individual paintings, contain in some way, in perpetuity, the emotions the artist put into them. If the emotions communicate to enough people, the result will be a successful design, pleasing to the accountants as well as to the stylist.

△ ▷ 1959 SELENA I SHOWCAR
Designed by Tom Tjaarda, son of the Lincoln Zephyr's creator John Tjaarda, the Ghia-built Selena made an effective use of space, with most of the length given over to the passenger-carrying cabin, and the engine at the back. However, as a prediction of what the future would bring, it was way off the mark.
PHOTO: GHIA SPA

Clues to the look of cars a few years hence can be gained from the annual shows at which concept cars continue to be exhibited. The open two-passenger sports car, of which the Corvette was the only representative for many years, was given a boost in 1989 with the Dodge Viper. Powered by a 400hp V10 truck engine, it was thought to be too way out, as well as environmentally unfashionable, for commercial sale, but it went into production in January 1992 and is still made in 1995. A GTS hard-top coupe version was planned for production in early 1996. Another possible candidate for the showrooms, also a Chrysler product, is the Plymouth Prowler with open-wheeled, hot-rod

BIBLIOGRAPHY

The American Car Since 1775 by the Editors of *Automobile Quarterly*, New York, 1971.

American Car Spotters Guides, 1920-1939 and **1940-1965** by Tad Burness, Motorbooks International, Osceola, Wisconsin, 1975 and 1978.

The Art of American Car Design by C. Edson Armi, Penn State Press, 1988.

Cadillac and La Salle by Walter McCall, Crestline Publishing, Sarasota, Florida, 1982.

The Cars of Lincoln and Mercury by George Dammann and James K. Wagner, Crestline Publishing, Sarasota, Florida, 1987.

The Cars of Oldmobile by Dennis Casteele, Crestline Publishing, Sarasota, Florida, 1981.

Chevrolet 1911-1985 by the Auto Editors of *Consumer Guide*, 1984.

The Classic Cord by Dan R. Post, Dan Post Publications, Arcadia, California, 1952.

Chrome Dreams by Paul Wilson, Chilton Book Company, Radnor, Pennsylvania, 1976.

The Custom Body Era by Hugo Pfau, A.S. Barnes & Co., New York, 1970.

The Dodge Story by Thomas A. McPherson, Crestline Publishing, Sarasota, Florida, 1976.

Dream Cars by Fred Horsley, Trend Books, Los Angeles, California, 1953.

Duesenberg, the Pursuit of Perfection by Fred Roe, Dalton Watson, London, 1982.

Encyclopedia of American Cars 1930-1942 by James H. Moloney, Crestline Publishing, Sarasota, Florida, 1977.

Fifty Years of American Automobiles from 1939 by the Auto Editors of *Consumer Guide*, 1989.

Ford, 1903-1984 by the Auto Editors of *Consumer Guide*, 1984.

Ford, the Men and the Machine by Robert Lacey, Heinemann, London 1986.

Great American Automobiles of the '50s by Richard M. Langworth, Chris Poole and the Auto Editors of *Consumer Guide*, 1989.

Harley Earl and the Dream Machine by Stephen Bayley, Trefoil, London, 1990.

The History of Holden Since 1917 by Norm Darwin, E. L. Ford Publications, Newstead, Victoria, Australia, 1983.

The History of Hudson by Don Butler, Crestline Publishing, Sarasota, Florida, 1982.

Packard edited by Berverly Rae Kimes, Princeton Publishing, Princeton, New Jersey, 1978.

The Plymouth and De Soto Story by Don Butler, Crestline Publishing, Sarasota, Florida, 1979.

Raymond Loewy by Paul Jodard, Trefoil Publications, London, 1992.

Rolling Sculpture by Gordon Buehrig, Haessner, Newfoundland, New Jersey, 1975.

Seventy Years of Buick by George Dammann, Crestline Publishing, Sarasota, Florida, 1973.

Seventy Years of Chrysler by George Dammann, Crestline Publishing, Sarasota, Florida, 1974.

Seventy-five Years of Oakland and Pontiac by John Gunnell, Crestline Publishing, Sarasota, Florida, 1982.

The Standard Catalog of American Cars, 1805-1942 by Beverly Rae Kimes and Henry Austin Clark, Jr., Krause Publications, Iola, Wisconsin, 1989.

The Standard Catalog of American Cars 1945-1975 by the Editors of *Old Cars Weekly*, Krause Publications, Iola, Wisconsin, 1982.

The Studebaker Century by Asa E. Hall and Richard M. Langworth, Dragonwyck Publishing, Contoocook, New Hampshire, 1983.

Mustang by Nicky Wright, Prion, London, 1994.

U.S. Military Wheeled Vehicles by Fred C. Crismon, Crestline Publishing, Sarasota, Florida, 1983.

Also numerous articles in *Automobile Quarterly* and *Special-Interest Autos*, epecially those by David W. Bird, Robert E. Bourke, Dan Burger, Jeffrey Godshall, Walter E. Gosden, Maurice Hendry, Beverly Rae Kimes, Mike Lamm, Richard M.Langworth and Strother McMinn.

INDEX

ACKNOWLEDGMENTS

Nick Georgano would like to thank the following people for their generous help with information. First, four stylists who gave their time to answer questions and supply illustrations: Dave Cummins, John Najjar, Bill Porter and Fred Schimmel. Among others, Dr Robert F. Croll, Norm Darwin, Eddie Ford, Mike Lamm, Karl Ludvigsen, Derek Maidment and Keith Marvin. He would also like to thank the Penn State Press for permission to reproduce interview material from *The Art of the American Car Design* by C. Edson Armi, and Jonathan Stein for permission to quote from an article on Howard Darrin in *Automobile Quarterly*.

Nicky Wright would like to thank the following museums and individuals for the special help they gave:

Auburn-Cord-Duesenberg Museum, Auburn, Indiana; Tom and Karen Barnes, for their help and friendship; Jack Beasley; Jim Bennett; Stan Block; Joe Bortz Dream Car Collection; Susan Boyd; Dan Brasch; Buick Motor Division, GM; William J. Chorkey; Carroll Clark; Keya Cositanes; Ronda Cositanes; Lonnie Crag; Dave Cummins; Mark Cuthbertson; Linda and Dale DeVine; Duke and Donna Davenport; Door Prairie Car Museum; Ward Gapper; John Gardner; Ford Motor Company/John Clinard; Leo Gephart; Gilmore Classic Car Museum, Kalamazoo, Michigan; Ed Grimes; Wally Herman; Blaine Jenkins; Larry Kensal, GM Archives; Larry Kislack; Lee Lephart; Glen Lueders; Robert A. Lutz, President of the Chrysler Corporation; Jeff and Janet May; Richard Mitten/Sanderson Ford, Glendale, Arizona; Bob Mason; John Najjar; Bill Porter; Gene Povinelli; Jim Powell and Michelle; Jim Ransom; Ron Redicki; Bob Rippy; Otto Rosenbusch; Allen C. Saffrahn, Hudson restorer; Charles Saatthoff; Fred Schimmel; Barney Smith; Ron Smith; Glen Staley; Studebaker National Museum, South Bend, Indiana; David Utter; Joe Whitney; Bill Woodke.

He would also like to thank Nikon, Pentax, Fuji Films, Accu-Color in Fort Wayne, Indiana, and Jack's Cameras in Muncie, Indiana.

Mirco De Cet would like to thank the following people and organizations for their help with picture research:

The Henry Ford Museum, Greenfield Village, Dearborn, Michigan; General Motors Media Archives, Detroit; Auburn-Cord-Duesenberg Museum, Auburn, Indiana; Chrysler Historical Photo Archives, Detroit; Chevrolet Photo Archive, Detroit; Ghia SpA, Turin, Italy; The David Burgess Wise Collection, England; The J. Baker Collection, England; and the National Motor Museum, Beaulieu, England.

629.231 GEO

Georgano, G. N.

Art of the American
  automobile : the
      1995.

OCT 1 9 1995

PENN YAN PUBLIC LIBRARY
    PENN YAN, N.Y.